THE
BONANZA
NARROW GAUGE
RAILWAY

THE STORY OF THE

KLONDIKE MINES RAILWAY

THE
BONANZA
NARROW GAUGE
RAILWAY

THE STORY OF THE
KLONDIKE MINES RAILWAY

ERIC L. JOHNSON
APRIL 1997

Published by

Rusty Spike Publishing

Vancouver, British Columbia, Canada

Copyright © Eric L. Johnson, April, 1997

Canadian Catalogue in Publishing Data:

Johnson, Eric L. (Eric Lennart), 1933-
   Bonanza narrow gauge railway

Includes bibliographic references and index.
ISBN number 0-9681976-0-4

1. Klondike Mines Railway. 2. Narrow gauge railroads--
Yukon Territory---History. 3. Gold mines and mining--Yukon
Territory--Klondike River Valley. I. Title.
HE2810.K58J63 1997 385'.54'097191 C97-910290-1

Layout and Editing by Lorne H. Nicklason

Printed by
   D.W. Friesen Inc.
   Altona, Manitoba

Front Cover: During the summer of 1908, engine No. 2, with box car No. 122 and coach No. 202, quietly steams away during a one-hour layover at Sulphur Springs, the southern terminus of the Klondike Mines Railway. The locomotive has already been turned on the wye, and is ready for the homeward trip northward to Dawson. No. 2 was the most-used engine in the KMR roster, a 2-8-0 Baldwin built in 1885, and acquired from the White Pass & Yukon Route in 1905. It now resides in the Dawson City Museum.

Passengers may at the moment be hiking up the slopes of King Solomon Dome—of which the southern slope is visible at the left side—or feasting at nearby "Dad" Hartman's Road House. Telegraph and telephone lines owned by the railway can be seen above the tender, leading to the communities on the creeks below.
   The Bancroft Library, University of California, Berkeley, 1905.1709 6264

TABLE OF CONTENTS

LIST OF MAPS

All maps were drawn by the author,
and cannot be reproduced without permission.

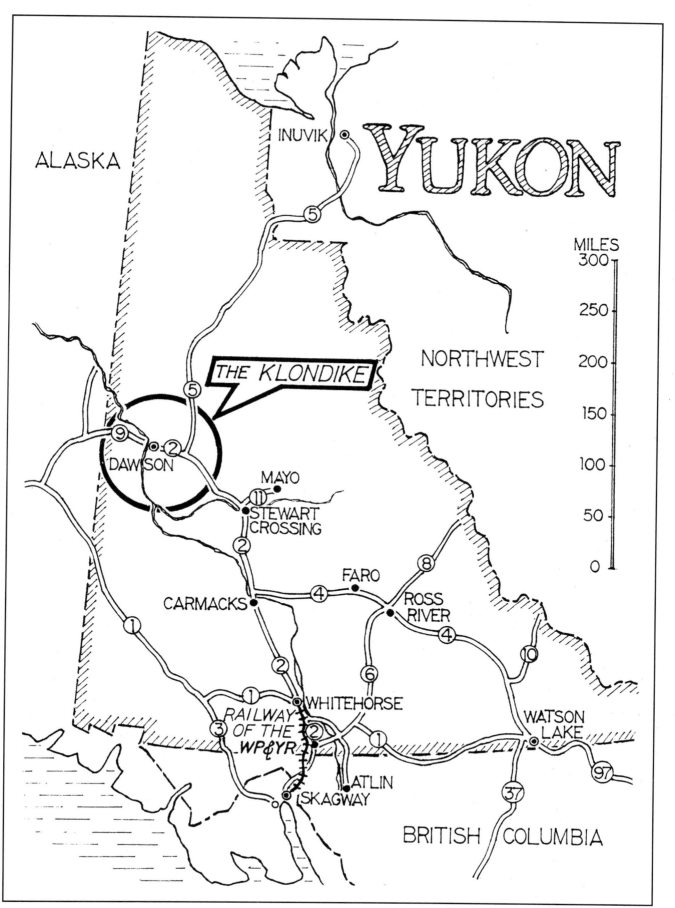

ACKNOWLEDGEMENTS

Little has been written about the Klondike Mines Railway, but a slim, tantalizing, chapter in Omer Lavallée's "*Narrow Gauge Railways of Canada*" dealing with this gold rush venture was the inspiration for a search for the specifics.

I had hardly begun gathering data when I was contacted by Bob Mitchell, a railfan, railway modeler and, by profession, a heritage recorder for Parks Canada. While working for Klondike Historic Sites at Dawson City, Bob had on his own time gathered information about the railway's physical plant. His generous help put me on the track to many sources of photos and the railway's history. At Dawson City I met Greg Skuce, who has done contract work for Parks Canada and the Dawson City Museum over the years. Greg, who has hiked the length of the Klondike Mines Railway's right-of-way, gave me a tour of the grade and pointed out the main remaining artifacts. I wish to give special thanks to both Bob and Greg.

I also thank many others who have contributed in various ways to the story of the Klondike Mines Railway—they include: David Burrell, Edmund Collins III, J. David Conrad, Harry Cooper, Frances Dwyer, John Gallagan, Denny Hilton, Robert G. Hilton, Barbara Hogan, William J. Husa Jr., Ken Hynek, George R. Kadelak, Arthur E. Knutson, David Krehbiel, Thomas Lawson, Jr., M.D. McCarter, Don Macintyre, Don A. Marenzi, Carl E. Mulvihill, Charles B. Porter, Victor Rafanelli, Art Schultz, Robert D. Turner, Harold K. Vollrath, David and Steve Wild, and Ronald W. Willis.

Organizations from which data, documents, and photographs were gratefully received are:
B.C. Archives and Records Service, Victoria, B.C.
Dawson City Museum, Dawson, Yukon
Dedman's Photo Shop, Skagway, AK
Glenbow Museum, Calgary, Alberta
MacBride Museum, Whitehorse, Yukon
National Air Photo Library, Ottawa, Ontario
National Archives of Canada, Ottawa, Ontario
Ottawa Public Library, Ottawa, Ontario
Parks Canada, Winnipeg, Manitoba
Provincial Archives of Alberta, Edmonton, Alberta
Railroad Museum of Pennsylvania, Strasburg, PA
University of Alaska, Fairbanks, AK
University of British Columbia, Vancouver, B.C.
University of California, Berkeley, CA
Vancouver Public Library, Vancouver, B.C.
Waterford Public Library, Waterford, WI
Yukon Archives, Whitehorse, Yukon

Since almost no business records of the company have survived, the greater part of the Klondike Mines Railway's story was gleaned from hundred of items from microfilmed copies of newspapers, in particular the **Dawson Daily News,** which was published continuously between 1900 and 1955. Other newspapers researched were: the **Klondike Nugget**, the **Yukon Sun**, the **Yukon World**, and the **Dawson Record**—all of which had succumbed before 1909; also searched were the **Whitehorse Star**, the **Vancouver Province**, Victoria's **Daily Colonist**, and Skagway's **Daily Alaskan**.

Finally, I would like to thank my editor, Lorne Nicklason, for his careful proofreading of the manuscript, and for laying out this book.

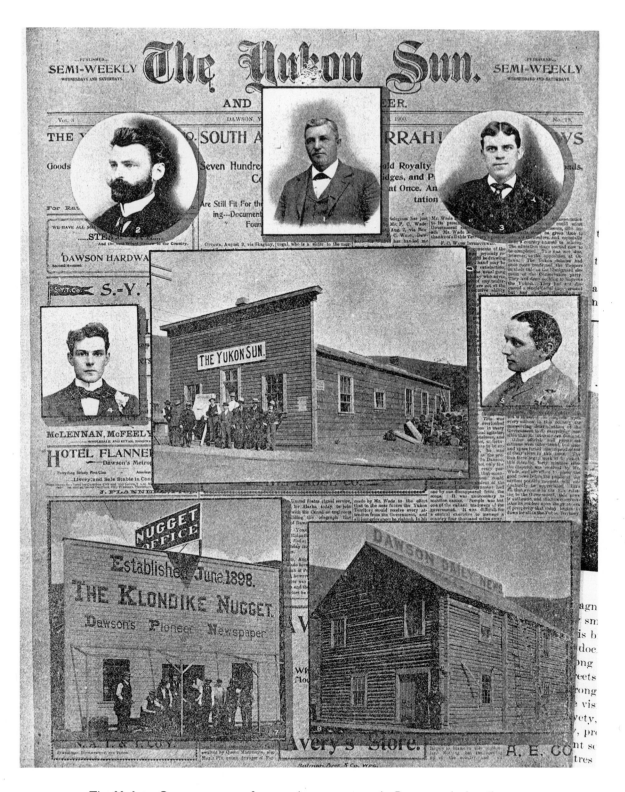

The **Yukon Sun** was one of several newspapers in Dawson during the Klondike gold rush. Owner Tom O'Brien, in the top centre photo, produced a booklet promoting his newspaper, the **Yukon Sun**, and also showing the **Klondike Nugget** and **Dawson Daily News**. All were important sources for the **Bonanza Narrow Gauge Railway**.
British Columbia Archives and Records Service, 81186 E-3017

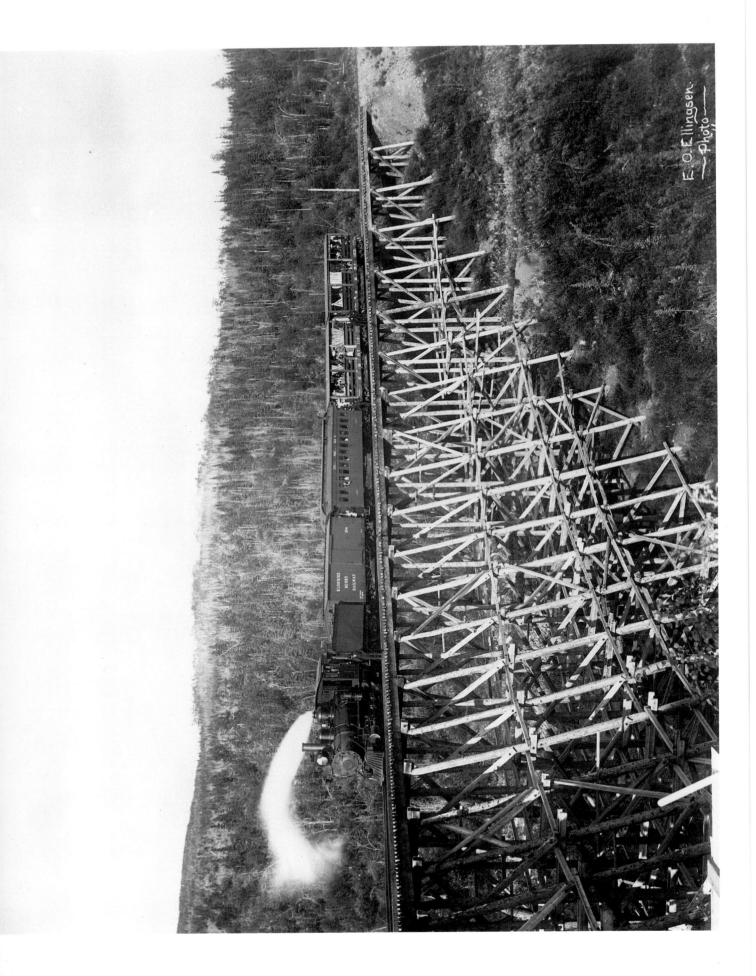

E. O. Ellingsen Photo

INTRODUCTION

The discovery of rich gold creeks in the Yukon in late 1896 created a stampede the like of which has not been seen since. Tens of thousands joined in the "rush" to the Klondike, although only a fraction of this number would eventually arrive at Dawson City, chief entry point to the goldfield. There, 1200 feet above sea level, where the Klondike River flows into the Yukon River, Dawson City, or simply Dawson as it was later known, sprang up within months of the discovery of gold. The gold creeks, however, were still some distance away. Central to the goldfield and about twenty miles to the south-east of Dawson is a lightly-wooded hill, over 4000 feet above sea level and the highest in the goldfield, appropriately named King Solomon Dome. Radiating from the "Dome" are five major creeks: to the north Hunker Creek and its tributary Gold Bottom Creek, to the east Dominion Creek, to the south Sulphur Creek, to the south-east Quartz Creek, and to the north-west Bonanza Creek. These creeks were the destination of the gold-seekers.

Encouraging prospects are said to have been found first on Quartz Creek and on a feeder of Hunker Creek, but it was George Washington Carmack's panning of very rich gravel on Bonanza Creek that started the great rush. Bonanza Creek flows generally to the north-west into the Klondike River barely a mile above the Klondike's confluence with the Yukon River. The valley of Bonanza Creek thus situated became the main traffic route to most of the workings, and the gravels of Bonanza Creek and its tributary Eldorado Creek quickly proved to be the richest in the Klondike. Within a year of the staking of the discovery claim the basins of all adjacent creeks were solidly staked. The discovery claim on Bonanza Creek was located about thirteen miles distant from Dawson; about one mile upstream Eldorado Creek flowed into Bonanza Creek, and here at 1600 feet above sea level a major camp named Grand Forks grew. By late 1897 settlements had been established on every one of the creeks surrounding King Solomon Dome.

Transportation of people and freight into the goldfield was a major problem, and early in the Klondike's development a railway appeared a necessity. A number of applications for charters were made, and among them the Klondike Mines Railway Company was granted a charter in 1899, but it languished for several years as gold production in the Klondike peaked, and then fell off. The delay in construction of the railway was not, as is generally believed, the result of right-of-way locational difficulties, although this created temporary set-backs. The company needed a million dollars to begin construction, but it appears that until 1901 no effort whatsoever was made to solicit investors. While one charter member, Thomas William O'Brien, made a real effort to mobilize the project, he didn't have the resources to carry it. The other charter members could better be called promoters and none, it seems, aggressively attacked the financing problem. When in 1902 an engineer eventually accepted the challenge, it was more than two years before he was able to drum up financial backers. During this time good wagon roads were built into the goldfield, and stage lines operated into all of the larger camps in the district. Whether the railway should have been built at all now was debatable, but in 1906 it was finally completed with, however, a line much shorter than had been first visualized. Equipped with rebuilt, secondhand, rolling stock, the railway never reached projected business levels, and after only eight years of seasonal operation in a gold camp now very much in decline, the railway ceased operation.

Many details of the Klondike Mines Railway's history are unknown. If any readers can add to the story—or correct errors in this story—the author would be grateful for their help. Should company documents, such as timetables and business records, be known they also would be of great value. Similarly, there must be many valuable photos of Klondike Mines Railway activity tucked away in old family albums. Anything provided me would, with the permission of the lender, be passed on to the Yukon Archives and the Dawson City Museum.

Eric L. Johnson
Vancouver, B.C.
April, 1997

Opposite: A mixed train/excursion in the early years of Klondike Mines Railway operation, on the photographer's favourite, the Homestake Gulch trestle. Behind engine No. 2 are box car No. 104, coach No. 202, and flat cars 113 and 103 fitted up as "open-air coaches".
Glenbow Museum, NA1466-33

CHAPTER ONE

THE KLONDIKE GOLDFIELD

It is believed that the first prospectors searching for gold in the Yukon came in the early 1870s, and their finds were sufficient to soon encourage others. In 1886 coarse gold was discovered in modest yields at Fortymile River, about fifty miles down the Yukon River from what was to become Dawson City, and by 1887 there were 250 prospectors in the Yukon. That year about $60,000 in gold was recovered. In 1894 the area now known as the Klondike (spelled Klondyke until 1898) was first prospected by a party of men including a Nova Scotian, Robert Henderson. By 1896 he had explored the major creeks to the south, east, and north of Hunker Summit. An acquaintance, George Carmack, had followed Henderson up Hunker Creek and crossed over the divide, descending Rabbit Creek (now Bonanza Creek) westerly, panning en route. On August 16, 1896, Carmack and his two Indian brothers-in-law, Skookum Jim and Tagish Charlie, made their famous discovery. Carmack made no secret of the exceedingly rich find, and by September 6, others had staked about 200 claims on Bonanza Creek. By November nearly every prospector in the Yukon had converged on the Klondike, and the rush from Outside was on!

By the spring of 1897 the non-native population of the Klondike had risen to 1500, and 700 claims had been staked; by January, 1898, the number of newcomers had grown to 5000 and claims also numbered 5000. The spiral continued with over 17,000 claims registered by mid-summer that year—the major creeks were blanketed. Although this was the height of staking activity, the population count continued to soar, and exceeded 25,000 by January of 1899, peaking at well over 30,000. By 1901 the count was down to 27,000 and by 1911, less than 8000. Gold production in the Yukon had risen from a quarter of a million dollars in 1896 to a maximum of more than twenty-two million in 1900. The decline that followed was a result of the gradual exhaustion of the richest of gravels, in spite of increasingly more efficient mining operations.

An individual miner was allowed to stake only one claim, except for the "discoverer" who was allowed the first two "discovery" claims on a particular creek; such was the case with George Carmack on Bonanza Creek, Andrew Hunker on Hunker Creek, and so on. Of course, individuals could buy any number of claims staked by others. Claims measured 500 feet along the creek, extending back to the base of the hill on each side of the creek, and were identified by their position above or below the discovery claim. For example: 25 Below on Bonanza was about 25 times 500 feet, or 12,500 feet (a little more than two miles), below Carmack's discovery claim. Claims on Eldorado Creek, which was judged a tributary of Bonanza, began with No. 1 on Eldorado at the creeks' confluence. The community of Grand Forks, later called Bonanza, was situated on Nos. 6, 7, 8, and 9 Above on Bonanza and just north-east of No. 1 on Eldorado. Hillside claims, those along the foot of hills and paralleling the creek beds, were considerably

> Gold found in nature is almost never 100% pure, being a natural alloy of gold and silver containing minor amounts of other elements. The purity of natural gold is measured by "fineness" which is the number of parts by weight of gold present in 1000 parts of the alloy. Fine gold, that is gold of fineness 1000, was until 1933 valued at $20.67 per Troy ounce (31.103 grams). In most North American placer goldfields, nuggets and gold dust was considered to be worth, on average, $17.00 per ounce, or fineness of about 820, and this is what a miner was credited with when settling accounts from his poke.

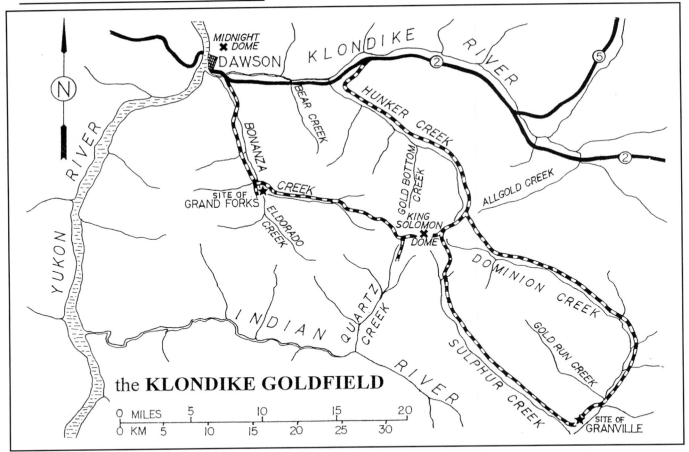

The heart of the Klondike gold country, showing existing access roads to the area.

smaller in area. Most claim stakers chose not to mine, instead soon selling their claims to others who were willing to undertake the organization and expense of mining.

Mining itself began with the staking of the first claims. The process of gold extraction in the beginning was one of manual labour: sinking shafts through permafrost, drifting, mining frozen ground, and stock-piling the "pay dirt" during the winter for washing to recover the gold in the summer. Fortunes were made by many miners, but the methods initially used could exploit ground only where higher gold values were found; much ground could not be profitably worked by individuals. Thus, partnerships or syndicates working groups of claims soon became the practice, the combined resources permitting exploitation by more complex and efficient operations.

The end of July, 1900, saw the completion of the railway of the White Pass and Yukon Route from Skagway to Whitehorse, which permitted lower cost freighting and the importation of considerably heavier mining machinery into the Klondike. With the increasing use of

machinery, there was a corresponding decrease in manpower required, but even extensive flume-work, steam-powered elevators, pumps, and large scale sluicing operations were only interim measures in the efforts to exploit less profitable ground. Among the many entrepreneurs in the Klondike were a few who saw the future much more clearly.

Arthur Newton Christian Treadgold came to the Klondike early in 1898, and realized that the very high-paying "dirt" would not last long. There were immense volumes of lower value gravels that could be exploited only with a grand scale operation, one which required a great deal of capital, control of the very limited supply of water, and acquisition of huge blocks of claims. Treadgold's personal resources were limited, but he was a most persuasive lobbyist and promoter. In 1901, Ottawa approved his plan to acquire claims which had been allowed to lapse, and additionally granted him the water rights needed to mine on a grand scale. The Treadgold Concession, as it was called, met with immediate hostility from the small operators, and in 1904 the government was forced to rescind the legislation. Treadgold, however, persisted and with declining gold production, his plan gradually gained acceptance, and with minor changes was sanctioned in 1906. Dredging would become the answer to sustained gold production in the Klondike.

Treadgold had assembled backers which included the wealthy Guggenheim family, and by 1908 the Yukon Gold Company was in full operation with dredges and hydraulic operations. To feed and power these mining operations, Treadgold had gained rights to water access, and in 1907 began construction of a hydroelectric plant on the Twelve Mile River. By 1911 the company had seven dredges at work on Bonanza and Eldorado Creeks, and two more on the other side of the divide. However, Treadgold was an unorthodox man who manipulated his backers, and due to the apparent illegality of his convoluted schemes he lost control of the company in 1910. But in 1911 the unstoppable Treadgold promoted another company, the Granville Mining Company, which he effectively managed and reorganized. He was also soon similarly banished from this company in 1916, returning to England, bankrupt, where he involved himself with extended legal battles against his opponents.

Because of problems arising during World War I, the major mining companies in the Klondike fell into debt, and as a result were reorganized in 1923 under one massive company called the Yukon Consolidated Gold Corporation (YCGC), which soon took almost complete command of the whole Klondike goldfield. In 1925, Treadgold returned, having gained control of YCGC. Under his autocratic rule the company gained strength but, as before, failure to disclose his promotional actions caught up with him, and in 1932 he was once more driven from the Klondike, never to return.

Treadgold was possibly the greatest promoter the Klondike has ever seen, but he was not the first to bring dredges into operation there, nor was he the only one to be granted concessions. Among about forty others granted concessions, Joseph Whiteside Boyle was equally successful as a promoter, and furthermore Boyle proved the better at bringing mining operations into production. As with Treadgold's companies, Boyle's company was in time also swallowed up by YCGC which, following Treadgold's departure, methodically worked over the gravels of the Klondike, year after year, finally ceasing operations in 1966.

> The Klondike District got its name from the river of the same name. First traders and prospectors into the area knew it as the Deer River, and it was so recorded by Lieutenant Schwatka on his momentous reconnaissance by raft down the Yukon River in 1883. But it was from the Indian word roughly transcribed as "Thron-duick", or "Tron-deg", meaning Deer River, that the name Klondyke was derived. In 1898, the officially-correct spelling became Klondike, although Klondyke was still extensively used for some time after.

A southbound mixed Klondike Mines Railway train steams upgrade at 90 Below on Lower Bonanza Creek. Engine No. 2 has in tow a box car, four flat cars—one loaded with lumber, and three empties—and combination coach No. 200. The small placer camp in the foreground is preparing for operation. This was a typical scene in the early days of KMR operation.

National Archives of Canada, PA 102890

CHAPTER TWO

TRANSPORTATION AND THE RAILWAY

Among the earlier arrivals in the Yukon Territory was Thomas William O'Brien, an Ontario-born adventurer, who had made a successful transport business in the budding Canadian West—his teams had been in the hire of General Middleton's Column fighting the Riel Rebellion of 1885. In 1887 O'Brien went to the Yukon as a prospector and trader, eventually to become a miner, steamboat operator, newspaper publisher (the *Yukon Sun*), and toll road operator. O'Brien was also an active member of the Yukon Order of Pioneers, for a time serving as president. When the news of Carmack's strike on Bonanza Creek reached Fortymile where O'Brien had been established for a number of years, he and many others were part of the first wave of stakers to reach the Klondike. By late 1897, O'Brien and his partner Billie Moran had built a large warehouse and store under the name of the Yukon Pioneer Trading Company on the bank of the Yukon River in Klondike City, although they still held property at Fortymile and at Circle City, Alaska. The O'Brien Brewing & Malting Company, subtitled the Klondike Brewery, was another partnership later established in Klondike City, coincidentally next-door to the Klondike Mines Railway engine house and O'Brien and Moran's store.

Although Dawson City, except for Government Reserve, had been developed by the private interests of the enterprising Joseph Ladue, Klondike City was from the beginning Crown Land, only leased to individuals. Early on, Klondike City developed an unsavory reputation and was referred to by most Dawsonites as "Lousetown" (historian H.A. Innis wrote in 1933 that in "polite" circles

it was known as Louisette town). For new arrivals, floating down the Yukon River on rafts, scows, and so on, Lousetown and O'Brien and Moran's store was the first evidence of the new boom town to greet their eyes. In 1899, a charter in the name of the Klondike Mines Railway was granted by the Canadian Parliament, and O'Brien's name headed the list of the applicants. Klondike City was to be the northern terminus of the railway.

From the beginning, trails and transportation from the riverboat landings at Klondike City or Dawson City to the camps throughout the goldfield were critical to development of mining. But, good roads to the mines could not be built immediately. In 1897 a scow was used to ferry freight across the Klondike River, from the boat landing at Dawson, and about a mile of road up the Bonanza trail was laid with corduroy. Initially pack horses were used to transport freight. The trail between the corduroy section and Grand Forks was swampy and difficult, while the section from the Forks to the Divide was drier but considerably more steep. By winter, sled-freighting on the Bonanza trail became practical, but the high cost of feed limited the use of horses. During this first winter, dog-teams were used extensively, hauling supplies into the distant camps. To improve freighting, $18,000 of federal government money was spent in 1898 on the road to Grand Forks. The *Klondike Nugget* of July 9, 1898, reported "An immense amount of work and money has been expended on the Bonanza Creek trail this spring and summer, and it is now a first class trail, corduroyed as far as the 70s. Messrs. McConnell,

At the time of the discovery of gold on Rabbit Creek, the area bordering the Yukon River was referred to as the Yukon District of the North-West (now Northwest) Territories, created by Dominion Government order-in-council on July 24, 1895. The Yukon Territory Act was passed by Parliament on June 13, 1898, establishing the Yukon Territory as an entity, separate from the Northwest Territories, with its own governmental institutions, although administered by the Department of the Interior in Ottawa.

Hamilton and Burrell are the promoters, operating a ferry at the mouth of Bonanza".

But the government road into the goldfield was still little more than a trail. Hill M. Henning, a contractor who had already completed a waterworks project in Dawson, saw the problem as an opportunity. In July, 1898, Henning applied to the Yukon Territorial Council for the right-of-way and timber privileges to build a tramway from Dawson City to Grand Forks, and he was referred to William Ogilvie, the territorial commissioner. In September, Ogilvie approved the franchise but refused special privileges, advising Henning to get the consent of the owners of claims over which the roadway would pass,

and that the government would then not step in and interfere with any mutual agreements made. Timber required, however, would have to be cut according to government policies, with a payment of royalties. Henning was issued a permit to cut timber from a plot three miles up the Klondike River valley.

Starting from Klondike City, Henning went to work, hiring about 150 unemployed miners to build the tramway, known then as the Bonanza Tramway. The project attracted little public attention until claim owners made complaints about Henning's crews "slaughtering timber" on Bonanza Creek—wood much needed in the mining operations. By early October, Henning reported

The "Officers of the Grand Lodge of the Yukon Order of Pioneers, Dawson, Y.T. 1910", Thomas William O'Brien seated in the president's chair. Tom was a charter member of the Y.O.O.P. having arrived in the Yukon in 1887. Seated on Tom's right is Robert Henderson, a Y.O.O.P. member since 1894, and considered by many to be the "real" discoverer of gold in the Klondike.
University of British Columbia, Special Collections, Western Miner Collection

Thomas Dufferin Pattullo in 1903 was elected alderman, one of six, of Dawson. In local politics Pattullo would become closely associated with O'Brien in 1904 as secretary of the Yukon Liberals, of which O'Brien was president. Pattullo become Liberal premier of British Columbia in 1933, holding office until 1941.

that the grades and bridges of the roadway to Grand Forks were complete, requiring only the addition of rails to make a complete tramway. "The railway will be of poles, and the cars will have the usual pole tramway wheels". But Henning was in trouble, for he still owed a considerable sum of money to the men who had worked on the road. About mid-October, O'Brien entered the picture with a bail-out and a controlling interest in the tramway. The partnership with Henning would prove to be an embarrassment to O'Brien for years ahead.

For a three-quarter interest—Henning holding the remaining quarter—O'Brien claimed to have paid off $30,000 in debts, $16,000 alone for unpaid wages.

Seeking an official charter from Yukon Council, the newly formed Pioneer Tramway Company made an application, dated October 31, 1898, for a number of concessions including: exclusive right-of-way until September, 1900, for a pole tramway over Bonanza, Dominion, Sulphur, Bear, and Hunker Creeks; freedom to cross all mineral claims; rights to cut, free of stumpage charges, timber and poles required for roadway, bridges, and buildings; right to take up government lands at points along the tramway; and exemption from taxation on the whole operation for a period of three years.

On November 3, 1898, Commissioner Ogilvie replied with a letter to Messrs. Henning & O'Brien stating that

Dominating this view of Klondike City, probably in the spring of 1898, are the warehouse and store belonging to Tom O'Brien and his partner "Billie" Moran. With businesses also at Fortymile and Circle City, Alaska, the partners were among the first to set up shop in the Klondike. Directly above the warehouse is the trail leading overland to Bonanza Creek, a mile and one-half distant. Tom O'Brien, one of many pioneer Yukon entrepreneurs, was a charter member of the Klondike Mines Railway and did his best to make Klondike City its base of operations. The engine house would eventually be built immediately to the right of the warehouse. Note the many tents and cabins of squatters, and the twenty-plus boats and barges tied up on this short stretch of waterfront—the gold rush is on!
Yukon Archives, T.R. Lane Coll'n, 1386

Thomas William O'Brien, Dawson City, circa 1898

British Columbia Records and Archives Service, HP81186

after discussion with Council the application had been granted, but with many limitations. First the company had to assume and pay the indebtedness of Henning incurred on account of the labour "on the said railway". Only then could control over the road, as it then existed, be granted. No monopoly or special privileges could be granted, due regard had to be paid to claim owners, and the company would be liable for any damages. Finally, the letter stated that "...the rights granted are only provisional, subject to ratification by the [federal government] minister".

Whether or not O'Brien and Henning intended to build a tramway in the coming year isn't known, but O'Brien now decided on a very unpopular means of paying off his investment—the Pioneer Tramway would become a toll road. The road was in rough condition, but by early October snow smoothed out the rough spots, and at once it became preferable to the old trail along the twisting bed of Bonanza Creek. O'Brien set up stations with toll collectors and scales, charging packers ten cents per pound for all freight passing over the route. Complaints went unheeded until mid-November when the *Klondike Nugget* under editor Gene Allen took on the fight, bringing O'Brien and the Pioneer Tramway Company to court. It is worth noting that O'Brien was also owner and publisher of a rival newspaper, the *Yukon Sun*; Allen, and his Nugget Express Company which had been subjected to the toll, took up the battle, ostensibly in support of the miners.

Representing the *Klondike Nugget*, in February, 1899, attorneys Pattullo and Ridley won the case, proving that the Yukon Council had no right to grant the Pioneer Tramway Company a franchise. Among Allen's arguments was the definition of a tramway: a tram is a railway car, while a tramway is a horse railway; and as yet neither a tramway nor rails were to be seen. As evidence the *Klondike Nugget* presented a toll receipt for $1.25 addressed Forty Mile, dated November 12, 189_ (sic), from O'Brien & Moran, Klondike City, Circle City, Forty Mile. On February 15, 1899, judgement was passed. The enterprise had plainly been a toll road, and the judge ruled that every dollar made was collected illegally. Permission to build the road had been granted by the local Council which had no power to do so, thus the Pioneer Tramway had no legal charter. In summing up, the judge was quoted, "no ordinance made by the governor in council, or the commissioner in council, shall appropriate any public money, lands, or property of Canada, without authority of parliament".

O'Brien petitioned the Yukon Council to recover money he had invested in the tramway, and in 1902 a committee recommended payment of $35,000 for his losses. In 1903 O'Brien was paid "compensation of $27,000 on account of the claim against the Dominion Government and the Government of the Yukon Territory for the construction of a road from Klondike City to Grand Forks in 1898". In 1906 a final payment of $8000 was made to O'Brien as "full settlement for principal and interest".

A report dated September 20, 1899, from Ogilvie, territorial commissioner, to the federal Minister of the Interior summarized the problems of road development into the goldfield;

> In the valleys of the creeks the miners naturally object to being interfered with in working their claims. To put a road across their claims almost insures its destruction within a few months. To my knowledge three roads have been constructed from Dawson up the valley of Bonanza to The Forks. The first was built in the spring of 1897, and was simply a pack trail. Ere many months it transpired that this road was broken up in places. Of course one interruption blocked the whole road. In the spring of 1898 I am assured that another road was constructed partly on the old site,

and on this the sum of $18,000 was expended. On my arrival in September, 1898, this road was pronounced impassable, or broken up in places, as had been the previous one. In September of 1898, a few weeks after my arrival, a wagon road was constructed up the creek, on which it was intended to put a tramway. This was known as the O'Brien Tramway [also the Bonanza Tramway, but records show the partnership was called the Pioneer Tramway Company]. It was a boon to the country at the time. Legal steps were taken to prevent Mr. O'Brien from collecting toll for passage over his road. These were successful and the result was Mr. O'Brien's connection with it ceased indefinitely. As he was not allowed to collect toll, he naturally gave up taking care of the road, and although the road at the time was pronounced a good one, it is today practically impossible to find more than bits of it here and there, the rest of it being under tailings or washed away in mining operation.

Ogilvie went on to say that any future road up the creeks, although clamored for, would undoubtedly suffer the same fate. It was necessary to cross over 100 claims between the mouth of Bonanza Creek and Grand Forks. The only option was construction of a trunk road following the ridges into the goldfield, with spurs leading down to the various workings along all creeks, and this was done in 1899. Ogilvie also added;

> I understand that Mr. O'Brien has been granted a charter to construct a tramway up the Bonanza Creek from Dawson [the Klondike Mines Railway Charter, granted July 10, 1899]. One of Mr. O'Brien's associates...proposed that I build a wagon road up the valley up the creek, making it wide enough to serve for wagon road and tramway, and that the railway company would make an arrangement with me to recoup the Government for the expense of building the trail.

O'Brien's associate had probably reasoned that official help in laying out the route would have been very helpful, however, Ogilvie declined. The conditions of the Klondike Mines Railway charter demanded that agreements with the creeks' claim-holders for damage compensation be made prior to start of construction;

"BONANZA - STUCK IN THE MUD - 30 BELOW"—probably about 1900. On Lower Bonanza Creek, at claim No. 30 Below, this scene typifies the problems experienced by early goldfield freighters. The teamster is digging out his wagon as his mules, ears laid back, wait passively. It was impossible to maintain roads along the creek bottom, prime mining ground which the miners worked regardless of traffic. Note how the hillside has been stripped of timber, all-important in early labour-intensive mining.

National Archives of Canada, PA 17038

Ogilvie realized this could not be quickly done, and so went on with the urgently-required ridge roads. In days ahead the right-of-way problem would also be a difficult one for the railway. The state of the road situation was exemplified by a report in the November 10, 1899, *Dawson Daily News*: "news from the Forks...The bridges on the old 'tramway' trail are in very bad condition and several valuable horses have already been lost".

Henning would, in September, 1902, apply for authority to build another toll road, this one along the west side of the Yukon River, but the Yukon Council wanted no more of toll roads and denied the right. O'Brien, however had bigger plans.

In July, 1899, he had gone to Ottawa seeking a franchise for a railway from Klondike City to the Forks (referred to in Ogilvie's report). The ever-sniping *Klondike Nugget* snidely headlined:

A Railroad for the Klondike—
Tramless Tom O'Brien the Father of the New Enterprise

Furthermore, "As described to the Nugget the railroad will be narrow gauge, from Klondike City to Grand Forks. The explanation advanced for not bringing the line across the river to Dawson is that it is to be operated, so far as possible, in the interests of the O'Brien & Moran mercantile establishment at Klondike City". Although O'Brien was believed to be the prime mover in the railway proposition, an American entrepreneur, John Hugh Mackenzie, was thought to be closely associated with him. Rumours also claimed negotiations were underway for two locomotives, and that the railway would be operating by fall.

*It is early summer at Klondike City, about 1900. On Klondike Island at mid-distance, the Klondike Mill is already in full operation. This island was privately-owned by the North American Transportation and Trading Company (NAT&TCo), and as such was not permanently settled with residences—the land was low, boggy, and subject to spring flooding. In the foreground is Klondike City; as federal land it was surveyed into streets and lots, but (as can be seen) squatters built cabins wherever an open patch of ground could be found. The long building fronting on the Yukon River is O'Brien and Moran's warehouse, their store just beyond it. In 1902 KMR engine No. 1 would arrive at Klondike City with six flat cars, but not until 1905 would construction of the railway begin. In 1906 the engine house would be built on the near side of O'Brien's warehouse, at 45 degrees to it and backed against the rock wall at right. The steamer **J.P. Light,** owned by Tom O'Brien and partners, is tied up at shore.*

National Archives of Canada, C 16324

CHAPTER THREE

THE KLONDIKE MINES RAILWAY
CHARTER AND EXPECTATIONS
1899/1901

Rumours do not make a railway, nor was O'Brien the only man with a vision. As in all developing regions, entrepreneurs from across the country made bids for the privilege of building a railway into the goldfield. Issues of the *Canada Gazette* for the years 1898 to 1900 list many applications made to the Government of Canada for railway charters, and the granting of a few:

February 23, 1898: An application was made to incorporate the Dawson Electric Railway Company, with powers to generate and sell electricity, to install telegraph and telephone lines, and to build electric railways or tramways within a fifty-mile radius of Dawson City, including along Bonanza and Eldorado Creeks and the Klondike River. Names of the applicants were not given.

November 12, 1898: Unnamed applicants asked Parliament to approve incorporation of a railway leading from Dawson City, up the Klondike River to Hunker Creek, up Hunker Creek, down Dominion Creek to the Indian River, following it to the Yukon River, and finally down the Yukon River back to Dawson City. The railway would also have branch lines. The applicants were represented by D.G. MacDonell of Vancouver.

November 19, 1898: The British Yukon Mining, Trading and Transportation Company applied to Parliament for an Act to authorize construction of a railway from Fort Selkirk to Dawson, then westerly. Other lines would also be built and the company name would be changed to British Yukon Railway Company. Representing the company was Chrysler and Bethune of Ottawa. This was in fact part of the White Pass and Yukon organization.

December 17, 1898: Unnamed applicants asked Parliament to grant rights to build a railway or tramway from Klondike City, up Bonanza Creek, down Dominion Creek to the Indian River and on to the Yukon River; the Yukon would be followed back to Klondike City. Representation was by MacCraken, Henderson and McGiverin of Ottawa. This is the route eventually specified in the Klondike Mines Railway's charter, and although unnamed, the applicants did include O'Brien.

January 7, 1899: Unnamed applicants asked Parliament to approve incorporation of a railway which will lead from Klondike City, up Bonanza Creek to Sulphur Creek and the Indian River, with branch lines in the vicinity. The applicants were represented by Eugene Lafontaine of Montreal.

February 4, 1899: Unnamed applicants applied to Parliament to approve incorporation of a railway which would run from Dawson to Grand Forks, and up to the headwaters of Dominion and Sulphur Creeks. The applicants were represented by Eberts and Taylor of Victoria. (D.M. Eberts was the attorney-general of the B.C. legislature).

April 15, 1899: Notice was given that the Yukon Mining, Trading and Transportation Company (Foreign) would apply to Parliament to revive the Act of the last session of 1897 incorporating the company, and to extend the time limit for construction of the railway. Representation was by MacCraken, Henderson, and McGiverin, Ottawa.

Harold Buchanan McGiverin, of the firm mentioned in the last application, was an up-and-coming lawyer who had been the junior partner in the law firm of MacCraken, Henderson and McGiverin of Ottawa. He now established the new firm of McGiverin, Haydon, and Greig which would become a very influential force in the Klondike. With the correct political connections he counseled many companies, opened doors for the granting of charters, and became director on the boards of many newly-chartered concerns. The record shows that both Treadgold and J.W. Boyle had used McGiverin's power and influence in obtaining Klondike mining concessions from the Ottawa government. McGiverin's advertisement running in the April 10, 1900, issue of the *Yukon Sun* read:

H.B. McGiverin -
solicitor, barrister; and parliamentary
departmental agent.
19 Elgin Street, Ottawa.

O'Brien and company had applied for a railway charter on December 17, 1898, it was granted in early July, 1899, and representation was by the new law firm.

On July 10, 1899, Canada Parliament assented to the incorporation of the Klondike Mines Railway in the names of Thomas William O'Brien of Dawson City, James Arthur Seybold of Ottawa, William D. Ross of New Glasgow, Nova Scotia, and Llewellyn N. Bate and Harold Buchanan McGiverin of Ottawa. Seybold was with the local firm, Ottawa Fire Proof Supply Company, Ross was a banker, and Bate was partner in a family grocery store called Bate & Company; all three men appear to have been entrepreneurs. Like O'Brien and McGiverin, none was wealthy enough to finance

construction of the railway by himself, and it seems likely that the three eastern partners were business acquaintances of McGiverin. In years ahead, O'Brien, Seybold, and all three of the law firm partners (McGiverin, Haydon, and Greig) would serve as executives of the railway company.

The Klondike Mines Railway charter described the route of the railway;

> ...from Klondike City along the Klondike River to Bonanza Creek, thence along Bonanza Creek to the Divide, thence along the Divide by the most feasible route to Dominion Creek, thence along Dominion Creek to the Indian River, thence along the Indian River to the Yukon River, and thence along the Yukon River to Dawson City.

That the charter listed Dawson City instead of Klondike City as the return terminus in this loop circuit was probably the work of McGiverin, blocking entry to the chief river port by other applicants. O'Brien, who controlled much of the Klondike City waterfront, had no

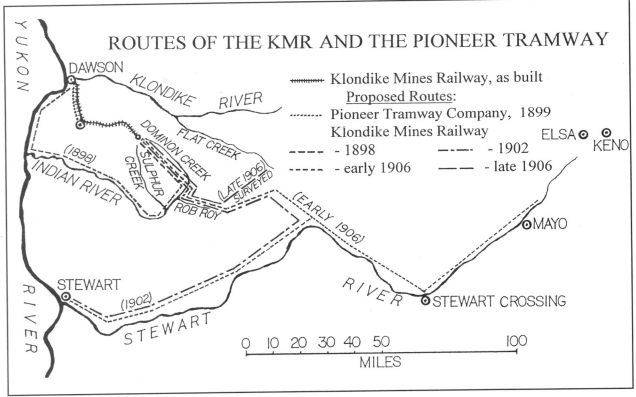

In the early years there were several routes proposed for the KMR. From the foot of Sulphur Creek, all four routes went southeast up Rob Roy, then diverged in four different directions. The 1898 route looped back along Indian River and the Yukon River to Dawson, the 1902 route went down the Stewart River to the Yukon River, the early 1906 route headed for Mayo, and even after construction was finished in 1906, a route was surveyed northeast to the head of Flat Creek.

intention of including Dawson City as the railway's northern terminus. The charter also spoke of the Klondike Mines Railway's right to build and operate tramways or railways on other creeks adjacent to its line. Among a number of other concessions, the company was also granted the right to develop telegraph and telephone services in the district covered by the railway. The terms of the statute initially limited capitalization to one million dollars. Additionally, if construction of the railway had not commenced, and if 15 percent of the capital was not expended by July 10, 1901, the enactment would be termed null and void; similarly it was required that the railway be completed and in operation by July 10, 1904.

The White Pass and Yukon Route was reported, in September, 1899, still planning an extension of its railway from Whitehorse to Selkirk. This northern terminus, defined in a charter two years earlier, might explain the choice of the "loop" circuit outlined in the Klondike Mines Railway charter; it effectively cut off any other railway's approach along the east bank of the Yukon River into Dawson City. O'Brien swung into action on October 3, 1899, applying to the Office of Crown Lands, on behalf of the Klondike Mines Railway, for;

> ...a 10-year lease on part of the waterfront at Klondike City for building wharves, quays, docks, for the purpose of the company's business. The part of the said waterfront applied for being 300 feet on the Yukon River opposite lots 6, 7, 8, 9, 10, and 11 in Block 1 of Klondike City.

A reply dated October 5 stated that lots 10 and 11 had already been applied for by others, and only lots 6 to 9 could be considered. There is little doubt that O'Brien did envision great personal benefit from both riverboat and railway terminals at his front door.

Newspapers frequently head-lined railway proposals, and on November 20, 1899, the **Dawson Daily News** read;

> There is a need for a railway to the Klondike. A railway between Fort Selkirk and Dawson is seen by a syndicate of British capitalists who have applied to parliament of Canada for an act to authorize them to construct and operate a line from Fort Selkirk to Dawson, thence westerly to the 141 standard meridian. The name of the company is the British Yukon Mining and Trading and Transportation Company...

—the original charter granted to the builders of the railway of the White Pass and Yukon Route.

Late in 1899 a survey plan of the Klondike Mines Railway route, from Klondike City to Grand Forks, was filed with the Board of Railway Commissioners in Ottawa; this survey prepared by O'Brien would be much criticized and modified before rail would ever reach "the Forks". On January 2, 1900, the **Yukon Sun** reported that Mr. T.W. O'Brien had left "for Ottawa on business with reference to his proposed railway", but nothing at all was done in 1900 towards starting of construction. The company was still trying to find backers to finance the road. O'Brien might have felt some satisfaction when in March and April, newspapers (rivals of the **Klondike Nugget**) noted that;

> ...the Nugget's Gene Allen has left town, whereabouts unknown, under suspicion of embezzlement regarding his Nugget Express Company...

and

> Gene Allen of the Klondike Daily Nugget and the Klondike Semi-Weekly Nugget was said to be in $30,000 debt primarily because of his Nugget Express Company. He is presently mushing to Nome, leaving behind the rest of his visible express assets: nine dogs (three in poor health), and his book accounts.

Harold Buchanan McGiverin, Ottawa, about 1910.
National Archives of Canada, PA 42505

*Tied up at the Klondike City waterfront, about 1901, are three steamboats:
the **Tyrrell** on the right, the **Lightning** on the left, and the **J.P. Light** behind.
O'Brien, who had a waterfront business and property in Klondike City, had
hopes of controlling shipping with his steamers, via the railway, into the
goldfield. He wanted Klondike City to be the northern terminus of the
railway, but competition from Dawson merchants, docks in Dawson, and the
powerful White Pass forced the railway into making Dawson the business
terminus while Klondike City became the railway's maintenance centre.*
Yukon Archives, VPL Coll'n, 2162

The November 9, 1901, issue of the *Canada Gazette* listed;
an application will be made to Parliament for a charter in
the name of The Dawson White Horse Navigation
Company (Limited) for the business of operating steamships
and merchandising. Applicants are: Edward M. Sullivan,
miner, Donald W. Davis, gentleman, Thomas W. O'Brien,
merchant, Roy B. Woodson, broker, and Charles G. Marsh,
gentleman, filed by solicitors Tabor, Walsh, and Hulme in
Dawson, through the agent for the solicitors in Ottawa,
H.B. McGiverin
—the omnipresent Mr. McGiverin.

A believer in diversification, O'Brien was not about to wait patiently for the Klondike Mines Railway to generate income. Victoria's *Daily Colonist* of July 4, 1900, read;

> A new shipping company to operate on the Yukon River has been formed by a syndicate headed by "Black" Sullivan and Tom O'Brien, proprietor of the Yukon Sun. Purchased from the British America Company were three sternwheelers: the Lightning and another for the upper river, and the Tyrrell for the lower river.

The new company was the Dawson White Horse Navigation Company—O'Brien's partner (actually, one of four other partners), Edward M. "Black" Sullivan, was a miner from Fortymile and an old acquaintance who in 1897 was described by writer E. Hazzard Wells as "a whiskey dealer". The British-America Corporation had been active on the Yukon River only during the 1899 season, and finding competition too fierce, sold its assets. The other steamer not named in the *Daily Colonist* report was the *J.P. Light*. Three new barges, the *Jean*, the *Louise*, and the *Margaret* (possibly named after O'Brien's youngest child), were built for the company. By August, a 40 x 150-foot warehouse had been built, clad in galvanized sheet metal, with a floating dock—said to the biggest on the river—on the Dawson waterfront. The syndicate would apply for a charter in late 1901, although the steamers were at work in the summer of 1900.

This new enterprise was not destined to be a money-maker. The White Pass monopolized shipping on the upper river, and on the lower river the NAT&TCo. (North American Transportation and Trading Company) and Northern Commercial Company, each with a large fleet of steamers, effectively overwhelmed most of the independent operators. While the *J.P. Light* and the *Tyrrell* remained with O'Brien and company until about 1904, the *Lightning* and the barge *Margaret* were sold in 1903 to James A. Williams of the Coal Creek Coal Company, and later to Dr. Grant of the Sourdough Coal Company, for hauling coal from the mines on Coal Creek. Until 1919 the *Lightning* was registered to the Northern Light, Power and Coal Company, successor to the Sourdough Coal Company.

While much had been made of O'Brien's Pioneer Tramway fiasco, O'Brien remained a popular man, and in August, 1900, a petition was circulated asking him and F.C. Wade to become candidates for Yukon Council.

In a letter from Commissioner Ogilvie to the Minister of the Interior dated March 8, 1901, he noted that T.W.

O'Brien recently gave the office of the Commissioner plans of the railway showing Klondike City as the terminus. The plans had been approved by the Department of Railways, but Ogilvie objected to the stated terminus saying that Klondike City had little land, no wharves, and no warehouses built while Dawson City had over one-half mile of steamboat landing. Later, the greater part of the route presented by O'Brien (covering only Klondike City to Grand Forks) would prove unacceptable to claim holders along Bonanza Creek, and would be revised several times before construction was finished. The March 14, 1901, issue of the *Klondike Nugget* opened with a story about the charter of the Klondike Mines Railway, and quoted an August 27, 1900, memorandum from the Minister of the Interior which stated that company intended to file new plans and profiles for a right-of-way on higher ground to avoid interference with creek claims, and to deliver a new line description. Somewhat more tolerant of O'Brien, the *Klondike Nugget* now listed George Allen as publisher. Protests from miners objecting to the location of the right-of-way had reached Ottawa, and the government reacted. A letter dated May 21, 1901, from the Secretary of Railways and Canals to the Department of the Interior (administration of the Yukon Territory) noted: "a portion of the railroad extending from Klondike City to Grand Forks, a distance of about $11\frac{1}{2}$ miles, has been located; plans, profiles, and a Book of References, etc., are on file here where they were filed on March 28, 1900". The Department of the Interior noted that the first plan, filed by O'Brien, showed a route following the Bonanza Creek bottom which the Department considered an unacceptable route—the grade would have to follow the hillsides to avoid interference with mining operations. O'Brien firmly objected saying, "the Klondike Mines Railway is unwilling to build except along the creek bottom...".

With the time limit for expenditures imposed in the charter approaching, the railway's directors asked Canada Parliament for an extension, which was granted; on May 23, 1901, the company was allowed a further two years for expending 15% of the capital stock, and five years for completing the railway. This apparent leniency was commonly extended to many other railways in the making.

A new route plan for the Klondike Mines Railway was filed by solicitor McGiverin, who wrote the Minister of the Interior, stating that an order-in-council dated September 4, 1900, had approved the planned rail route and granted the right-of-way, and that a patent would be granted. McGiverin asked assurance that the patent be granted. However even the new plan would raise objections, and in 1905 the right-of-way was once more challenged. The Minister had been unable to give McGiverin the assurance he wanted.

O'Brien was a very active businessman, still making plans for the development of the railway terminus at Klondike City, and in June he applied once again for leases on lots 1 to 5, and lots 6 to 9, along the Yukon River waterfront. Looking ahead to increased traffic leading from Dawson City to Klondike City, he and his associates bought the Klondike River toll bridge for $4000 and opened it to free passage. Partners in the venture included Joseph Segbers, manager of the Klondike Mill Company and proprietor of the Yukonia Hotel, and John R. Howard.

A letter dated July 16, 1901, from the Director of (Railway) Surveys to Commissioner Ross summarized the state of affairs. He noted that the present Klondike Mines Railway right-of-way interfered on its right limit (west side) of Bonanza Creek with very few claims being worked, but crossed numerous undeveloped claims. The left limit of the right-of-way would interfere with a larger number of working claims, from tailings, pumping plants, and so on. Also, the railway would cross and re-cross the present wagon road a number of times. From an engineering point-of-view it would be much cheaper and shorter to build along the creek bottom, but relocation, with extensive trestle work, was advised. The Klondike Mines Railway also asked for yard and station ground at 8 and 9 Above Discovery (the upper, east end of Grand Forks), and for 14-1/2 acres on the banks of the Klondike River east of Klondike City (near the junction of Bonanza Creek with the Klondike River) for a wye site. Acquisition of land at the latter site would be a problem since it was settled by many squatters who had rights in applying for land ownership, but more importantly the ground was within the boundaries of placer mining claims presently in good standing.

By mid-summer of 1901, two years after having been granted a charter, the Klondike Mines Railway was still nothing more concrete than a bulky file in Ottawa and a proposed route through the Klondike goldfield.

CHAPTER FOUR

PROMOTION, HAWKINS ARRIVES
1901/1902

As the charter of the Klondike Mines Railway languished, activity on another railway to the south had proceeded post haste. Under three separate charters granted by the Government of the United States, the Province of British Columbia, and the Government of Canada, the railway of the White Pass and Yukon Route (the White Pass) had been pushed from Skagway, Alaska, through the north-west corner of British Columbia, to the Yukon Territory. The White Pass railway was built in three stages, and the first, the Skagway to Bennett section, was completed on July 5, 1899. Until then, much freight bound for the Klondike had come by way of either Brackett's wagon road over the White Pass, or over the Chilkoot Pass, both routes converging on Lake Bennett. There, steamboats transferred cargoes via Bennett Lake, Nares Lake, Tagish Lake, and Marsh Lake (referred to as the upper lakes) to reach Canyon City; at Canyon City all freight and passengers were unloaded and forwarded over a five-mile tramway, which by-passed the treacherous waters of Miles Canyon and the Whitehorse Rapids, to reach the burgeoning village of Whitehorse.

Whitehorse grew at the lower end of the rapids, and this became the northern terminus of the White Pass railway, and the transfer point to all northbound steamboats. On July 8, 1900, the White Pass completed the second section of track work between Whitehorse and Carcross (called Caribou, or Caribou Crossing, at that time), located on the short river connecting Bennett Lake with Nares Lake. However, steamboats were still needed to transfer freight and passengers between Bennett and Carcross until July 29, 1900, when the final, third, section of the railway along Bennett Lake was finished. With the completion of the 110-mile railway, almost all of the upper lakes steamboat traffic, except to Atlin, ended.

As the White Pass railway was being built, the company had bought out transportation opposition, including the Brackett wagon road, the Chilkoot Pass tramlines, the

Whitehorse tramway, and the Canadian Development Company, all with the intent of eliminating competition.

During the summer shipping seasons of 1898 to 1900, a considerable tonnage of freight reached the Klondike via the lower Yukon River route. From St. Michael, at the mouth of the Yukon River on the coast of western Alaska, several well-organized, long-established, trading companies operated many steamers through Alaska into the Yukon Territory. By this route freight was shipped from Seattle, Victoria, and Vancouver by steamships up the British Columbia and Alaska coastline, at least 1800 sailing miles farther north than Skagway, and then up the Yukon River from St. Michael by sternwheeler for another 1500 miles to Dawson. The White Pass route, by railway and sternwheelers from Skagway to Dawson, was in total about 500 miles. The completion of the railway of the White Pass meant significantly lower freight rates, much shorter in-transit time of freight, and the capabilities for hauling far greater tonnage during the short shipping season on the upper Yukon River.

The completion of the White Pass railway was welcomed by O'Brien and company. Besides not yet having found investors, the charter members of the Klondike Mines Railway were aware that bringing in the thousands of tons of supplies prior to the completion of the White Pass would have been prohibitively expensive. Heavy equipment could now be brought to the Klondike quickly and more cheaply, and since construction of the railway was completed, the White Pass also had a number of excess pieces of rolling stock in which the promoters were interested. Furthermore, a surplus of railway construction talent was also now available.

Chief engineer during construction of the White Pass railway was Erastus Corning Hawkins, a civil engineer, who on completion of the road became general manager of operations for the White Pass. He had worked closely with Michael J. Heney who had been the construction contractor of the whole project, and manager of interim transportation. Heney was now unemployed, but financially comfortable. In late July, 1901, Hawkins, Heney, and Samuel Haughton Graves, president of the White Pass, visited Dawson, staying a few days. The visit aroused little comment at the time, but on September 3, 1901, the *Klondike Nugget* announced Hawkins' resignation from his position as general manager of the White Pass.

Hawkins returned to Dawson again in late September, and confirmed his resignation, saying he was "here working on a proposition for construction of a railway to the Forks and Eldorado Creek"; he stayed a few days. Victoria's *Daily Colonist* of Tuesday, October 10, 1901, reported;

> Mr. E.C. Hawkins, formerly general manager of the White Pass and Yukon Route, has secured an option on the O'Brien charter for a railway from Dawson to Grand Forks, Eldorado and Bonanza Creeks, and he says he will have the railway in operation by September next. Construction will start at Klondike City, where the holders of the charter have valuable waterfront rights, and will pass through the recently-discovered coal lands which will supply fuel for the locomotives. In time the road will be extended to all the creeks in the district.

The coal lands referred to were in the Tantalus area along the Yukon River, ten miles below Five Finger Rapids—hardly on the rail line. The *Klondike Nugget* added;

> Hawkins has secured an option on the O'Brien franchise depositing the sum of $40,000 in escrow, pending the consummation of further arrangements...steam instead of electricity will be used on the Klondike Creeks Railway. Arrangements have already been made for an engine and rails. Mr. Hawkins is going to Ottawa to secure the right-of-way directly, without being liable to the claim-owners for indemnity.

Hawkins had already formed the Hawkins Construction Company with the head office in Seattle, at the Dexter Horton Bank Building, where a year earlier Hawkins had been listed only as a civil engineer. A document dated March 21, 1905, on file at the Dawson Museum, indicates there was some friction in organizing the Hawkins Construction Company, and that Hawkins had for unknown reasons excluded O'Brien from the list of stock holders in the new construction company. The general plan was, of course, for Hawkins and his associates to promote the sale of Klondike Mines Railway stock, and then profit in the building of the railway.

With the release of information connecting Hawkins with the Klondike Mines Railway, rumours appeared in outside newspapers. The *Vancouver Province* of November 14, 1901, reported;

> It was stated this afternoon, on good authority, that the firm of Messrs. McLean Brothers of this city, contractors for the Chilliwak (sic) dykes and other large government works, are interested in the construction of a new railway line which will be built in the Klondike early next season. This winter all the preliminary arrangements will be made, and it is expected that everything will be in readiness for starting of work on the road, so that it will be finished and in good working order next season. The line will be 12 miles in length and it is estimated that it will cost in the vicinity of $600,000. The railroad is the same in which E.C. Hawkins, late president and general manager of the WP&YR, is interested. It will be built under the charter granted to Thomas O'Brien of Dawson.

The *Klondike Nugget* further embellished the rumour,

> Vancouver; McLean Brothers announce they will commence work on the Klondike Creeks Railway early in the spring.... The main line will be built up Bonanza and Eldorado, across the divide to Indian River, subsequently extending to the Stewart River and on to the mouth of the Pelly River. The McLean Brothers have been associated with Mackenzie & Mann, and talk of links with their lines would make this an all-Canadian route.

All of this was only speculation, and similar and wilder stories would crop up during the next five years.

Meanwhile, the energetic O'Brien now surprised Dawson with another application for a charter; the January 11, 1902, issue of the *Canada Gazette* included a notice of application to Parliament for incorporation (charter) of The Dawson City Electric Railway Company (Limited), with the right to organize a power company, to build rail lines within a three-mile radius of Dawson, to build a bridge over the Klondike River, and to operate an electric railway or tramway with the head office in Dawson. The solicitor was, of course, H.B. McGiverin. In July, O'Brien applied to the Yukon Council for a franchise to operate the street car system in the area.

The year 1902 looked promising for concrete effort towards construction of the Klondike Mines Railway, as McGiverin, O'Brien, and Hawkins made news. On January 6, McGiverin applied for waterfront on the Yukon River in Klondike City, asking for a total frontage of 550 feet, at $5 per foot rental. The *Daily Klondike Nugget* of January 17 reported that O'Brien had received a telegram from Hawkins, McGiverin, and Tabor in

Ottawa saying the Canadian Bank of Commerce would release $10,000 held in escrow for transfer to the Klondike Mines Railway. O'Brien expected a spur from the railway would run up Victoria Gulch to a gold-quartz prospect there. The line would also run towards the Stewart River, where there was low-grade placer ground, and on to the Indian River valley, where there were also other quartz prospects. A letter dated January 18 from Clifford Sifton, Minister of the Interior, to H.B. McGiverin noted that route plans and profiles provided by the Klondike Mines Railway had been approved by Commissioner Ross, and that land use was authorized, allowing beginning of construction.

On January 20, Hawkins forwarded a letter to the Department of Railways and Canals including a contract signed between the Klondike Mines Railway and the Hawkins Construction Company, Limited, providing for the construction and equipment of a railway from Klondike City to Grand Forks, distance about 13 miles. McGiverin, still wary of right-of-way problems, asked the Minister of the Interior to investigate beforehand the Klondike Mines Railway's land purchase applications to "save complications".

Hawkins' full plan was revealed when, on Thursday, February 17, 1902, the *Klondike Nugget* analyzed a prospectus developed by Hawkins. The headline read:

Prospectus Reaches Dawson
Passenger Fare to be $2 to Grand Forks - Freight Charges in Proportion - Will be Completed 12 Miles by July 1.

Since no copies of the prospectus survive today, the *Nugget's* detailed commentary is the best available alternative; the whole story as it appeared is reproduced in Appendix A.

The story noted the essential points: on September 25, 1901, an agreement between Hawkins and the provisional directors (the five charter members) of the Klondike Mines Railway provided for construction and operation of "a railway" between Dawson and the Forks, at the junction of Bonanza Creek and Eldorado Creek—no immediate plan was given for extension of the line beyond the Forks. The *Nugget* contradicted itself in saying that this first section of railway, twelve miles to the Forks, was to be completed before July, 1903, and later September 1, 1902. It was clear, however, that as soon as the first section was completed, arrangements would be made to extend the railway another twenty miles south-easterly.

The directors agreed for the consideration of $18,000 cash and 2,200 shares of the capital stock of the company of the par value of $222,000, to furnish the right of way, terminal grounds, etc., and subsequently to hold a meeting in Ottawa for the purpose of transferring to Mr. Hawkins the shares, stock and all rights, title and interest of the charter possessed by them, to elect new officers and pass a bylaw changing the head office of the company from Ottawa to Dawson.

In compliance with the terms of the agreement Hawkins had already secured subscribers of 2,500 shares of stock and deposited in the Canadian Bank of Commerce in Ottawa $25,000;

> The agreement...was supplemented by a formal contract approved by the board of directors January 10, 1902, in accordance with which a construction company was incorporated and a contract entered into for the building of the road, furnishing the necessary buildings, equipment and all appurtenances, the construction company to accept shares of the company's stock in payment therefore. This stock of the par value of $100 a share is offered to investors at $80 a share and the belief is ventured that when the road has reached the Forks the stock will be above par. The capital for the first section of the road is $1,000,000, divided into 10,000 shares of $100 each, is fully paid up and non-assessable.

One of the principal sources of revenue was expected to be passenger traffic; an estimated 300 patrons per day and special excursions would yield a yearly revenue of $220,000. A huge business was also seen in the shipping of fuel and mining timbers into the goldfield, since the hillsides for miles in the vicinity of the creeks had been practically denuded of timber for some time. In 1900 more than 100,000 cords of fuel and timbers were consumed on Eldorado and Bonanza and their tributaries. Annual revenue for haulage of cordwood alone was estimated at $160,000 and lumber of all kinds would generate another $16,000. Revenue from freighting merchandise was estimated at $142,000 and various other earnings at $37,000 for an estimated total of $575,000 in yearly earnings;

> The total expense of operation, including general expenses, is estimated at $245,000, which deducted from the estimated earnings, leaves a surplus of $330,000 upon a capital stock of $1,000,000 and it is considered by Hawkins safer to assume that the road will pay an annual dividend of at least 25 percent.

The **Klondike Nugget** concluded this highly optimistic report saying that Hawkins would arrive in Dawson over the ice next month, that actual work of construction would begin at the earliest possible opportunity, and the building of the road would "give an impetus to business in general second only to the days of '98".

A notice placed in the March 15, 1902, **Canada Gazette** by McGiverin called for a meeting of the shareholders of the Klondike Mines Railway to request parliamentary authorization for increasing capital stock from $1,000,000 to $2,500,000. A petition by the company to the Parliament of Canada was consented to on May 15th, 1902, allowing the increase. Additionally the loop route first described was dropped; the road would now be constructed as an "extension of its railway from a point at or near Grand Forks to the Stewart River, and thence to a point at or near the source of the Stewart River and to a point at or near the entrance of the said river into the Yukon River".

The proposed routes had not been surveyed, simply scouted, possibly by O'Brien himself. If the amendment correctly stated the railway's latest intent, the mileage of the road would be greatly increased. The loop circuit first proposed, going no farther south than the Indian River, measured approximately 130 miles. Still originating at Klondike City but running as far south as the Stewart River, the revised route would reach the Stewart at its confluence with the Yukon River, 60 miles upstream from Klondike City; mileage of this route would have measured at least 200 miles. It appears that at this stage the railway had already firmly defined only the Klondike City to Grand Forks section.

On May 13, 1902, O'Brien got bad press again when it was reported fees charged for use of his toll bridge had angered a number of people, and a petition was being circulated to question the legality of the operation; O'Brien and his associates had bought the bridge in 1901 and announced at that time that the bridge would be open to free passage.

In Skagway, on May 15, Hawkins told reporters that 10,000 tons of equipment for the railway would move by June 1, and that there would be plenty of work for men. Curiously, the report referred to the railway as "the Creek Railway". A day later, 141 men from Seattle were said to have arrived at Skagway, bound for work on the railway. On May 31, 1902, O'Brien spoke confidently to **Dawson Daily News** reporters, who wrote;

...everything is in readiness for the road grading as soon as scrapers, horses, and general grading equipment comes from Whitehorse. While it has been appearing as though we have done little at this end, says Mr. O'Brien, we have no equipment with which to grade. Railroads cannot be built simply with picks and shovels...we must wait for the river to open. All the rails for the first 23 miles have been at Whitehorse for some time. ...and I suppose that scrapers and everything of that kind also is there. Contracts have been let for sufficient ties to build through to Indian River...and I should not be surprised if we build that far this summer. We shall get at least as far as the summit. Captain Campbell has the contract to get out 30,000 ties and N.A.T.&T. has a contract to get out 85,000. The N.A.T.&T. has 3,000 ties ready. I have not heard from Mr. Hawkins, general manager, of late, and don't know exactly where he is, but expect he will be here soon.

O'Brien was never at a loss for words when speaking to reporters.

Yukon Territorial Commissioner, James Hamilton Ross, who had recently come from Victoria and Seattle, was told by Michael Heney, the grading contractor, that the Klondike Mines Railway would begin construction shortly. In conversation with Hawkins, general manager and chief promoter of the road, Ross learned the Canadian Bank of Commerce had underwritten one million dollars worth of bonds for work, and that Heney, no longer affiliated with the White Pass and Yukon Route, was expected to grade forty miles that year, and another forty the next. While Heney may have initially been involved in plans to build the road, it is likely he was only a stock-holder in the Hawkins Construction Company, and in fact he had nothing to with the eventual construction. Another rumour later that month had Heney as contractor in construction of a standard gauge railway, the proposed Valdez, Copper River and Yukon Railroad Company, running an all-American route to the Klondike.

Also in June, William White, of White, McCaul & Davey, local solicitors for the Klondike Mines Railway, had received a telegram from Hawkins authorizing the appointment of John W. Astley as chief construction engineer. Astley had already started on the Klondike City to Grand Forks section, and would locate a line to King Solomon Dome. He had been in the Dawson area for some time and was junior member of the firm of Jephson & Astley, Dominion Land Surveyors and mining engineers. On behalf of the railway White also applied for purchase of 14.61 acres of land for railway repair shop, to be located on Lot 265, Group 2 (near the Ogilvie

Bridge) east of Klondike City. This site would become the location of the railway's only wye at the northern end of the line. While Astley surveyed the route of the railway, Alfred A. Williams, formerly in the employ of the White Pass with Hawkins, was appointed chief engineer of the Klondike Mines Railway. In Seattle in mid-June, awaiting Hawkins' arrival, Williams assured reporters;

> The first spike is expected to be driven June the 29th. The stock is practically all disposed of and we have sufficient backing by Ottawa and Chicago capitalists to carry the work through without a break. It is expected the first section will be in operation by September 1st.

Wishful thinking!

In sessions of the Yukon Council in July, two applications for franchises to operate street railways in Dawson were discussed, but a decision was deferred pending the arrival of Hawkins, who had objected to any such competition. Still in Seattle, Hawkins was expected to further advise Council upon his arrival. One of the street railway applicants was not named, the other was "O'Brien, Bruce, et al". Was O'Brien showing displeasure over not having been included in the Hawkins Construction Company?

In August, 1902, the *Valdez Prospector* circulated a new rumour, that "the Valdez, Copper River & Yukon Railroad has secured control of the Hawkins road, or as it is better known, the 'Dawson and Indian River' road. This road is to start from Dawson and will run to the Indian River country, a distance of 80 miles toward the American territory...". Not only did reporters have the name of the railway badly mangled, they also exhibited poor knowledge of geography. The *Dawson Daily News* of August 8, 1902, quickly dispelled the nonsense saying, "A rumour started by the Valdez contractor, Helm, implied that the 'Creeks Railway' would be sold out to the 'Valdez Road' is false". But the *Dawson Daily News* then contributed a new rumour saying Williams, former surveyor of the White Pass, would survey the Creeks Road and then move on to survey the Valdez Road.

In early August, Yukon Council discussed the terms of a franchise for the entry of the Klondike Mines Railway into Dawson City, but no decisions were made since Hawkins, who was to have been present, had not yet arrived in town. He had on August 6, 1902, signed another contract for the Hawkins Construction Company, Limited, for railway construction and supply of equipment. On August 30, Hawkins finally arrived, but at first declined to comment to reporters. However, he did say that the company had earlier let a contract for

railway ties, and 40,000 were now stacked up at the Klondike Mill. Hawkins' reticence was explained a few days later when he was interviewed by local newspapers.

The September 1, 1902, *Klondike Nugget*, explained Hawkins' reasons for the delay in construction of the Klondike Mines Railway. In Ottawa until May, dealing with legislators for the increase of capitalization originally allowed under the charter, Hawkins then unavoidably spent considerable time in New York and Chicago before travelling to the west coast, and then back east again, all in attempts to organize finances. While Canadian government officials, in particular Commissioner Ross, had been most co-operative, the much-subdued Hawkins ran into one most unexpected stumbling block;

> It might surprise you if I told you that one of my greatest difficulties in the east was in overcoming the prejudice against the name of our company, the Klondike Mines Railway. The fact is the name is a hoodoo and if there had been any other way of changing it except by act of parliament I would have renamed it long ago. You see it associates mining with railroading and the last thing an eastern investor or a firm of brokers wants to hear of is a Klondike mine. Several years ago when the charter was first procured it was all right, but it is different now. The greatest calamity that has ever happened to this country was the unloading during the boom days on the eastern market of a lot of worthless wildcat properties, not one of which ever returned a dollar on the investment made. Anything pertaining to mining in the Klondike the investors are shy of, and will not touch at all. I have personal friends who have every confidence in my judgement tell me to recommend anything but Klondike securities and they would handle them. I could have floated any old sort of a scheme in Mexico, in the southern states or even in some of the revolutionary South American states quicker and with less effort than I have this, and one cannot write enough literature to alter their opinions.

Hawkins then went on to reiterate the need for the railway, and its benefits, that some equipment would likely be shipped soon, but that it was too late to begin construction this year. In response to concerns about railway service into Dawson, Hawkins stated emphatically that his plan included a bridge over the Klondike River, and extra trackage into Dawson. Other rival companies had applied for a franchise for a street car railway in Dawson, and this was opposed by Hawkins who then asked Council for a deferment of decision pending his arrival here. The railway would put a request for its franchise before Council.

With this disclosure by Hawkins, the nature of his contract with the railway became more clear. He was to build only the section between Dawson City and Grand Forks, and it is clearly evident he had taken on the role of promoter also, soliciting investors to generate the necessary cash. It is certain that the original charter members had only minimal cash in the company, expecting others to take the risks—typical of other such ventures.

Two quartz miners, George Campbell and his son-in-law H.O. Fleming announced they were tired of waiting for the Klondike Mines Railway, and would apply to Ottawa for a charter of their own.

In early September the *Dawson Daily News* gave details of the reimbursement to O'Brien in respect to his Pioneer Tramway of 1898;

> The committee of the Council, having in charge the petition of Thos. O'Brien regarding the tramway which flourished in the early history of the camp, had spent much time studying books, vouchers, papers pertaining to construction of the tramway, its cost of maintenance, and the profits derived from its operation, and they recommended that Mr. O'Brien be indemnified for the two-and-one-half months the road was not in operation, at the rate of $6000 per month = $15,000.

Council also recommended that;

> ...he be paid an additional $12,000 for expenses incurred in construction of the grade, bridges, and culverts which the public afterward appropriated for its own use. The committee considers that the government really owes Mr. O'Brien $35,000, but they only recommend $27,000. The recommendation of the committee is not equal to payment, as the appropriation will have to be voted upon. The report was adopted unanimously.

Following this recommendation, O'Brien was paid $27,000 "on account of claim against the Dominion Government and the Government of the Yukon Territory for the construction of a road from Klondike to Grand Forks in 1898". Not until 1906 was the balance of $8,000 paid "in full settlement for principal and interest for the construction of a road from the Klondike River to Grand Forks". The Department of the Interior had accepted absolute blame for the demise of the operation.

O'Brien's partner in the tramway scheme, Hill M. Henning petitioned Council in September, 1902, for "a right and privilege of constructing a toll road from West Dawson along the left bank of the Yukon River to Swede Creek and other creeks in the Fortymile area". An attempt was made to avoid calling the subject of Henning's petition a toll road, but Council, badly burned once, would not approve the venture.

In spite of his difficulties, Hawkins pushed on, applying to the Crown Timber and Land Agent for an amendment to an original application to include only Lots 1 to 8 of Block 1 (in Klondike City), and to ask for a waiver of the rental fee until the 1903 season. The amendment was approved and a waiver of the rental fees was allowed until May 1, 1903. Hawkins, identified now as general manager of the railway, also asked for use of the 66-foot-wide street laid through the bed of Bonanza Creek at the town site of Grand Forks (Bonanza) for the railway tracks; Hawkins did not wish to use city lots. The previously chosen station grounds were adequate there (on 8 and 9 Above on Bonanza). Hawkins also began assembling supplies and equipment for construction start-up. On leaving Dawson in mid-September, Hawkins reiterated his many difficulties in floating the enterprise, and the rigid conditions imposed by the government and by those who would provide the capital.

From Skagway on September 11 came the news that Engine No. 1 was ready to ship to the "Klondike Creek Mines Railway". At Bennett, B.C., the White Pass began the loading of eleven cars of rail and fastenings, 140 tons—said to be enough for four miles of track—bound for Dawson. This mileage was rather optimistic since 140 tons of 45-lb rail is only 18,700 feet of rail, or less than two miles of track. The *Yukon Sun* also reported that in the White Pass shops at Skagway, former White Pass engine No. 63 had been fitted up and repainted, lettered **"Klondike Creeks Mines Road"** (yes, that's what the *Sun* wrote) with No. 1 in gold, and it would be rushed to Dawson.

On September 16, forty tons of rail arrived, and within one week a section of track, long enough for a loco-motive and six flat cars, had been built at Klondike City. The track was only temporary, for storage of the rolling stock which was on the way. About 100 yards of tracks were laid from the river's edge, on ties widely spaced, although not yet solidly spiked. The course of the railway around the Klondike River bluffs was partly staked although no further work would be done until the next spring.

On September 27, 1902, Klondike Mines Railway engine No. 1 and some flat cars arrived on the sternwheeler *Mary F. Graff*, and were unloaded the following day. (At 544 tons, the *Mary F. Graff* was at that time the

*A builder's photo of Brooks construction number (c/n) 522, built in 1881 as No. 7, the "**Sidney Dillon**", for the Kansas Central which was controlled by the Union Pacific (at the time Sidney Dillon was president of the UP). After service on other western railways, c/n 522 arrived in Skagway in 1900 and went to work as WP&YR No. 63. In 1902 it was refurbished and shipped to Klondike City for the Klondike Mines Railway as engine No. 1.*
Harold K. Vollrath, Kansas City, MO

largest carrier on the upper river fleet.) A tender and flat car arrived next day on the **Bonanza King**. The **Dawson Daily News** reported Klondike Mines Railway No. 1 as being the first locomotive to come so far north in North America. Next day the rival **Yukon Sun** countered, saying it was in fact the second locomotive to come to the Yukon interior, although the first in Dawson; the first into northern Yukon was the locomotive belonging to the Cliff Creek coal mine, 58 miles downstream from Dawson, on the Yukon River. By the 29th, Klondike Mines Railway engine No. 1 and tender had been off-loaded on the track built to water's edge at Klondike City. They were hauled from the steamers using a heavy rope and the ship's capstan. On October 9 the **Mary F. Graff** arrived with several more flat cars.

Records suggest that the rolling stock was supplied by the White Pass on credit, likely approved because of Hawkins' past association with the White Pass. A post-1906 White Pass property account does show locomotive No. 63 as being sold for $3882.36 in 1902, but the buyer is listed as the DGF&SRRy (Dawson Grand Forks and Stewart River Railway Corporation) which did not come

into existence until late 1904. In total, six flat cars were purchased, numbered 51, 53, 55, 57, 59, and 61, but all were later retrieved by the White Pass. When railway contractor Jerome Chute took command in early 1905 he was reported to have ordered twenty-three freight cars, comprising thirteen box cars and ten new flat cars; the flat cars were then numbered in the 101, and up, series.

Why was narrow gauge (36-inch) chosen over standard gauge (56½-inch) in construction of the Klondike Mines Railway line? On leaving Skagway in 1902, promoter Hawkins was on good terms with the WP&YR, which upon completion of its railway had a number of idle locomotives not suited for mainline duty. Most of the first locomotives acquired by the WP&YR were old and smallish, but had provided adequate service as construction locomotives. When, in 1898, the WP&YR had begun shopping for used rolling stock there was a plentiful supply available—a number of 36-inch gauge railways of the western United States had been standard-gauged in the 1890s, and there was then little demand for the surplus "slim gauge" equipment. With limited funds, initially, the WP&YR acquired many pieces of rolling stock at bargain prices. For these same reasons, the KMR in 1902 acquired narrow gauge stock from the WP&YR: it was cheap, and it was available.

To the WP&YR, however, construction of a narrow gauge railway had also offered the great advantage of lower costs: in building the grade, narrower cuts would suffice (rock-work was considerably reduced), tighter curves and steeper grades could be laid out, snaking along the mountain sides (less cut-and-fill, smaller trestles), and light-weight rail could be laid (locomotives were proportionately lighter). These were very important factors to the WP&YR whose first twenty miles of grade was largely blasted out of the solid rock of precipitous mountain buttresses. To the KMR, however, these factors were not nearly so critical, but were of some consequence in keeping line construction costs down. Most of the KMR's narrow gauge grade, carved out of overburden with horse and scraper, could have been built to standard gauge requirements almost as cheaply, but at the three gulches above Grand Forks, and in the Flannery area, considerably greater costs would have resulted. At these points surveyor Astley was able to lay out a number of 17½ degree curves—curves too sharp for larger

standard gauge locomotives—and in so doing kept cut-and-fill to a minimum, and permitted construction of shorter, lower, trestles.

It appeared as though 1903 would be a busy year, but there were still some details to iron out. In mid-October, 1902, engineer Astley approached the Dawson Council, on behalf of Hawkins, with a proposal to lay Klondike Mines Railway tracks along Front Street (paralleling the Yukon River) into Dawson. A bill was introduced by Council, but there was considerable opposition by a number of property holders along that street. Although a petition was circulated opposing the bill, Council met with railway representatives O'Brien and W.H. Parsons (manager of Ames Mercantile Company of Dawson, with an interest in the railway), and in late December granted the company a franchise. Hawkins had stressed that he wanted a terminal facility in Dawson for a railway, and wanted no competition from a street railway. It appears that O'Brien had laid aside his street railway plan. Perhaps his motive in floating the scheme had been to head off competitors.

CHAPTER FIVE

STAGNATION
1903

In early January, Chief Isaac of the Moosehide reservation asked Council to have the Klondike Mines Railway extended northward through Dawson to the village of Moosehide. But tracks of the railway would not be laid in Dawson in 1903, or even in 1904.

The *Klondike Nugget* of February 18, 1903, reported that:

> The railroad promoter Mr. Hawkins is coming, bringing a capitalist from New York willing to invest. When Mr. Hawkins was here last he had difficulty in securing subscriptions to the stock of the new railroad—just sufficient to go outside and show how much the local merchants were interested in it. He has no such trouble now, from the last account of his financial doings in New York.

But when Hawkins arrived a week later he brought no "capitalist;" accompanying him were Michael J. Heney, George McLaughlin, representative of the Ministry of Railways and Canals, and J.H. Rogers, agent with the White Pass.

The three visiting railway men, and W.H. Parsons and O'Brien, made a three-day inspection tour of the creeks, and on their return to Dawson, Heney was quoted as saying, "the railroad will be very easy to build and of much lower cost than was the White Pass railroad". The promoters were building up another pitch for investors, and in early March a report on the state of quartz mining properties in the Klondike was presented them. Additionally statistics regarding cordwood utilization was requested; an enormous amount of wood was cut annually just for heating purposes. At the time hillsides through the immediate area were stripped of trees, and wood had to hauled up the creeks to a number of camps. Such data would be included in a new prospectus.

There were ominous signs of financial difficulties now, in spite of the flurry of late 1902 activity. By May the rental fee had not yet been paid on frontage property in Klondike City. However Commissioner Congdon intervened in any forfeiture, extending the fee due date to September 1, 1903, contingent upon the railway making interest payment on the fee. With no construction yet done, the company once again applied to Parliament to amend the charter, extending the time limit for construction.

Hawkins and Heney were now applying political pressure, for the Yukon Council released a memo recognizing the depletion of wood resources in the area, and urged Ottawa to "grant aid to the Klondike Mines Railway which is needed for transportation". To fortify the request Yukon Council telegraphed Ottawa, "unanimously resolved memorialize Government Ottawa grant subsidy or guarantee interest on Mines Railway Company bonds to assist immediate construction railway. Memorial being forwarded by mail. F.T. Congdon". On June 25, 1903, Parliament granted a further two-year extension of time, details exactly as granted in the extension of 1901.

Opposite: Downtown Dawson City about 1904, before the arrival of KMR tracks: the ferry tower is located a few yards upstream (to the right) from the foot of Queen Street, and situated halfway between Queen Street and Princess Street is Boyle's Wharf. Originally home of the Seattle-Yukon Transportation Company, this building would in 1906 become the KMR's Dawson City depot. Note the rafts of wood tied up at the lower right, destined to be sawn into cordwood for local heating fuel. This area of the waterfront would become the railway's Dawson yard, where thousands of cords of firewood would later be loaded onto flat cars bound for dredge sites on Bonanza Creek.
University of British Columbia, Special Collections, Western Miner Collection

It was early autumn in the Klondike and nothing at all had been done in 1903 towards a start of rail construction. Finally Hawkins arrived on September 12, and when the *Dawson Record* asked him about the success of his Klondike railway scheme he replied, with a hint of weariness;

> The time of the present session of parliament is practically all taken up with the government bill regarding the extension of the Grand Trunk to the Pacific. That question is paramount to all others and until it is settled no other railroad proposition, no matter how small or comparatively inexpensive, will be taken up for consideration.

Asked if he had hopes of his subsidy bill being passed at this time;

> Yes, I am hopeful and confident that so soon as the Grand Trunk question is settled the matter of the Klondike road will receive favourable consideration. The capital is all ready to proceed with work so soon as the government acts favourably on the matter of granting the desired subsidy. Owing to the lateness of the season, no work would be done in 1903, but early in 1904, still according to original plans.

Hawkins had spent the previous two months in Ottawa, New York, and Seattle before setting out for Dawson, and he was once more off for the financial centres of New York, Ottawa, San Francisco, with much work yet ahead. It is apparent that a good deal of Hawkins' sale pitch now involved both government grants and the plans of the Grand Trunk. Hawkins left the Klondike, never to be seen here again. His venture into promoting was a near-disaster; although discouraged he would eventually find the backers he had been searching for and become involved, in ways more suited to his talents, in another railway venture. Hawkins went to work for the Union Pacific Railroad until 1907, when he rejoined his old White Pass partner, Michael Heney, in building the Copper River and Northwestern Railway in Alaska. Coincidentally, when financing was finally found, a map was released by the Grand Trunk Pacific Railway showing a proposed trans-Canada route with a branch line extending right to Dawson.

By late September, 1903, rails were being laid on the beach opposite the courthouse in Dawson, but this was the work of a coal company, not of the long-awaited Klondike Mines Railway. In April, 1903, the Coal Creek Coal Company had surveyed a twelve-mile, narrow gauge, railway from mines leading to loading docks on the Yukon River not far from Fortymile, and fifty-four miles down-river from Dawson. With a force of 100 men the company had the railway on Coal Creek completed in July, and by August had locomotives and cars on the property. At Dawson, railway tracks led from coal barges, at the docks, for about 2000 feet to the powerhouse of the Dawson Electric Light & Power Company; there an inclined trestle ended at the coal dump. This was in fact a tramway, for horses pulled cars along the better part of the road as far as the trestle, where cables pulled the cars up the last incline. The *Yukon Sun* later reported that some coal might also be shipped to Dawson from "Miller's Mine" near Carmacks, some 200 miles upstream on the Yukon River.

On October 24, 1903, the Canadian Parliament passed an act to authorize the granting of subsidies in aid of the lines of railway therein mentioned; the Klondike Mines Railway was only one of several dozen railways that could apply for this assistance. In defining limits in granting subsidies, the Klondike Mines Railway had to specify its proposed mileage and route, which had changed once more; it was now simply defined, "for a line of railway from Dawson to Stewart River, passing at or near Grand Forks, not exceeding 84 miles". In November the *Yukon Sun* speculated that construction of the railway could cost about $30,000 a mile, and that this assistance would no doubt start "active work" next spring. The *Dawson Record* similarly noted the passage of the new railway subsidies act, and the newspaper complimented Hawkins for his effort and labour, expecting work to start in spring. Aid was in the sum of $6400 per mile, but since construction costs were estimated at $30,000 per mile, this was hardly the answer to Hawkins' problems. Perhaps he had expected the subsidy to be greater, thus encouraging prospective investors. Exemplifying the fortunes of the railway, O'Brien totally ignored letters from the Crown Timber and Land Agent requesting that the lease fees for the Klondike City frontage be paid, and his application was ultimately cancelled.

While both *Poor's Railroad Manual* and the Department of Railways and Canals (Poor's data taken from reports to the Department) state that two miles of track had been laid to June 30, 1903, this was not so. The company did have 45-lb rail sufficient for two miles of track, but as of December 31, 1903, only a few hundred feet of temporary line had been laid at Klondike City, and no more would be added in the immediate future.

CHAPTER SIX

FINANCING AND ACTION
1904/1905

Dawsonites were becoming cynical over the lack of railway action, whether from local lines or outside lines. A cartoon from the front page of the January 12, 1904, *Dawson Daily News* captioned:

The Railroad Situation
as It Would Appear to Dawson

Shown are five railways converging on Miss Dawson: on four tracks are locomotives labeled Dawson & Kittimat (sic) RR, Grand Trunk, Whitehorse & Alaska, and Valdez; on the fifth track is a tram labeled Dawson & the

Forks Ltd.; at the tram control is Tom O'Brien, manager, and towing the tram are a rabbit and a husky. O'Brien had in fact worked as conductor and motorman on streetcars in the city of Toronto twenty-five years earlier.

In early January, 1904, the *Yukon Sun* noted that no work had been done towards construction of the Klondike Mines Railway during 1903, but announced the ever-enterprising O'Brien was about to grace the Klondike with a brewery. By February it was nearly ready for production, only awaiting the arrival of hops

THE RAILROAD SITUATION AS IT WOULD APPEAR TO DAWSON

Dawson Daily News, Page 1, January 12, 1904

In the early 1900s prostitutes were banished from Dawson City to settle in Klondike City where they were allowed to practice their trade; their numerous, tidy, two-room cabins can be spotted easily. Wooden boardwalks connect businesses and dwellings, and on the waterfront rail line is a single Klondike Mines Railway box car. It is spring of about 1908; breakup on the river has taken place only a couple of weeks ago, but slabs and blocks of ice can still be seen on both shores of the Yukon River. Across the Yukon River a number of steamboats and barges are gathered at Camp Easy (properly known as Sunnydale), a wintering site used by many shipping companies.

Yukon Archives, MacBride Coll'n, 3879

from San Francisco. As the **Yukon Sun** worded it;

Klondike City will soon have another attraction added to those it now has, for the brewery will be installed in the O'Brien buildings; at that point a sidetrack will be run to them from the Klondike Mines Railroad.

(Two years earlier all prostitutes in the Dawson area had been banished to Klondike City; they were the first "attraction" that the writer had in mind.) The brewery occupied the basement, main floor, and upper level of the old warehouse, while the principal building was the O'Brien Store at the end of Main Street. Brewery capacity would be 15,000 gallons per day. The **Dawson Daily News** contradicted the latter statement saying capacity would be only 1,200 gallons per day—a more likely figure—adding;

...a contract was let to G.F. Mero to transform the three O'Brien & Moran buildings into a brewery. The founders of the O'Brien Brewing & Malting Company are applying to Ottawa for a letters patent, capitalized at $200,000...the license (local) has already been granted.

O'Brien's brewery would soon influence political party nick-naming in the Yukon. Early in April there developed a rift in the Yukon Liberal organization headed by Commissioner Congdon—a split which resulted in two feuding groups. The Liberal Association group re-elected O'Brien as president with "Duff" Pattullo as secretary, and Alfred Thompson became their

Until the early 1950s, there were all sorts of "collectibles" for the taking in Klondike City. In 1946, YCGC employee Don Macintyre picked up this label near the site of the brewery.

Eric L. Johnson, label courtesy Don Macintyre, Burnaby, B.C.

candidate. This wing quickly became known as the "steam beers" because of the brewing process used in the Klondike Brewery owned by O'Brien and Thompson. The other group, headed by Congdon, became the territorial wing, better known as the "tabs" because of the Commissioner's refusal to pay bribery debts (i.e. the tab) after the previous election. This group included Dawson mayor James MacDonald and many civil servants. The terms "tabs" and "steam beers" were first printed in the May 7 issue of the **Dawson Daily News** and would be used for years to come.

In spite of skeptics, the hopes of Yukoners for a railway from the outside were not waning. The front page of the May 9 **Dawson Daily News** featured a map of the Grand

Trunk's route across Canada to Port Essington, British Columbia (near modern-day Prince Rupert), showing a proposed 800-mile spur from Hazelton north to Dawson.

In early summer, O'Brien received a telegram from Ottawa, dated June 10, 1904, saying, "Have received several cables from Hawkins. Construction whole railway will assuredly be completed". signed H.B. McGiverin. Skagway's **Daily Alaskan** reported, "Information is received from Seattle that the Klondike Mines Railway will surely be built..". A week later Michael Heney was in Skagway, having just returned from London, where he had been with Hawkins, "...the railroad is an assured fact!"

O'Brien's brewery was officially in business when the February 5, 1904, issue of the **Canada Gazette** declared;

> Public notice is given that under The Companies Act, 1902, letters patent have been issued under the Seal of the Secretary of State of Canada, bearing the date the 1st of February, 1904, incorporating Thomas William O'Brien, merchant, of Klondike City Addition to Dawson, Yukon Territory, Alfred Thompson, physician, John Robert Howard, merchant, Daniel Hugh MacKinnon, barrister-at-law, Tyra Frank Lawson, miner, Alexander John Gillies, dentist, and Hector Allan Stewart, farmer, all of Dawson, in the Yukon Territory.

The company was named *The O'Brien Brewing and Malting Company (Limited),* with a total capital stock of $200,000 divided into 2000 shares of $100 each, and with the chief place of business to be in Klondike City. The public notice also listed a number of clauses which permitted the company to engage in brewing, malting, bottling of a variety of drinks, and numerous associated credit, real estate, and promotional ventures.

Heney had become interested in a proposal to build a railway from Prince William Sound on the south coast of Alaska into the mountains north-easterly, where an extremely high-grade copper find, the Kennecott mine, was being developed. Heney's visit to London was explained in Lone E. Janson's book *The Copper Spike*, in which she detailed events leading up to construction of the Copper River and Northwestern Railway by Heney; the road would be many-fold more difficult to build than the White Pass.

In 1904 Heney had visited London and paid a call on his old friends and associates at the Close Brothers offices. The Close Brothers had financed construction of the White Pass. Heney had heard of the difficulties they were having in building the seaport at Katalla, which was to be the foot of the road to the Kennecott mine. After some research Heney wired Siegley, his secretary and confidential advisor, telling him to contact all of "his boys", those who had worked with him on the White Pass, and to put them on the payroll immediately. Back in Seattle he finalized his plans and took a coastal steamship to Juneau where he filed plans for the "Copper River Railway", to be financed by the Close Brothers. The year 1905 was spent in preliminary work, and construction of the Copper River and Northwestern began in 1906. While Hawkins may have been an accessory to Heney's plans, he was not officially a member of the construction team until July, 1907, when he was appointed chief engineer.

Meanwhile, The Dawson White Horse Navigation Company was in trouble; in July the steamer *Tyrrell*, owned by O'Brien and partners, was seized by a sheriff for wages due to Captain McLean. He had been the steamer's master, and claimed $184 was due him.

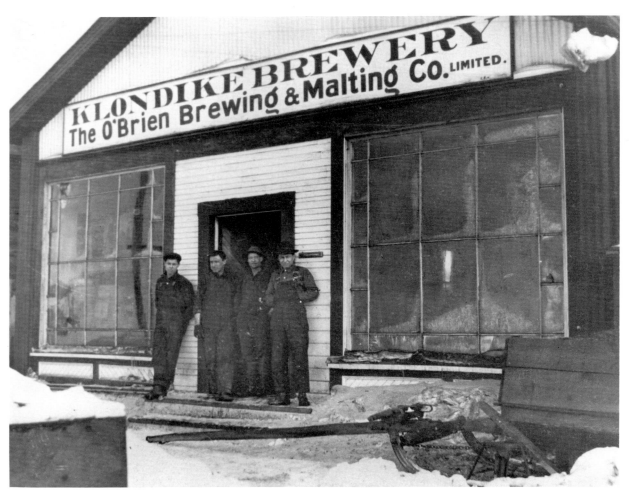

From a postcard of about 1912, this winter scene shows the employees of Tom O'Brien's brewery—the young man on the left is possibly O'Brien's oldest son Henry.
Eric L. Johnson Coll'n, courtesy Frances M. Dwyer, Seattle, Washington

Another winter arrived in the Klondike, and details of Hawkins' efforts, and his departure from the Klondike Mines Railway, became known. Filed with the Department of Railways and Canals on October 1, 1904, was a new railway survey for the line between Klondike City and Grand Forks, done by civil engineer F.C. Lightfoot, and signed by E.C. Hawkins, engineer, and H.B. McGiverin, vice president. This plan was the first to show the Klondike Mines Railway crossing a bridge over the Klondike River, entering Dawson City as far as Third Street. (In December, 1902 the railway, represented by engineer John Astley, had received authority from Council to enter Dawson and run along Front Street (First Avenue).)

But of greater import was news of Hawkins' selling job. On November 1, 1904, the Dawson, Grand Forks and Stewart River Railway Corporation Limited (DGF&SRRCo) was incorporated—company number 82440—in London, England. Capital was listed as 10,000 shares at one English pound per share, 9,993 of these issued to Lawther, Latta & Company as commission on business obtained from the Klondike Mines Railway. Robert Allan Lawther and John Latta were partners in the firm of Lawther, Latta and Company, ship owners and merchants of Ayrshire. They had just become almost sole owners of the Klondike Mines Railway, and their newly formed corporation would become the construction company. On November 11, a contract between the Klondike Mines Railway Company and the Dawson, Grand Forks and Stewart River Railway Corporation was signed providing for the construction and equipment of a railway from Dawson to Grand Forks, a distance of thirteen miles in all.

As part of Hawkins agreement of 1902 with the Klondike Mines Railway, he would sell the stock and then gain the contract for building the first section of the line—Dawson to Grand Forks. The Hawkins Construction Company, of Seattle, had been formed for this purpose. However, instead of finding the many investors he had hoped for, and profiting from the construction job, the railway stock was sold almost entirely to Lawther and Latta who, under their DGF&SRRCo, chose to contract out the line work themselves. The sale agreement eliminated Hawkins' further involvement, invalidating his contracts of January 20, 1902, and August 6, 1902. The terms of the termination of Hawkins' contract were not revealed, but there were hints that he was "cheated" when mining developer Jerome Amandren Chute was given the construction contract instead. Chute, a native of Wisconsin, had been mining in the Klondike from the early days and was now

about to become a general contractor. His mining company, Chute and Wills, had in 1901 and 1902 been one of the most important individual mining enterprises in the Yukon, and had operated on Gold Run Creek with fifteen creek claims and a number of bench claims. Chute was also said to have had many years of railway construction experience.

It might seem hard to believe that overseas investors would finance railway construction when population and gold production in the Klondike were now on the decline. But it was well known that there was still much gold in the Klondike to be mined—enormous volumes of lower value gravels in the Dawson area, and in the valleys of the Indian and Stewart Rivers. Additionally, the outlook for lode mining in the district was still hopeful. At the time, the scale of development of dredging was not foreseen, and it appeared that both placer and lode mining would require a large labour force scattered throughout the goldfield. This translated into prospects of a healthy freight, express, and passenger business for the Klondike Mines Railway—as Hawkins had outlined in his prospectus of 1902.

This was also the age of great railway schemes. While many were speculative, there were a few northern railways of unqualified success. Construction of the Trans-Siberian Railway, Chelyabinsk to Vladivostok, began in 1891 with work commencing at both ends of the proposed line. The 5787-mile line was completed in 1905, and opened the country to colonization, mining, and agricultural development. In Canada the Temiskaming and Northern Ontario Railway (T&NO) began construction northward in 1902 from North Bay, Ontario, into silver and gold camps. The railway was instrumental in developing several rich mining camps, and in opening northern land to agricultural colonization. The T&NO, renamed the Ontario Northland Railway in 1946, would today be referred to as a "resource railway". Chartered in 1899, the Algoma Central Railway had similar beginnings.

Of more relevance to the Klondike Mines Railway was the Grand Trunk Pacific Railway, chartered in 1903 as a subsidiary of the Grand Trunk Railway. Wholly owned and managed by private British investors, the Grand Trunk had been expanding in eastern Canada since 1853, but was now looking at building a railway westward from Ontario, across the northern prairies, to reach the Pacific Ocean at what would become Prince Rupert. Although construction did not start until 1909, and was not completed until 1914, plans of this initially well-heeled concern were getting much publicity in 1904. Prospects included exploitation of the Peace River country of Alberta, and an ambitious and highly speculative all-Canadian branch line from Hazelton, British Columbia, into the Yukon Territory—and in particular to the Klondike. Travelling in the same financial circles as the Grand Trunk backers were Lawther and Latta, and without doubt they were party to first-hand knowledge of the Grand Trunk's schemes. From the late 19th century and into the 20th century, England had provided funding for many railway projects around the world, and as one writer put it, British investors had "seemingly unbounded enthusiasm for railway ventures". Lawther and Latta had become Hawkins' saviours.

Several significant notices then appeared in the *Canada Gazette*;

December 3, 1904: Notice of an application to be made to the Parliament of Canada to amend the Klondike Mines Railway charter yet again, allowing the line to commence at Dawson City, permitting the company to build a bridge across the Klondike River, and to extend the time for commencement and completion of the railway.

February 1, 1905: McGiverin & Haydon, solicitors for the Klondike Mines Railway Company, were informed the company had qualified for the government construction subsidy made available by the 1903 enactment.

February 4, 1905: Notice is hereby given that a meeting of the shareholders of the Klondike Mines Railway Company will be held at the office of the company, No. 19 Elgin Street, in the city of Ottawa, on Tuesday the 28th day of February, 1905, at 11 a.m., to consider and if thought expedient to pass resolutions authorizing the directors to borrow money for the purposes of the company, and to issue bonds securing repayment thereof as the directors think fit, and authorizing the execution of mortgages upon all or any of the assets and property of the company securing the repayment of the same.

Signed, Andrew Haydon, Secretary.

(No. 19 Elgin Street was the business address of McGiverin, Haydon and Greig.)

In mid-February, 1905, the Yukon Territorial Commissioner called for a meeting of Council to discuss an application to lay tracks on Front Street in Dawson. Presented by Astley and Chute, the plan which was accompanied by a map dated February 15 showed the line (which was eventually built) running down Front Street, with a terminal yard between Duke and Albert (Fifth and Sixth) Streets. Council had in December, 1902, already approved Astley's request for the railway's entry into Dawson City, but now, more than two years later, felt the request had to be reconsidered. The request was not greeted wholeheartedly, but on February 23 a petition of Front Street property owners generally approved railway access. A number of concerns were expressed: no switches should be allowed at the entrance to the fire hall; tracks ought to be planked to permit normal street traffic; spark arresters would be required if wood-burning locomotives were used (Dawson had experienced several disastrous fires); the speed of locomotives should not exceed eight miles per hour from the Klondike River north to the terminal; and Front Street, especially between King and Queen (Second and Third) Streets, must not be used as a freight yard. Although two or three property owners did not approve at all, merchants generally welcomed the rail entry.

With no decision from Council three weeks later, Chute fired off a huffy letter to the Commissioner saying that if approval of the rail route into Dawson was not to be granted he would advise the company not to build a railway at all. Two days later, on March 11, the Klondike Mines Railway was officially granted the right, subject to the above conditions, to enter Dawson.

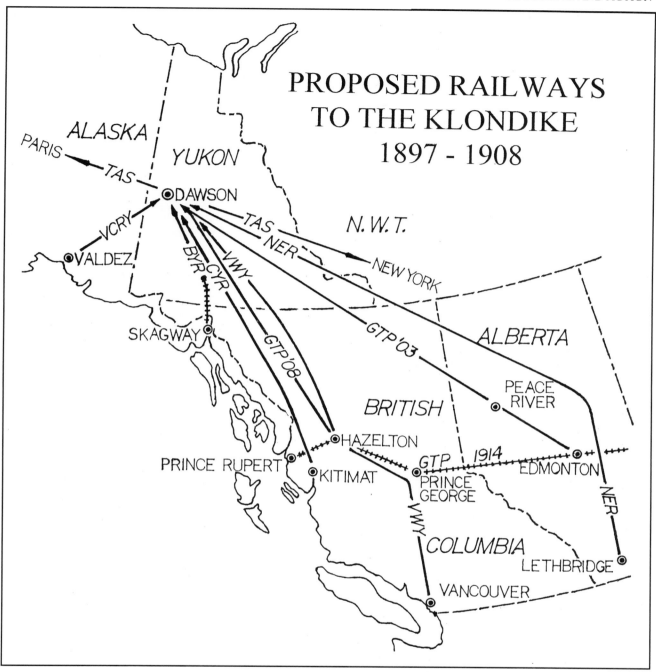

PROPOSED RAILWAYS TO THE KLONDIKE 1897 - 1908

The turn of the century saw a flurry of railway speculation, and Dawson, the heart of the spectacular gold rush, was a prime target. Here are some of the dreams of the railway visionaries.

BYR	**British Yukon Railway (WP&YR)**	*1897*
CYR	**Coast Yukon Railway**	*1903*
GTP	**Grand Trunk Pacific Railway**	*1903*
NER	**Northern Empire Railway**	*1908*
TAS	**Trans-Alaska-Siberian Railway**	*1902 (proposed)*
VCRY	**Valdez, Copper River & Yukon Railroad**	*1901*
VWY	**Vancouver, Westminster & Yukon Railway**	*1901*

...and many others.

Smoke from a Klondike Mines Railway locomotive in 1944? Neglected engine No. 2 at Klondike City had a visit from Ron Willis and friends. They lit up some oily rags in the firebox, and for the first time since 1913, smoke came out of No. 2's stack.
Ron W. Willis, Vancouver, BC

CHAPTER SEVEN

CONSTRUCTION STARTS, AND FALTERS
1905/1906

March 12, 1905: the *Yukon World* quoted Jerome Chute, contractor, who already had fifteen men at work;

> We shall make camp on the N.A.T.&T.Co.'s island in the Klondike [River] for 100 men. Fifty men will work on the rock cliff on the other side of the Klondike, and we will prepare for bridge construction. On N.A.T.&T.'s island we will have a blacksmith shop, other shops, and the construction camp. The Yukon sawmill is now working on bridge timbers. The track, after coming south from Dawson, will cross the Klondike then onto the island and will cross a channel [Klondike Slough] to join the track to be built from the waterfront at Klondike City, right at Potter's Store. From there on to Grand Forks the route is not definitely fixed. A pile driver is being built at the Yukon Iron Works. We have one locomotive here and some 45-lb rail, but 52-lb is needed, and an order for 1100 tons has been placed. The White Pass is building for us at Skagway twenty-three new freight cars, and is re-building its best locomotive; it is also building two fine passenger cars. That is all the rolling stock for this season. Rail laying will probably start in June with arrival of the 52-lb rail.

Passing through Dawson at the time was Falcon Joslin, chief promoter and builder of the railway on Coal Creek, and now driving hard for completion of his new Tanana Mines Railroad. With him was Charlie Moriarty, long-time roadmaster with the Great Northern, about to become gang boss on construction of the forty miles of rail grade between Chena and Chatanika. Joslin said he had read Chute's optimistic comments, and "thought he would like to race his old friend Mr. Chute as to which could get his railway in operation first". While Chute had just placed a large order for a locomotive and twenty-three cars from the White Pass shops in Skagway, Joslin had also placed a substantial order: "...the sale of fourteen cars of various kinds including two coaches, six flat cars, six hand cars, and a locomotive and other material".

Reports made by the Klondike Mines Railway to the Department of Railways and Canals inferred two miles of track had been laid by mid-1903, and although rail for a little less than two miles of track had been delivered in late 1902, it was apparent that tracks had never left the banks of the Yukon River in Klondike City. The route had only been staked out eastward around the Klondike Bluffs, along what then was no more than a rough and narrow trail leading to Bonanza Creek. Chute's men had not yet begun blasting these rock cliffs along the Klondike River, situated only 4000 feet east from the Yukon River, to cut a right-of-way sufficiently wide for a rail bed.

Charles Boyle, older brother of Joe Boyle, announced that ties and timber for the Klondike Mines Railway were being cut from the Boyle timber berth, yarded out by horses and stored near the Old Inn at the Ogilvie Bridge. The first lot of 12,000 ties had been cut already, with a contract for 35,000 more, and cutting of telegraph poles and big timber had begun, also for the railway. Ties were to be spaced at twenty-four inches, thus the Boyles would provide ties sufficient for almost eighteen miles of track.

On behalf of the Klondike Mines Railway, contractor Chute applied for purchase of fifteen lots in the Addition to Klondike City; this block of land just east of the Klondike Slough became the site of the junction of the Dawson City line with the original main line to Klondike City. While the lots had cost only $387.50 there was still some question about squatter's cabins, some inhabited, on the property and who would remove them.

Solicitor McGiverin, now also vice-president of the Klondike Mines Railway, continued to churn out charters. To his already overflowing briefcase he had only recently added the charters of the Northwest

Telephone Company, the Vancouver, Victoria and Eastern Railway and Navigation Company, and the Kaslo and Lardo-Duncan Railway Company. He would in all likelihood also hold executive positions with these concerns.

At the mouth of the Klondike River contractor Chute was rushing to completion four piers for the railway bridge by early April, 1905. On site were two boilers with tall smoke stacks, thawing ground for the piers. At Klondike Slough, a little farther east and on the opposite side of the same island was another bridge construction scene. A little farther on, was a third construction site where men were blasting out a grade at the foot of the rock bluff along the Klondike River. The four piers at the mouth of the Klondike River were to be finished soon, while the two piers on Klondike Slough were not far behind. All the bridge work would have to be done before the spring melt and rising river levels. The railway had about eighty men at work, one-third of them at the rock bluff near Klondike City. When grading commenced later that spring many more men would be needed.

While driving piles through the ice on the Klondike River, it was found that the ground was frozen to only eight feet below river bottom, and this seemed strange, since on the gold creeks ground could be frozen to depths of 200 feet or more. The bridge piers rested on piles driven deep into the ground. When completed, the bridge across the Klondike River would consist of three structural steel spans of 100, 140, and 80 feet in length, from north to south, with timber trestle approaches resting on pilings on both sides of the river. The southern approach was a particularly long, curving, trestle. Bridge piers were framed of timber, bolted, and filled with boulders from the river bed. Labourers were paid $5.75 a day deducting $1.75 a day for board, and the company ran a mammoth mess house, feeding the men "fine square meals that gets the most out of them", according to Chute.

Farther up Bonanza Creek, near Joe Nee's roadhouse at 60 Below, the railway company put up a large tent to accommodate 100 men. In a few days it was expected that 75 men would be at work cutting through a point of rock that jutted into the creek there; a blacksmith shop for sharpening steel for rock work had already been installed.

O'Brien was once more making news. In early April, Yukon Council pre-election speeches were being delivered by the candidates which included O'Brien. The *Dawson Daily News* read; "Tom O'Brien made the speech of his life. Although not often on a platform, he talks with the assurance of a man of affairs, a wide experience, and a great deal of local and political knowledge". His speech included his recent and not-so-recent activities: the steamer company with which he nearly went broke because he was boycotted in favour of American-owned boats (the Northern Commercial Company and the North American Transportation and Trading Company on the lower Yukon River); he had mined at Fortymile nineteen years ago; he had run the first store in the district in opposition to the big companies; he had put in the first telephone from Dawson to the Forks; and he had started the railway, "and it would now be finished were not some jealous of me making a dollar...the railroad would have been a great advantage here". His newspaper advertisements read simply, "Vote for T.W. O'Brien".

Under attack in pre-election debates, O'Brien defended himself; "I had nothing to do with the building of the tramway to which Fowlie [a political critic] refers. The job was done by Henning, and I had to pay for it, and pay dearly, when I bought Henning out". O'Brien said he had started the scheme, made a trail, reduced freight rates, and when he took it over he paid $29,000 of bad debts, himself indebted to $52,000, and was left in the air when the government failed to protect his interest. The indemnity award of $27,000 was held up. The controversy over the toll bridge which O'Brien and two partners built had cost $19,000—and it had been for the public benefit. The *Dawson Daily News* praised O'Brien, saying his speech was the best presented. In the election which ran on Wednesday, the 12th of April, O'Brien won more votes than any other candidate, defeating Clarke, to become member of the Yukon Council for a two-year term, representing South Dawson.

In the first week of May a gang of men extended the railway tracks another 1000 feet beyond those recently laid along the Klondike Bluffs This extension would be only temporary to allow use of an engine and cars to commence full-scale grading. After almost three years of inaction at Klondike City, Klondike Mines Railway locomotive No. 1 was about to be fired up. Chute then re-applied for lease of 425 feet of water frontage in Klondike City—the same lots applied for in late 1903 by O'Brien, and relinquished. The lease would run for twenty years at a rate of $1.00 per foot per year.

When the shipping season opened on the Yukon River, supplies for the railway began arriving; in mid-June the steamer *Columbian* brought in a load of spikes and other material labeled for the Dawson Grand Forks and Stewart River Railway—the construction company. The

Cheechaco Hill on the right and Gold Hill in the distance on the left--Grand Forks is just at the base of Gold Hill—are seen in this view of Bonanza Creek facing south about 1900, when gold production peaked. The hills have been stripped of trees, the wood needed for mine lagging and firewood. George Carmack's discovery claim is on the left of Bonanza Creek at the foot of the ridge which sweeps down from Cheechaco Hill. With the jumble of individual mining operations strung out along the creek bottom it is little wonder that roads could not survive long—note the public road on the hillside to the left. The KMR met claim interference problems head-on in trying to locate a right-of-way through this no-man's-land. University of British Columbia, Special Collections, Western Miner Collection

Klondike Mines Railway had lost the honour of having the first locomotive in the district to the railway serving the Cliff Creek coal mine, and now the Tanana Mines Railroad brought the first passenger coach through Dawson. Along with the Tanana's engine No. 50 and four flat cars, the coach was unloaded from a barge pushed by the *Columbian*, to be transferred to another carrier sailing for Tanana. The next steamer brought in the first new order of Klondike Mines Railway cars and track material, and more was on the way.

Grading was well under way with track work not far behind, but ominous signs of right-of-way problems began to appear. In late June the Superintendent of Works and Buildings requested information from the railway on where the right-of-way interfered with the Government Road. Chute responded with sketches showing only three locations: 1) on creek claim 50 Below—road very close, above rail; 2) on creek claim 46 below—road crossing; and 3) on creek claim 36 Below-road crossing. Then, on July 1, protests from claim owners were answered when the first injunction against the railway was granted to the McDonalds at 43 Below on Bonanza. A week later some construction men had to be laid off when Treadgold and several other claim owners were also granted injunctions.

But Chute had a contract to complete and for the moment considered the injunctions simply as nuisances. The *Dawson Daily News* of July 22, 1905, gave the following play-by-play;

Treadgold and the railway people met this morning. Mr. Treadgold didn't like the railroad crossing one of his claims in the 90s, so removed one of the rails. When the track crew arrived on a car drawn by a locomotive it stopped; Mr. Treadgold disputed their right and stood in the middle of the track and demanded the authority of the party. Jerome Chute, contractor for road construction, politely picked up Mr. Treadgold and lifted him off the track, depositing him some feet away. Mr. Treadgold tried again, but the more skookum Mr. Chute did as before, holding Mr. Treadgold this time as the crew re-laid the rail. When let go, Mr. Treadgold returned to the tracks refusing to let the engine pass onto his claims, but this time Mr. Dave Curry, crew foreman, took Mr. Treadgold 'in charge' and knelt across his chest until the train had passed. Injunctions are continuing.

The injunctions were, of course, binding, and work soon came to a stop.

Before the Klondike Mines Railway had any working track laid, three short 36-inch gauge mining railways in the district had already been built and were in business. When the Klondike Mines Railway charter was granted in July, 1899, the NAT&TCo's coal mine at Cliff Creek was already operational, and the 1¾-mile railway leading to the mine was completed a month later. Cliff Creek is a tributary of the Yukon River, fifty-eight miles downstream from Dawson, and nine miles below Fortymile. The NAT&TCo's Porter 0-4-0 saddle-tanker was the first locomotive in the Klondike; it would later work on the Coal Creek railway when coal ran out at the Cliff Creek mine, and it was subsequently sold to the Tanana Mines Railroad in Alaska.

In January, 1903 the Coal Creek Coal Company was granted a charter, and by late 1904 the company had completed a twelve-mile railway leading from the mines to the Yukon River. Coal Creek empties into the Yukon River only fifty-four miles downstream from Dawson, and four miles above Cliff Creek. The first locomotive on the property was the Cliff Creek Porter, bought from the NAT&TCo, followed a few days later by two larger Porters brought to Coal Creek from the outside. Although coal veins at the Cliff Creek mine were worked out by late 1903, coal had been stockpiled at a load-out on the Yukon River and provided an adequate supply for Dawson until the Coal Creek mine began shipping in 1905. Chief promoter of the Coal Creek Coal Company was Falcon Joslin, who in 1904 incorporated the Tanana Mines Railroad, and was its president.

Closer to Dawson, the Detroit Yukon Mining Company also had a mining railway in action. Incorporated in

Michigan in 1902, the company owned placer gold claims on Bear Creek which drains into the Klondike River six miles east of Dawson. Four brand new Porter 0-4-0 saddle-tankers, very similar to the Cliff Creek Porter, arrived on the property in mid-1904. In the latter part of 1904 and the early summer of 1905 these locomotives and twenty-four side dump cars hauled gravel down to a washing plant, for gold recovery, on the Klondike River. In the meanwhile the Detroit Yukon Mining Company acquired a large mining concession in the immediate region, and reorganized to form a new concern called the Canadian Klondyke Mining Company (the officially-correct spelling for that region of the Yukon Territory was Klondike). Construction of a very large dredge, and start of operation in August, 1905, eliminated the jobs—which were relatively unproductive—of the company's little Porter locomotives.

On the Tanana River in Alaska, gold had been discovered in 1902, and by 1903 there was a rush of prospectors and miners into the area. This newest gold rush proved genuine, and hundreds flocked into "the Tanana", many having left from the Klondike which was now in decline. The Tanana River empties into the Yukon River near Circle City, Alaska, about 200 miles below Dawson, and it was navigable by smaller steamers, thus making for easy access and rapid development. Falcon Joslin had his Tanana Mines Railroad incorporated in 1904, and by fall the line was surveyed. In early June, 1905, the NAT&TCo's ex-Cliff Creek Porter was already on its way to the Tanana, and by July trains were hauling revenue traffic.

It was almost six years since the Klondike Mines Railway had been incorporated, and now, when it seemed construction here had begun in earnest, injunctions stalled progress. It was a long gestation period.

But the backers pushed on. The *Canada Gazette* of August 5 notified readers that a mortgage and deed trust had been deposited with the Secretary of State by John Carlisle and Robert Allan Lawther, trustees of the Klondike Mines Railway Company, securing bonds to the extent of $30,000 per mile for the first section of the railway. Financing of construction was assured.

Although construction had halted in mid-1905, supplies on order continued to be delivered. At the Klondike City headquarters a short spur was built, jutting off from the main line leading to the coal bunkers, out over the Yukon River. There, rail and rolling stock could be landed. On August 9 the steamer *Canadian*, pushing the barge *Pelly*,

Baldwin c/n 7597 on construction duty during its first winter on the White Pass. It would become KMR No. 2 in 1905.
Yukon Archives, E.A. Hegg, 2740

arrived at Klondike City carrying rails, two cars, two coaches, an engine, and lumber for the railway. All of the rolling stock was ex-White Pass equipment refurbished at Skagway. Engine No. 2 had begun service in 1885 as Columbia and Puget Sound No. 8 before being sold to the White Pass as their No. 5, later renumbered as No. 55. The passenger cars, in fact a combination baggage-coach and a coach, numbered 200 and 202, had been acquired by the White Pass from narrow gauge lines to the south which had been standard-gauged in the 1890s. White Pass property accounts show that engine No. 55 was valued at $6500, and that the coach and combination coach sold for, respectively, $1691.50 and $1763.50. Although no records prove the exact date of arrival of the freight cars, photos indicate that most of the thirteen box cars, even-numbered from 100 to 124, and ten flat cars, odd-numbered from 101 to 119, arrived in September and October, 1905.

To begin sorting out right-of-way injunctions which had stalled construction of the Klondike Mines Railway, the Dominion Land Surveyor at Dawson made a report to Frank Oliver, Minister of the Interior, clarifying the changes the railway had made from initial route plans to the latest plan. Three-quarters of the present Klondike Mines Railway location was now on hillsides, resulting in twice the grading costs. The distance of deviation from the initial survey did not exceed more than 150 feet except at two points: 1) 600 feet to reach the hillside near the mouth of Bonanza Creek, 2) 600 feet at 61 Below to avoid a mining operation—a 27-foot rock cut was necessary here. The region of greatest problems was in the 40s Below on Bonanza where active placer mining was being done. By mid-August the Dominion Board of Railway Commissioners in Ottawa dispatched a railway engineer to investigate the injunctions, and on September 5 Judge Craig released a long written decision regarding the problem. Changes to the route were minor, but since construction crews had been disbanded several weeks earlier, no further work was done that fall.

Some of the rail bed graded that summer had to be abandoned, but almost three miles of track had been laid and was acceptable; grade had been advanced to 30 Below, and rail had been laid as far 90 Below. To inspect progress, Lawther and Latta had sent their London-based solicitor, Charles Granville Kekewich, to Dawson. On Labour Day, Monday September 4, he organized an excursion—the first passenger train to run on a portion of the new road. The train went only as far as 96 Below on Bonanza, although inadequately-ballasted track ran beyond there. Utilizing the single day coach, the excursion party consisted of a few selected guests. Under the direction of road construction superintendent Dave Curry, engineer McIntyre let engine No. 1 "out a bit and for a short distance good time was made", thrilling the guests.

Contractor Chute's crews had built the piers for the bridge over the Klondike River, and now in mid-September, 170 tons of bridge steel arrived. Fed up with construction progress gone sour, Chute quit, transferring property, over to the Dawson, Grand Forks and Stewart River Railway Corporation. The attorney signing the agreement was solicitor Kekewich of Kekewich and Company, London, England. Chute would catch the next steamer out. Hereafter work would be supervised by the DGF&SRR under J.W. Astley.

With the Klondike autumn turning into winter, Kekewich organized another, less selective, excursion. The

Dawson Daily News covered the event;

On September 30 a substantial group of about 75 guests assembled at the south end of the Klondike City bridge at 8:00 am this morning, and in spite of a light snow covering on the ground, the second Klondike Mines Railway excursion of the season was arranged by Dawson visitor Kekewich. The train consisted of engine No. 1, a tender, a coach, and two flat cars fitted with stakes, sideboards, and seats.

The ancient Brooks locomotive chuffed out of Klondike City, going as far as 96 Below on Bonanza. At this point

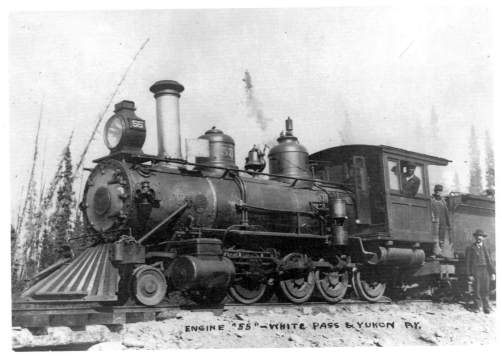

Upon being overhauled by the WP&YR in 1902, Baldwin c/n 7597 was re-numbered from 5 to 55. Now in revenue service on the WP&YR, No. 55 is flying white flags, and has been fitted with classification lamps and a more up-to-date headlight.
Dedman's Photo Shop, Skagway, AK

Opposite top: September 30, 1905: although this photo is labeled **"First Excursion on the KMRy"** *it was in fact the second such tour. Seen here at 96 Below on Bonanza are engine No. 1, coach No. 202, an unidentified flat car, and flat car No. 119 (the latter hastily-equipped pair were referred to as observation cars). Over the years the KMR ran many excursions with these "observation cars". On the right is a "sourdough", an old-timer in the Yukon, and on the train are "cheechacos", that is, new-comers (the wording on the rear railing was later added to the photo print by the photographer). After pausing here for the photo session the train backed up to the wye at Old Inn to turn around and head back towards Klondike City.*
National Archives of Canada, C 18651

Opposite bottom: September 30, 1905: taken by the same photographer, this photo is captioned **"First Train over the K.M.Ry., Dawson"**. *The train is seen on the east leg of the wye at Old Inn Station near the Ogilvie Bridge, probably backing in to turn around for its return to Klondike Island. In the left background is Bonanza Creek. The cabin to the right was part of a fair-sized settlement in the area; behind the cabin are box car No. 100 and two others in temporary storage.*
British Columbia Archives and Records Service, 77049

THE CHEECHACO

FIRST EXCURSI... SEPT 30TH 190... ADAMS & CO PHOTO.

TRAIN OVER THE K.M. RY DAWSON

a sourdough on foot emerged from the hills with a bed-roll on his back, immediately to be photographed with the train—a significant picture of what was, and of what was to be. Engineer Bob Thompson piloted No. 1 back to the Klondike City yards where in "the big mess house of the company" the guests were treated to "a dainty lunch and various drinkables".

Upon departing Dawson, Kekewich advised the Department of Railways and Canals;

> ...one steel bridge on one arm of the Klondike River [the Klondike Slough] has been built, the other bridge work is advanced but cannot be completed this winter. The line to Grand Forks is now being surveyed, and with minor line changes the claim owners have been satisfied; Mr. Treadgold, the main claim owner, now approves of the line. New plans will be sent to Ottawa. After leaving Grand Forks the railway will run higher above Bonanza Creek.

Kekewich also requested permission to use 45-lb instead of 52-lb rail on the section beyond Grand Forks, although subsidy specifications called for 52-lb rail. On October 25 a telegram from Ottawa reached Dawson, "Plans Klondike City to Grand Forks approved by government in council and Minister of the Interior".

Even at this late date there were still other entrepreneurs with dreams of railways in the Klondike. The January 2, 1906, issue of *Canada Gazette* included the following;

> A notice of application to the Parliament of Canada to incorporate a company to construct and operate a railway, and other ventures, up the Indian River from its confluence with the Yukon River, along the valleys of Hunker and Quartz Creeks, to the Klondike River and down it as far as the mouth of Bonanza Creek.

This route would have encircled the existing Klondike Mines Railway territory; neither the names of the applicants nor the city in which the office of the solicitor, J. Langlois Bell, were named. Considering the Klondike Mines Railway's charter rights, this application had little hope for approval.

Early January, 1906, found O'Brien once more actively involved in the "Creeks Railroad", now as a contractor and general manager; he and John Hugh Mackenzie had been awarded the construction contract following Chute's departure. O'Brien's partner, Mackenzie, had been in the Klondike since the early days, and had been involved in one of the first applications to the Parliament of Canada for a railway charter there—a charter which had not been granted because, so it was said, he was an American, not a British subject.

On January 29, came word from the Department of the Interior, "T.W. O'Brien is arranging claim difficulty problems". In Seattle in early February he was interviewed by the *Post Intelligencer*;

> O'Brien, general manager of the Klondike Mines Railway, says construction is to start again. The building of the railroad was for two years postponed, for various reasons. Two years ago the project was first taken up and the contractor Jerome Chute had graded eight miles of roadway, however only four miles of this will be available; the other four miles in litigation. O'Brien is just back from London, England, where he succeeded in raising the money, and a federal subsidy in Ottawa. O'Brien estimates the thirty-mile road will cost $1 million—greater than estimated since government standards are more rigid.

O'Brien may have stretched a few points: construction was hardly "postponed" (the delay was more like five years); Chute had accepted the contract only one year ago; Hawkins had in fact raised the money to begin work; and Hawkins had also applied for the federal subsidy. Modesty was not one of O'Brien's weaknesses.

Back home in Dawson on February 21, O'Brien, sticking a little closer to facts, spoke to newsmen. They reported the following;

> With a contract that means the spending of half a million dollars in the Klondike this summer for wages and supplies, Tom O'Brien, member of the Yukon council, head of the dominant Liberals of the Yukon, and a multitude of business interests, arrived last night. Mr. O'Brien says: Work of construction of the Klondike Mines Railway will be pushed this summer so that we shall have the line in full operation to Sulphur Springs on the Dome by October. ...For his contract he will open an office in Klondike City, and an uptown office in Dawson. Albert Williams who ran the preliminary Klondike Mines Railway survey while Mr. Hawkins was here will be engineer for O'Brien; Williams had worked for the White Pass. Mr. Astley who made the surveys will be the corporate engineer. The stock of the Klondike Mines Railway is owned by a small body of London men, all intimate acquaintances. None of the stock is for sale, nor does White Pass own any of the stock. The railroad plans to get coal for its operation from the Tantalus Mine. All engines and cars needed for some time are here now. Mr. Kekewich who was here last fall was solely a council for the shareholders.

Despite the comforting telegram of October 25, 1905, all was not yet well with the railway's right-of-way, for as John Astley wrote, "less than 5% of the mining claims along the line are surveyed, and it is difficult thus to assure that there will be no right-of-way infringements". On March 24, 1906, partner Mackenzie wrote O'Brien a letter warning him of impending trouble. Mackenzie had put up a $100,000 bond in gaining the construction contract, then later discovered that legal problems were far from solved. Latta and Kekewich had failed to disclose just how tenuous the railway's position was, and passed the seemingly insolvable right-of-way questions on to the new contractors.

Leading the opposition to the railway was Treadgold, who controlled the greatest number of claims along Lower Bonanza. Following discussions with Treadgold, Mackenzie related how Treadgold denounced Chute, Latta, and Kekewich "as idiots and rascals", vowing not to allow railway construction over any of his claims. The confrontation of the previous July had obviously incensed Treadgold even further. Mackenzie also added that although O'Brien had always been against Treadgold (with respect to mining concessions and the railway right-of-way), Treadgold was "very kindly disposed" towards O'Brien, who was "honourable and square". In closing, Mackenzie advised O'Brien to visit Ottawa, "procure the best legal advice and follow it, and after doing this you conclude our case is hopeless, do not throw good money after bad".

But good legal advice O'Brien had, and political influence, in H.B. McGiverin. The following sequence of events defined the problem and solution: April 12, the Klondike Mines Railway presented its new line to Ottawa seeking approval from the railway commissioner—the application was opposed by Treadgold who said the grade would injure his property. The railway was represented by attorneys McGiverin and Haydon. On May 12, the Clerk of the Privy Council rescinded part of the 1902 order-in-council (in respect to the railway's route and right-of-way) and substituted a clause limiting the railway's access to right-of-way over mining claims and access to Crown lands, holding the railway responsible for damage to claims, and requiring plans of further routes for approval by the Board of Railway Commissioners. June 28: the Klondike Mines Railway was ordered to post money as security for possible damage before crossing certain claims. With that, construction could continue unhindered.

Klondike City, June 1906: a temporary spur has been built out over the Yukon River for unloading of rails and bridge timbers just arrived on a barge. A donkey engine powers the derrick now at work, and a second derrick in the foreground will be used to hoist coal from barges into the bunkers seen in the right foreground--one man is at work here now. The distant building with the tall stack, and with a pile of beer kegs against the wall, is The O'Brien Brewing and Malting Company (also known as The Klondike Brewery). The KMR engine house and the tracks to it have not yet been built; a few months later it would occupy the lot on this side of the brewery. On the main line can be seen engine No. 2 and four flat cars, and on the siding are the coach and combination coach. Set off to the side (not set on rails) are two box cars which, during this construction period, are not yet in revenue service.

Yukon Archives, J. Johnson Coll'n, 82/341 #1

Opposite: This photo was likely taken on the same day, in summer of 1908, as were the ones on pages 48 and 69; the photographer was perched on the roof of a box car (with its catwalk removed, metal flashing covers the ridge). Engine No. 2 is parked in front of O'Brien's brewery, having just arrived with its short consist at the Klondike City yard. The three box cars are on the main line leading to the coal bunker, while two flat cars loaded with cordwood are on the siding. To the right, two tracks lead to the engine house, out of the picture.

The Bancroft Library, University of California, Berkeley, 1905.1709 6253B

CHAPTER EIGHT

COMPLETION, AND OPTIMISM
1906

The right-of-way question no longer held up progress, and O'Brien began work by moving his home and office to Dawson in late February. In late March the Yukon Saw Mill was awarded a contract for cutting 45,000 ties to be delivered by July 10—enough for seventeen miles of track—and the first span of the bridge over the Klondike River was in place; all three spans were up by April 3. With snow off the ground, construction began in full. Rail was laid along Front Street in Dawson, running to the north end of town. O'Brien spoke of construction of cars barns and car yards between Duke Street and Albert Street, but none were ever built there.

The Klondike Mines Railway informally started business when the first cargo was shipped from O'Brien's Klondike Brewery. Determined to open the railway in a memorable way and on a memorable day, Empire Day, May the 24th, O'Brien sent a load of lager to Dawson. However the Klondike River was in full flood, with water nearly to the level of the rails on the railway bridge, flooding the track to a depth of two to three feet at the south end of First Street in Dawson. The railway had one engine back the loads across the bridge, where the cargo was transferred to Orr and Turkey wagons which carried the brew to a point in front of the courthouse—here another locomotive took the beer for the remaining distance to vendors. A day later the brewery shipped not only lager, but also "bock" and a "fine brew of porter".

By early June, O'Brien guaranteed the railway would reach the Forks for the celebration of the First of July. By the end of June track had been laid two-thirds of the way to the Forks, and 300 men were working. It was also announced that the line would be completed beyond the Forks to King Solomon Dome where a station called Sulphur Springs would be built.

Building of the right-of-way had been straight-forward grading done with men using pick and shovel, and horse and scraper. While several deep gulches had been bridged, there had been a minimum of rock work. Blasting was confined to the Klondike River bluffs, a short section on Lower Bonanza, and the Sulphur Springs wye; all were simple, shallow, cuts. It was unspectacular railway building, particularly when compared with the difficulties on the grade of the White Pass, which might explain the absence of any photographic record of the work—no photos of O'Brien and Mackenzie's construction progress have yet been found.

Although most of the order for 30-foot, 15-ton, box cars had been delivered in late 1905 (including box car No. 122—the highest number), three more arrived in late June along with a barge load of bridge timber. Coal bunkers were now in place on the most southerly high ground of Klondike City, and on June 27 "a barge-load of coal arrived from the Tantalus mine, consigned to T.W. O'Brien of the railway".

By Dominion Day, July 1, 1906, rail had not yet reached the Forks, in spite of O'Brien's assurance. Here in the Klondike, where over half the population was American, both the First of July and the Fourth of July, and the two days between, were days of celebration. On Monday, July 2, O'Brien scheduled special excursion services to open the new line to Grand Forks. Although the track work was complete only as far as 25 Below on Bonanza, that did not faze the enthusiastic crowd, as stages took the passengers the remaining two miles to the Forks for the festivities. Three trains ran that day, leaving Dawson at 9:45, 14:30, and 19:30, and the consist was Engine No. 1, the tender, a coach, a combination coach, and an "observation car", which, despite the name, was just a flat car fitted with side boards and seats. Newsmen reported;

> ...Tom Beveridge at the throttle, Joe Stengle at the firebox, and Billy Rogers with the ticket punch. Many were evidently keen for a ride on the new-fangled contrivance and some of the sourdoughs who had not seen a train in ten years had to be fitted with blinders and backed into the coaches. The latter were soon comfortably filled and with a salute from the whistle in rag-time they were off.

The explanation of the sourdough/blinders spoof was that backwoods mules or horses unaccustomed to, or frightened of, trains or steamers could not be led onto these contraptions; they had to be blind-folded and then could be backed on, apparently having no qualms about this approach.

Immediately after the early July celebrations, work began on the Grand Forks to Sulphur section with the establishment of several camps: 1st—at 35 Above, which had moved up from 46 Below; 2nd—at 51 Above, moved up from 25 Below; and 3rd—still farther up-line was a camp moved from 4 Below. Work to the Forks was soon completed and limited freight service started.

On July 6, the first serious accident occurred in construction of the railway;

> A flat car loaded with telegraph poles which were being distributed from the slough bridge on, was near 65 Below when the standards of the car gave way, and instantly poles rolled down the embankment carrying three men along. George Ward suffered a broken leg and was badly bruised. Joseph Mayo and Thomas Johnson suffered numerous contusions, and were badly shaken up.

The coal bunkers which had been built for the railway in Klondike City were increased in capacity to hold 1000 tons. O'Brien had got the contract to handle Tantalus coal in Dawson and on the Creeks, but coal was delivered to Klondike City by White Pass steamers, not by O'Brien's steamer company, which had since gone under.

The *Whitehorse Star* of July 7 reported, "Mrs. E.A. Murphy is on her way to Dawson where her husband is employed as a conductor on the Klondike Creeks Railroad"; evidently a misquote—or was it? Eugene A. Murphy was at the time Skagway agent of the Pacific Coast Steamship Company. Murphy was in fact visiting Dawson, and possibly interested in a position with the railway; a year later he would become general manager of the Klondike Mines Railway.

A Dawson City depot for the railway had been selected by mid-July. Renovations were being made to the old Boyle Warehouse on the waterfront just south of the ferry tower. The warehouse was first used by the Seattle-Yukon Transportation Company which had operated on the lower Yukon River with the steamers *Seattle No. 1* and *Seattle No. 3*. Boats and barges with long gangplanks could reach the back side of the depot which fronted on First Avenue (Front Street) a little south of Queen Street. At the south end of the building were two waiting rooms, one of 16x28 feet for general use, and one of 14x14 feet for women. Offices faced the river, the main one 16x20 feet, of which one end, 12x12 feet, was set apart for train dispatcher, telegrapher, and ticket agent. The baggage room was 14x20 feet with its floor three feet above street level, and the entire north end of the building, 33x30 feet, was reserved for freight—the floor here was also three feet above the street for easy loading onto drays. On July 28, the *Dawson Daily News* reported that the "**Grand Central Depot**" in Dawson was open with trains running only to the Forks, carriages taking over from there. Dawson City had the most northerly railway depot, ever, in Canada!

Right-of-way complaints were now out of federal hands, the Klondike Mines Railway having agreed to compensation where challenged, and through July and August hearings were held without construction stoppage. Various Bonanza Creek claim owners, plaintiffs in the matter of bench mining claims versus the Klondike Mines Railway Company, the Dawson, Grand Forks and Stewart River Railway Corporation, and T.W. O'Brien and J.H. Mackenzie, the defendants, were heard before Mr. George Black, Justice of the Peace; the subject: compensation from the company for crossing of the claims and damages incurred. The hearings were rather informal, with court questioning only, and Mr. Black handed down amicable settlements. Not all settlements were handled with such legal representation. O'Brien avoided litigation in settling with miner Fred Maier whose heavy operation on Gold Hill would be "damaged" by the railway. O'Brien's willingness to pay (and avoid construction delays) led to a mutual agreement where an experienced miner was chosen to arbitrate, and very quickly Maier was "paid $650 for damages to three claims and the destruction of a cabin."

On July 16 Grand Forks was at last connected by rail, and now that frost was out the ground, grading was proceeding at a faster rate. By August 1, O'Brien and Mackenzie had built 12½ miles of track to the Forks, and 350 men were working on the 18½ mile section from the Forks to Sulphur. Grading as far as the Forks had been largely hillside cuts in gravel or soil with a minimum of rock work; the grade was slight with a gain of only 300 feet between Dawson City and Grand Forks. Grading was no more difficult from the Forks to the Dome, again only a minimum of rock blasting was needed, although the grade was considerably steeper, at a maximum of 3.48 percent. Following the valley of upper Bonanza Creek as far as Carmack Fork, the route climbed towards the ridge, and near Flannery roughly followed the old

KLONDIKE MINES RY. CO.
Good for one continuous passage
FROM
GRAND FORKS, Y. T.
TO
DAWSON, Y. T.
If presented on date stamped on back.
H. D Weeks, Gen. Agt.
No. D..................

Not Good If Detached

KLONDIKE MINES RY. CO.
Good for one continuous passage
FROM
DAWSON, Y. T.
TO
GRAND FORKS, Y. T.
If presented within 15 days from date stamped on back.
H. D. Weeks, Gen. Agt.
No. D..................

Dawson City Museum, Dawson, Yukon

Government Ridge Road right to Cook's Roadhouse near Sulphur Springs. The elevation gain between the Forks and Sulphur was about 2000 feet. Running mainly along the divide between Bonanza Creek and the Klondike River watersheds, the route would be subject to fierce winds and drifting snow in the winter months ahead.

Wooden trestles were under construction, or already built, at Homestake Gulch, Gauvin Gulch, McKay Gulch, and four in a bunch at Flannery. The trestles on the gulches were each 400 feet long. The trestle at Homestake Gulch (21 Above on Bonanza) was the highest of all at 65 feet. None of the railway's bridges and trestles had concrete footings; all, including the Klondike River bridge, were built on wooden pilings. About 100,000 board feet of timber went into construction of the three Upper Bonanza trestles. The heaviest work on the line was reported to be between Carmack Fork and McCarty.

Meanwhile, Treadgold had been very active, acquiring claims for consolidation of all properties on Bonanza Creek under a new company, and preparations were being made for the construction of three dredges on

Bonanza and a hydroelectric plant to provide power for the dredges. The backers of the "new company" were made known in early August, when representative members of the Guggenheim family arrived in Dawson for an inspection of their properties. The head of the family, Meyer Guggenheim, had come to America in the early 1800s and had made a fortune in the embroidery business, and then prospered from Colorado mining properties, further adding to his wealth and experience. Meyer's sons Daniel and Solomon were the principals of the Guggenheim Exploration Company which was now about to begin operations in the Klondike—this would become the Yukon Gold Company, and the company headquarters near the junction of Bonanza Creek with the Klondike River would quickly become known as "Guggieville." Daniel and Solomon had also brought their wives along to visit the Klondike, and for the occasion Treadgold chartered a special excursion train. On the 9th;

> the Guggenheim party...took a ride over the gold-paved route of the Klondike Mines Railway. They left at 9:30 am on a special train comprising one coach and an observation car splendidly fitted out for the comfort of guests. In addition to the Guggenheim family were A.N.C. Treadgold, Tom O'Brien, Bloomfield Smith, Chester A. Thomas, S.H. Graves, and George Coffey. The train left Dawson from opposite the N.A.T.&T.Co. store and went to Grand Forks and Beyond.

Track between Dawson and Grand Forks was now spiked in place and ballasted. A sworn statement given August 16 by Herbert Bloomfield Smith, engineer for the Klondike Mines Railway, certified that he was familiar with the work on this fifteen miles of track, and that he had inspected the line, stating it was ready for use and for inspection by the government inspector. The inspection was immediate as Charles W. MacPherson, Board of Railway Commissioners, approved the track work, declaring it ready for business. A full statement followed on August 29, listing a number of features:

- cost in excess of $28,000 per mile.
- 1200 feet of wyes.
- 3200 feet of yard and minor sidings.
- steel bridge over the Klondike River, 3 spans of 140 feet, 100 feet, and 80 feet.
- steel bridge over Klondike slough, 1 span of 80 feet.
- at Dawson City, a 26 x 80 foot combined passenger station and freight shed, of corrugated sheet iron, containing: general waiting room, ladies waiting room, general offices, warm storage and baggage room, and general freight shed.
- at Grand Forks, a 26 x 46 foot station house of corrugated sheet iron, containing: general waiting room and ticket office, ladies waiting room, warm storage and baggage room, and general freight shed.
- 20,000 gallon (450 barrel) tanks for water supply from steam pumping plants at 12 miles apart.
- 800 ton coal bunkers at Klondike City.
- telephone and telegraph facilities at Dawson and Grand Forks and at a through siding about six miles from Dawson.

On August 19 the first commercial excursion train ran directly from Dawson to Grand Forks, departing at 9:30 a.m. to return by 4:30 p.m., and the fare of $3.00 included a dinner at the Golden Hill Hotel. Although trains were running daily, passenger service was neither scheduled nor regular yet. On September 8, 1906, the *Dawson Daily News* ran the first advertisement, a public time table, to be published by the Klondike Mines Railway:

Klondike Mines
RAILWAY
BETWEEN
DAWSON AND GRAND FORKS.

Daily	Daily
Leave Dawson.	Arr. Grand Forks.
8:30 a. m.	9:30 a. m.
4:00 p. m.	5:00 p. m.
Leave Grand Forks.	Arrive Dawson
9:45 a. m.	10:45 a. m.
5:30 p. m.	6:30 p. m.

Opposite: A mate to the photos on pages 45 and 69, this photo shows engine No. 2 with box car No. 122 and coach No. 202 on the Homestake Gulch trestle. Two ditches, one above the other carried water from a dam on Upper Bonanza to hydraulic-mining operations downstream. Beneath the far end of the trestle is the lower ditch, and at track level in the foreground is the second artificial water course utilizing an inverted siphon to connect the ditches on either side of the gulch.
The Bancroft Library, University of California, Berkeley, 1905.1709 6263

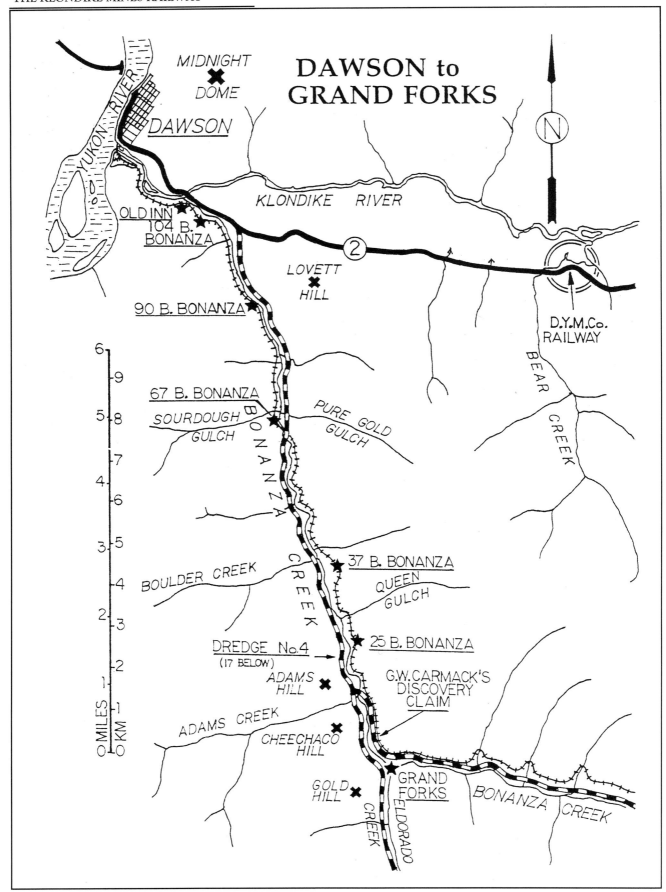

DAWSON to GRAND FORKS

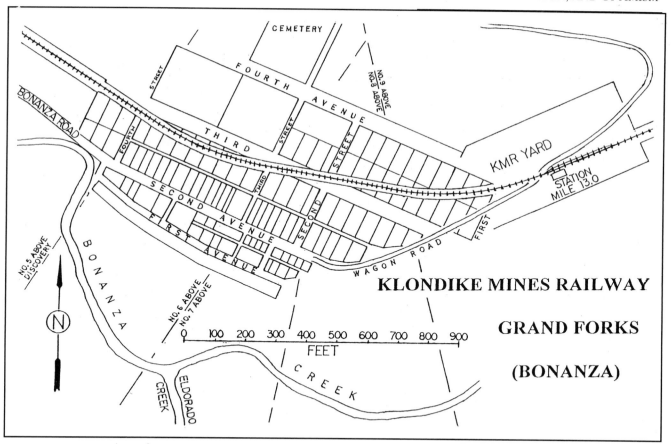

Businesses in Grand Forks were concentrated along First Avenue and Bonanza Road. Survey plans showed the above neat townsite, but in fact no streets were built above Second Avenue, which lay at the foot of the hillside. A number of cabins and shacks were built on the lower side of the railway grade, but only footpaths served these dwellings. What in reality existed can be seen very well in the photo showing dredge No. 8 under construction on Bonanza Creek (on Claim No. 6 Above), taken August 11, 1911 (see photo on page 80). Grand Forks was practically abandoned when the Klondike Mines Railway was shut down.

This schedule was in effect until November when time tables were revised to include Sulphur Springs, often referred to simply as Sulphur. Official approval permitting the railway to engage in general traffic came in late August when tariffs and rates had been approved and published. The railway still had only sixteen miles of track completed, but the *Yukon World* waxed optimistically;

> By the middle of September one can ride to Sulphur Springs. A year from now the trip can be extended to the vicinity of Australia Creek, and two years from now in all probability the headwaters of the Pelly and McMillan will be virtually brought to one's door.

At the time, Montreal was the financial headquarters of Canada, and from the *Montreal Gazette* came the most bizarre misnaming yet seen for the Klondike Mines

Railway. August 23, 1906: "Work is well under way on the Atlin, White Horse and Dawson Railway which is to give communication between the capital of the Yukon and the mines and perhaps ultimately with the outside world." The paper also reported that several cargoes of rail had been sent north and it was hoped the line would be completed by winter. The rails, a thousand tons, were purchased from Illinois Steel Works; this was 45-lb rail, enough for over twelve miles of track. The railway had got approval to use only 45-lb instead of 52-lb rail between the Forks and Sulphur.

To avail themselves of the soon-to-be-finished railway, miners on adjacent creeks petitioned for government roads. Seventy-five to eighty men worked during September to complete good wagon roads, leading down from the railway on the ridge to the creek bottoms. Work was straight-forward hillside grading with no rock-work

On Upper Bonanza Creek, not far from Grand Forks, is a dam, power house, and sluicing operation. On the right the grade of the KMR begins its climb away from Bonanza Creek, heading for Flannery. This photo was probably taken in 1908.
Yukon Archives, Schellinger Coll'n, 5965

needed. The community of Readford, situated on Lower Quartz Creek, was formerly accessible only via Bonanza and Eldorado Creeks, southward; it was now reached by a new road which crossed the rail line about one-half mile west of Sulphur Springs. Hunker Creek and the community of Gold Bottom had until now been reached via the valley of the Klondike River, but a new road down Gold Run Creek, commonly called Soap Creek, from Sulphur Springs gave down-hill freighting all the way. A new section connected the Sulphur terminal with workings on lower Sulphur Creek and the camp known as Sulphur. On Dominion Creek were the communities of Caribou, Paris, Jensen Creek, Gold Run, and Dominion, and at the confluence of Dominion Creek with Sulphur Creek was Granville, the largest camp south of the divide. None of these settlements survived more than a few decades.

Steel-laying was far from done, but at the end of August, 120 rail graders were laid off, with their work complete to Sulphur, right on the Divide between Gold Bottom and Sulphur Creeks and one-half mile beyond Cook's Roadhouse. Grading had been indeed easy, especially

when compared to the work which had been necessary on the route of the White Pass. Rail was laid as far as Homestake Gulch where a big trestle, the highest on the line, was just being completed. Four days later track had been advanced to McKay Gulch. On September 14 the *Yukon World* reported that the last trestle work on the line, four short ones at Flannery, located on the upper branches of Carmack Fork, were being completed. From here it was ten more miles to Sulphur, where the company had already built a train shed, a station with a heated waiting room for passengers, a warehouse for warm storage, a stall for the locomotive, and a wye for turning engines around. The Sulphur wye was a last-minute addition to the route plans. Not shown on earlier plans submitted for approval, this wye was in fact a full one mile west of King Solomon Dome, and its location was authorized only in late August. The full intentions of the company prior to this development are uncertain, but the initial survey plan indicated the line would end, for the time being, one-half mile farther on, at the very head of Sulphur Creek (Sulphur Springs) on the south-western slope of the Dome.

The Sulphur wye may or may not have been intended as a permanent fixture. On September 17 Herbert Bloomfield Smith, Dawson representative of the London stockholders backing the railway, received instruction to make preparations for extending the rail line. Surveyor Astley had a crew working beyond Sulphur for some time, and the plan was to now read;

> The route from the Springs will be down Caribou Gulch, to Caribou City, on Dominion Creek; thence along the right limit of Dominion Creek, to 98 Below Lower on Dominion Creek; thence along the left limit to Rob Roy, opposite the mouth of Gold Run and Granville; thence up Rob Roy for four miles; thence into Melba, and up Melba to the head of the divide between the Flat Creek and Dominion basins. An easy grade then will lead into Flat Creek. . . . it is yet a question whether only thirty or fifty miles will be constructed next year.

Smith anticipated no problems in crossing mining claims on any of this section.

On September 24, C.W. MacPherson sent a plan, provided by the Klondike Mines Railway, to Ottawa. The survey, dated August, 1906, and signed by J.W. Astley, engineer, and H.B. McGiverin, president, asked for approval of land for stock yard grounds and repair shops-

land near the Ogilvie Bridge where the railway had its only other wye. The railway was "squatting" on this land, on which a mining company had prior surface rights. As O'Brien oversaw construction progress, his partner Mackenzie arrived from the Outside and was interviewed by the local press. With some scrambled facts, the ***Dawson Daily News*** of October 1 reported;

> He is a San Francisco capitalist with mining interests. He expects the Grand Trunk Railway within a few years. The Klondike Mines Railway is the initial link in what may become a system of vast importance here. Mr. Mackenzie is the original projector of the railway up Bonanza from Dawson. He came in 1898 and surveyed the first route. He and O'Brien...secured the franchise for the road, but conflict with others seeking similar franchises and entanglements over the rights of way and the like tied up the road indefinitely, even after material was ordered at the beginning. Mr. Hawkins later took an interest in promoting the company, but finally English capital took hold of the road and is backing the enterprise.

It was October 1, and rail to Sulphur was still not completed. Regular coach service to the Forks was temporarily stopped to allow completion of the line as both engines No. 1 and No. 2 were working full time,

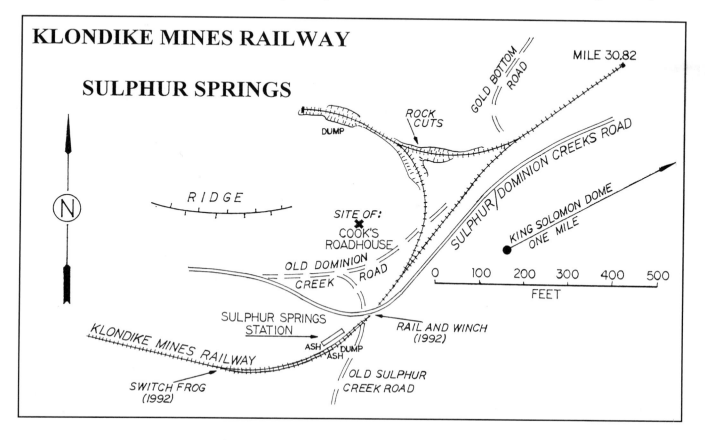

KLONDIKE MINES RAILWAY

SULPHUR SPRINGS

NO. 7-A COMPOUND ENGINE ON THE WHITE PASS & YUKON ROUTE

Brand new, WP&YR's No. 7 poses at Bennett, B.C. Built in January of 1899 by Baldwin as c/n 16456, this compound, outside-framed, locomotive was in 1900 relettered as WP&YR No. 57, and in 1906 was sold to the Klondike Mines Railway as engine No. 3.
Dedman's Photo Shop, Skagway, AK

with the coaches left on a spur in Klondike City. Another engine was on the way, but it would arrive too late to help in construction. Shoving a barge, the steamer ***Bonanza King*** left Whitehorse on September 30 with freight, including one locomotive for the "**Grand Forks Railway**". Although low water on the Yukon River was impeding steamer movement, the ***Bonanza King*** arrived on October 4 with Klondike Mines Railway locomotive No. 3. Bought secondhand from the White Pass, as were No. 1 and No. 2, this engine valued at $12,000 was the newest and biggest on the roster. An 1899 Baldwin Vauclain compound engine, it was one of two identical models bought new for the White Pass, first numbered 7, then re-numbered 57 in 1900. It was to be placed in commission shortly.

At about the same time, O'Brien, Mackenzie, and Astley left on a trip to Flat Creek, scouting the extension route for the railway, going down Caribou Creek, down

Dominion to Granville, up Rob Roy, and around the head of Melba, and into the Flat Creek country.

With snow already flying, rail to the summit was finally finished on October 12, although some ballasting was still needed. Compliments came from the ***Yukon World***;

A large force of men have been employed all season, many of them having been on the payroll since beginning of work in the spring, and they speak in praise of the treatment that had been accorded them by the contractor, the wages paid, the character of the table, and general accommodations furnished.

The road was examined by Charles MacPherson, Inspector of Railways, who accepted the work and turned the road over to the company for business. The railway's Klondike City office was moved to Dawson, where engineers Williams and Rendell occupied the depot, which was in the charge of agent Harold D. Weeks. Rail extension work would begin next spring.

On October 25, 1906, the final inspection report by M.J. Butler, Dawson City, for the entire line included:

- ruling grade 3.48%, sharpest curve 24 degrees.
- first 15.64 miles 52-lb rail, remainder of line 45-lb rail.
- 1500 feet of wyes.
- at Klondike City, a 80 x 30 foot roundhouse* and repair shop, covered with corrugated iron sheet, to accommodate three locomotives and one passenger coach.
- at Sulphur Springs, a 66 x 24 foot station house covered with corrugated iron sheet containing: general waiting room, ladies waiting room, general office, baggage room, warm storage room, and a freight shed.
- wye accommodations for locomotive and four cars at end of track at Sulphur Springs.
- frame roundhouse* for one locomotive at Sulphur Springs.
- coal bunkers at Klondike City enlarged to 1500 tons capacity.
- water tank at seven miles beyond Grand Forks.
- telegraph facilities the full length of the line.

Total cost of construction was estimated at one million dollars.

With over thirty miles of track, three locomotives, two passengers cars, thirteen box cars, and ten flat cars the Klondike Mines Railway Company was now ready for business.

---

*Although often referred to as a "roundhouse" the Klondike City engine house had no turntable—only two parallel tracks, over service pits, onto which the locomotives and tenders were backed. The Sulphur Springs engine house was a single track shelter.

MONTH		
Jany		
Feby		
Mar.		
April		
May		
June		
July		
Aug.		
Sept.		
Oct.		
Nov.		
Dec.		

ad. 1906

№ 2392

George Pringle

CONDUCTOR'S CASH FARE SLIP.
PASSENGER'S RECEIPT FOR CASH PAID CONDUCTOR.

Klondike Mines Ry. Co.

First-Class Fare—Baggage—100 lbs. Half Fare—Baggage—50 lbs. Excess Baggage Rates, 50 per cent. 1st Class Fare per 100 lbs. or Fraction thereof.

BETWEEN
DAWSON AND

Klondike City	$ .25
Old Inn	.50
60 B. Bonanza	1.00
25 B. Bonanza	1.50
Grand Forks	2.00

BETWEEN
GRAND FORKS
AND

25 B. Bonanza	$ .50
60 B. Bonanza	1.00
Old Inn	1.50
Klondike City or Dawson	2.00

BETWEEN
KLONDIKE CITY
AND

Dawson	$ .25

Local Distance Tariff

MILES		PASSENGER FARE PER MILE
OVER	NOT MORE THAN	
0	4	20c ....$.
4	8	18c 1.50
8	12	17c 2.00
12	16	17c 2.75
16	20	17c 3.25
20	25	17c .... 4.

| 26 | 27 | 28 | 29 | 30 | 31 |

MacBride Museum, Whitehorse, Yukon

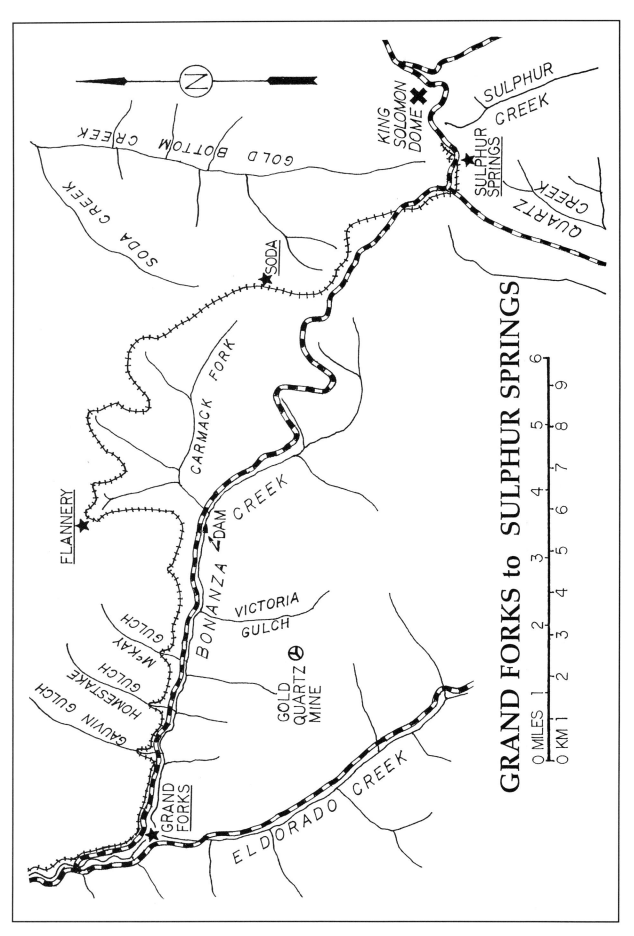

GRAND FORKS to SULPHUR SPRINGS

0 MILES 1 2 3 4 5 6
0 KM 1 2 3 4 5 6 7 8 9

CHAPTER NINE

REALITY
1906 AND 1907

Officially operational, the railway got off to a miserable start, and things would get worse—far worse. Although trains left Dawson promptly at 8:30 a.m., return times were irregular because delays were encountered in unloading freight, and in the inevitable problem of snow. By late October a flanger and snow plow of "new design" was being built for the railway; this was in fact a basic wedge plow, not a rotary plow.

On November 1, 1906, a new public time table appeared, for the first time listing service to Sulphur Springs. Signed by John W. Astley, chief engineer, and H.D. Weeks, superintendent and traffic manager, the schedule included one return trip per day, seven days a week: Train No. 1 southbound from Dawson at 8:30 a.m. arriving at Sulphur Springs at 11:30 a.m., then returning as Train No. 2 northbound from Sulphur at 12:30 p.m. to reach Dawson at 3:30 p.m. Both trains made the usual ten minute stop at Grand Forks, and averaged about 10 mph. With winter conditions worsening, trains handled by engine No. 1 frequently ran very late. Manager Astley reported that the schedules would be adhered to when engine No. 2 could be put back in working order. Although rebuilt by the White Pass before arriving here, No. 2 was having steaming troubles, and was in the shop. Engine No. 1, the ancient Brooks, was a light-weight engine, and for reasons soon explained, engine No. 3 which had just arrived a month ago could not be used either.

The railway had made arrangements with Orr and Turkey Stage Lines, long-time freighters on the creeks, to haul all freight and passengers to points on Dominion, Sulphur, and Gold Run Creeks from the Sulphur Springs terminal. Tickets were sold by the railway for through trips using the stage service. Sunday service was apparently little patronized for on November 10 a reduction of service to six days per week was announced. The *Canada Gazette* of November 24 carried the railway's "Notice of Standard Freight and Passenger Tariffs", submitted by H. Bloomfield Smith, C.E.M. Inst., General Manager, and H.D. Weeks, General Freight and Passenger Agent, effective November 19, 1906. (See Appendix B)

Although passenger service was not heavily patronized, it was appreciated. The *Yukon World* detailed one sourdough's viewpoint;

His First Ride on the Train:

A miner of Lower Dominion coming to town yesterday had his first ride on a train of cars in twelve years. He was a grizzled old veteran, the hero of many stampedes, and had been in the Birch Creek country before the Klondike was discovered. When the train pulled into the station at Sulphur Springs and he climbed the steps, before entering the car he looked around in a sort of mystified way, muttering to himself that it did "beat all—the change that had come over the country". "D'ye see that trail running down that hogback", he said to a fellow passenger, pointing to a narrow streak scarcely visible meandering through the sparse underbrush, "that's the trail I took when I stampeded to Sulphur with the first outfit that planted stakes on the creek in June '97. It took us three days to make the trip from Dawson, packing our grub, frying pan and coffee pot. Now they tell me they make the trip in three hours. It do beat—" and he passed into the car, the look of wonderment increasing as the train rounded the head of Cormack's (sic) Fork and a half hour later swung into the Forks.

Trains may not have been running according to schedule, but the comfort of passengers was well looked after. Waiting rooms and storage rooms for perishables at Sulphur and the Forks were heated, of course, and "the passenger coach now in use has been equipped with storm windows, and with a stove in each end it is as warm and comfortable as any of the palace cars on the transcontinental lines". Not only passengers enjoyed the new service; freight was now being delivered to Sulphur

KLONDIKE MINES RAILWAY CO.

DAWSON .... 191 ....

Capacity of Siding	Miles from Dawson	Train No. Conductor Engineer Engine STATIONS		Telegraph Calls	Telephone Calls
	0	DAWSON		DS	1R
		1			
25	1	KLONDIKE CITY	w.c.		2R
		1.6			
10	3	OLD INN	y		1L2S
		1			
6	3	104 B. BONANZA			
		1.4			
4	5	90 B. BONANZA			
		2.2			
4	6.6	67 B. BONANZA			
		3			
	9.6	37 B. BONANZA	w.		
		1.2			
	10.8	25 B. BONANZA			
		2.2			
4	13	GRAND FORKS		GE	1S1L
		6.75			
	19.75	FLANNERY	w.		4R
		7.25			
8	27	SODA			5R
		4			
4	31	SULPHUR SPRINGS	y	SU	3R

A re-creation of part of a Klondike Mines Railway dispatcher's train sheet. Note the discrepancies in mileages from Dawson versus the mileages between stations; also note that both water and coal were available at Klondike City, and that there were only two wyes: at Old Inn and Sulphur Springs. The other part of the train sheet included blanks for: dispatcher's names, weather reports, train consists, and operating details.

Dawson City Museum, Dawson, Yukon

*An excerpt from the **Dawson Daily News** of November 6, 1906, showing the Klondike Mines Railway passenger schedule. The KMR was not the only transportation company to advertise in Dawson.*

at 1¼ cents per pound—in the summer of '98 the rate was 40 cents per pound.

The Yukon winter now took charge and the *Dawson Daily News* of November 27 read; "Drifting snow and gales are the worst in years. Special snow clearing gangs are ready, plus a plow and flanger, built at the Yukon Mill, which it is believed will handle the snows. It has been necessary to pull up the planking between the rails on First Avenue in Dawson...snow gets packed in and there is no room for the wheel flanges." One day later the *Yukon World* continued, "One of the worst snow storms, a blizzard, in many years is here; with drifting snow and the snowplow yet unfinished, a locomotive is stuck in snow." On the 29th the details were known: "The train is blocked four miles from Sulphur; it left Dawson yesterday morning, and spun out with snow on the track, it then gave out of water and died, and the fire had to be pulled." There were three passengers in the coach; two men who mushed on, and a woman who stayed on, but the coach had a coal stove at each end so she kept warm and comfortable. The railway company sent up sheet metal workers to build tanks for melting snow for the engine. The water tanks at Sulphur were frozen solid, and there was no other supply here in deep snow near the Dome.

Engine No. 2, over the years the most-used locomotive on the roster, was in the shop being overhauled. Engine No. 1 was a light machine intended only for construction and maintenance work, and it was now locked in snow drifts on a wind-blasted ridge. Although engine No. 3 was the most powerful engine of the three locomotives on the roster, it immediately proved a disappointment. Even before snow began to pile up it was discovered that it was too wide to get past some of the few rock cuts. Engines No. 1 and No. 2 were about seven feet in width at the cylinders, but No. 3 was fully nine feet wide—the bulk of the massive compound cylinders and an outside frame accounting for the difference. In the coming year the grade would be widened where necessary, but in the meanwhile, engine No. 1 was dug out from the drifts and resumed operation within three days.

This appears to be in the late winter of 1906-07, when the train is being shovelled clear of hard-packed snow drifts near Soda Station. Several times during the winter, crews of men were packed into a coach with supplies in a box car for attempts to open the line to Sulphur Springs—more than ten miles of the route ran along the wind-blasted divide separating the valleys of Bonanza Creek and the Klondike River.
MacBride Museum, 93-28 X901.3A.28

With railway operation back to normal by mid-December a few changes in personnel and operations were made. M.E. Bennett replaced Weeks as traffic agent at Dawson. Weeks went out on holiday, and never returned, going to work for Hawkins, and A.J. Dewar, who had been agent at Sulphur, was transferred to the Forks where he became office manager. The company also set up a new water station at Soda, where snow-melting boilers were installed. Spring water from Flannery contained so much silt and alkali as to interfere with locomotive boiler operations, but a different source there was apparently tapped, for in later years Flannery would be listed as the only water tank between the Forks and Sulphur.

By the new year, Klondike Mines Railway shop men, although hampered by inadequate locomotive shop equipment, had nevertheless rebuilt engine No. 2 with complete success. Now back in service with an enlarged firebox for greater heating surface, and towing the tender

from engine No. 3, which held 800 gallons more than No. 2's tender, service to Sulphur Springs was once more back on schedule. While engine No. 2 was being overhauled, engine No. 1 had been pressed into service, but with its limited tractive effort trains ran slower, and consists were limited to a single freight car or coach. The result was that passengers occasionally had to ride in box cars laden with express items. Engine No. 1 was now in the shop being completely rebuilt—it had been driven hard during the road's construction stages. Newly-arrived engine No. 3 was for the moment relegated to the engine house in Klondike City. While No. 2 could now carry more water, the company had also set up snow-melting tanks at Bush's Fork four miles beyond Flannery.

To combat drifting snow, snow fences were built for a distance of three or four miles along the ridge southward from the summit at the head of Soda Creek, and additional snow fences were built surrounding the wye at the

the Sulphur Springs terminal. In spite of these noble efforts the Yukon winter continued to stall operations. On January 12, plow-equipped No. 2 became stuck in snow two miles from Sulphur. Twenty men with horses were sent to clear the track, and engine No. 1 was sent up at midnight to bring supplies to the stranded train; drifts were up to six feet deep on the tracks. One week later the long-stalled train had been finally dug out and the whole line cleared. The train returned to Dawson a little more than a week after its departure.

Sunday service had been discontinued in November, and a new schedule was published on February 12, 1907. Changes in departure and arrival times were minor, and one round trip per day was listed for six days a week. The resignation of Weeks was reflected in an announcement of management changes, as Astley became local manager and superintendent, and M.E. Bennett became agent.

Located at the very north end of the Dawson City line, the Yukon Saw Mill was ready to ship timber to a new power dam, financed by the Yukon Gold Company, to be built at 60 Above on Bonanza. On March 14 the unused track north of the railway station leading to the Yukon Saw Mill had to be opened up through deep snow drifts.

With winter now weakening, the railway advertised an excursion to Sulphur Springs on St. Patrick's Day, Sunday March 17th. The round trip cost $5.00, including dinner at Sulphur Springs, with the train leaving the depot at Front Street at 9:00 a.m.

In late March, O'Brien returned to Dawson after a three-month trip which included visits to Ottawa, London, and Seattle. In Seattle in January he had talked of plans to extend the railway south, connecting either with the White Pass at Whitehorse or with the Grand Trunk now being built. Three days from Vancouver to Dawson! At home again he spoke confidently of extending the line to the Stewart River. Notwithstanding these brave words,

A.S Wyman who arrived from London with O'Brien to act as assistant manager and chief accountant, cautioned that rail work this year was only a "perhaps." O'Brien did become the railway's general manager immediately, succeeding Astley. The appointment was announced a week later when a new time table was published, basically unchanged, still listing Train No. 1 southbound, and Train No. 2 northbound, six times a week.

On April 12th, 1907, Parliament consented to a further extension of time for completion of the line, as defined in its charter. The two-year expenditure clause of the 1902 amendment had been fulfilled by 1904 but, now in 1907 the five-year line-completion clause was not satisfied.

Development of the North needed an efficient transportation system. The White Pass' Skagway to Dawson route was hardly satisfactory; steamboats were adequate in summer but haulage of any large amount of freight in winter was impossible. Entrepreneurs saw the need for an all-season, all-land route, to the Yukon. Among others railway companies, the Grand Trunk Pacific's proposed line from Hazelton to Dawson, an all-Canadian route, was one of the earlier schemes which, of course, never materialized. Another idea, which had been around since the mid-1800s was a railway connecting Siberia with Alaska ("Paris to New York," via Dawson) with a tunnel beneath the Bering Strait. With the evolvement of the Klondike goldfield, promoters picked up this plan and began studies, and by 1904 none other than John J. Healy, who until now had shown remarkably good business sense, became seriously involved. He spent the last of his earnings gained through the NAT&TCo in promoting the "Trans-Alaska-Siberia Railway." He had hoped to gain funding from the Czar of Russia, but by late 1907 the plan was killed, leaving Healy dead broke. Still the promotions continued; in 1908, yet another railway (among many others) was to reach the Yukon, albeit a more modest plan--the Northern Empire Railway out of Lethbridge, Alberta--was to be in Dawson within four years.

KLONDIKE MINES RAILWAY CO.
TIME TABLE
MONDAYS, WEDNESDAYS AND FRIDAYS

No. 2 North Bound -		No. 1 South Bound
2.15 p m Ar	DAWSON	Lv 7.00 a m
1.15 p m Lv	GRAND FORKS	Ar 8.40 a m
1.10 p.m Ar		Lv 8.10 a n.
12.00 n	SULPHUR SPRINGS	Ar 10.30 a m

TUESDAYS, THURSDAYS AND SATURDAYS

No. 2 North Bound -		No. 1 South Bound
1.15 p m Ar	DAWSON	Lv 7.00 a m
12.15 p m Lv	GRAND FORKS	Ar 8.00 a m
12.10 p m Ar		Lv 8.10 a n.
11.00 a n Lv	SULPHUR SPRINGS	Ar 10.30 a m

JOHN W. ASTLEY,
Local Manager and Supt.

M E BENNETT,
Agent

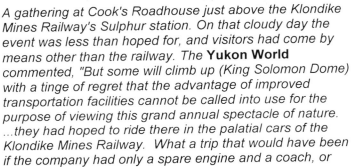

A gathering at Cook's Roadhouse just above the Klondike Mines Railway's Sulphur station. On that cloudy day the event was less than hoped for, and visitors had come by means other than the railway. The **Yukon World** *commented, "But some will climb up (King Solomon Dome) with a tinge of regret that the advantage of improved transportation facilities cannot be called into use for the purpose of viewing this grand annual spectacle of nature. ...they had hoped to ride there in the palatial cars of the Klondike Mines Railway. What a trip that would have been if the company had only a spare engine and a coach, or even a little public-spirited enterprise." Cook's Roadhouse was a popular destination for many excursions. On the right horizon one-half mile distant is King Solomon Dome, a popular destination for day-hikers. The gentleman on the wagon is probably J.D. "Dad" Hartman, proprietor of the hotel and eatery. Only two others have been identified: fourth from left is Mrs. Mary B. Dwyer, sister-in-law of Tom O'Brien, and third from right is Tom's wife, Anna Josephine O'Brien.*

Eric Johnson Collection, courtesy Frances Dwyer, Seattle, Washington

Whether or not the railway had actually planned to continue track work, or whether the extension was petitioned for solely to ensure forthcoming subsidies, isn't certain. As in the two earlier time extensions, the same terms applied. In re-applying for further construction subsidies, the Klondike Mines Railway once more redefined the line of completed and planned track work, which was detailed in a parliamentary act dated April 27th, 1907:

a) for a line of railway from Dawson to a point at or near Sulphur Springs, not exceeding 31 miles;

b) for a line of railway from a point at or near Sulphur Springs to a point at or near the divide between Dominion and Flat Creeks, not exceeding 45 miles; and

c) for a line of railway from a point at or near the said divide to or towards the Stewart River, not exceeding 8 miles.

In fact no further work was ever done beyond Sulphur Springs.

Passenger patronage of trains had not been satisfactory, and O'Brien made a short-lived attempt to encourage residents of communities beyond Sulphur to better utilize the service. For the three weeks between May 20 and June 7, 1907, he scheduled Train No. 1 northbound from Sulphur at 8:00 a.m. to arrive at Dawson by 10:30 a.m. A six and one-half hour lay-over in Dawson would allow

KLONDIKE MINES RAILWAY CO.

TIME TABLE.

Daily Except Sunday.

No. 1 North Bound.		No. 2 South Bound.
Lv...... 8:00 a. m.	SULPHUR SPRINGS	Ar...... 8:00 p. m.
Ar...... 9:30 a. m.	**Grand Forks**	Lv...... 6:05 p. m.
Lv...... 9:35 a. m.		Ar...... 6:00 p. m
Ar......10:30 a. m.	DAWSON	Lv...... 5:00 p. m.

Connecting at Sulphur Springs with Dawson Transfer Co's stages for Sulphur, Gold Run, Quartz and Dominion Creeks.

Stages leave Granville and 33 B. L. Dominion, 5 a. m., every week day (giving creek residents a chance to come to Dawson and attend to business and return same day.)

The above change in schedule will go into effect on and after the 23rd May. T. W. O'BRIEN, Gen. Mgr.

the visitors a chance to shop and attend to business before leaving at 5:00 p.m. on the No. 2 Train southbound. This arrangement must have proven no more popular, for the schedule soon reverted to the previous routine. Train crews would certainly not have appreciated the overnight stay at Sulphur. The May 20 time table and its follow-up noted that stages of the Dawson Transfer Company made daily, except Sundays, connections between Sulphur Springs and Sulphur, Gold Run, Dominion, and Quartz Creeks. The June schedule remained in effect until the end of the season.

During the days of mixed train operations, which were day shift only, locomotives were always parked at the Klondike City shops—except, of course, for the three weeks in late spring of 1907 when trains remained overnight at Sulphur Springs. At Klondike City, where the locomotives had been backed into the shop tracks, trains were taken past the Dawson City-Klondike City junction and backed more than one mile, across the Klondike River bridge, into the Dawson City station. After picking up loaded flat cars and box cars at the

dockside warehouses, and loading of passengers, the train pulled out for Sulphur Springs and way stops.

At Sulphur Springs passengers were dropped off, the locomotive was turned on the wye, and loaded freight cars were dropped off and empties picked up. After a short layover, the train steamed for the Front Street line in Dawson City. After possibly dropping off empties there, the locomotive, coach, and cars backed across the Klondike River bridge, to the wye at Old Inn station, more than two and one-half miles from Dawson City, where the locomotive was turned. The train was then backed into the Klondike City yard, one and three-quarter miles away, where the cars and locomotive were parked for the night.

The federal construction subsidy, of which so much publicity had been made, was paid to the railway prior to June. The maximum allowed subsidy of $6400 mile for 30.81 miles amounted to a total payment of $197,184— or less than 20 percent of the construction cost, which was said to have exceeded one million dollars.

On Lower Bonanza Creek, about 1907, engine No. 2 with a light box car/combo consist is southbound. Here (probably Queen Gulch in the foreground) Bonanza Creek has not yet been attacked by dredges, and the cabins of many individual mine operators can be seen alongside the creek. Two or three bench claim groups on the hillsides are also being worked.
National Archives of Canada, PA 44650

Winter of 1906/7, or late fall of 1907 or 1908: engine No. 2 with combination coach No. 200 is steaming over the Klondike River bridge into Dawson--the railway had no cabooses. This abbreviated consist was typically seen in winter operations. In returning from Sulphur Springs, the engine has not been turned around on the Old Inn wye, as would have been done during the shipping season in order to bring freight cars in to the Dawson City docks. The long trestle in the foreground is on Klondike Island which was subject to annual spring flooding. The photographer's viewpoint is the public road crossing of the rail grade where the Government Bridge from Dawson touched down on Klondike Island. The buildings with the smoke stack houses the coal-fired or wood-fired, steam-powered, generators of the Dawson Electric Light and Power Company. The power house is still at this location today, except generators are now driven by diesel engines.
Dawson City Museum, Cribb's Drugstore, 984R-50-76

Lawther, of Lawther, Latta and Company, major stock-holders in the Klondike Mines Railway, visited Dawson in late June and told reporters that the extension of the line was now uncertain;

> The railroad is not altogether satisfactory from the amount of business done. When it was projected we did not know that the Guggenheims were coming in. That has altered the situation and the basis of calculation very much. But no doubt we shall have a large business from that company. We have the roadbed in first class shape and ready to haul the heavy machinery the company will need.

Lawther was referring to the recent consolidation of nearly all claims along Bonanza Creek under the name of the Yukon Gold Company, formed with Guggenheim money only last year. The Guggenheim's plan—or really Treadgold's plan—was taking shape; smaller mining operations using a good deal of manpower would be replaced by the much less labour-intensive dredging method, resulting in a coincidental drop in population and railway business along the line. Three Bucyrus dredges with five-cubic yard buckets were put into operation before the summer was out, and more and bigger machines were in the offing.

In early July, Lawther talked to the Dawson Board of Trade about extending the railway to link up with trans-continental lines, saying he favoured such an extension southward. The day before his departure from Dawson, July 21, Lawther ran a special excursion train over the line inviting a number of local powers, including general manager O'Brien.

Leaving Dawson a week earlier were John W. Astley and wife; he had accepted a position as consulting engineer on the new Hudson's Bay Railway. Astley had been replaced as manager by O'Brien only in late March, and now on August 19, 1907, O'Brien in turn was about to be replaced. Eugene A. Murphy arrived in Dawson a year earlier to join the Klondike Mines Railway, and now he took on a role which would last until the railway was finally shut down in 1913. He had been with the Pacific Coast Steamship Company as the Skagway agent for several years. Previous to that, Murphy was with the White Pass, and he had first come to Skagway from the Great Northern Railway seven years before. Now Murphy received an offer from the Klondike Mines Railway which he accepted, and he took full operational control of the railway. The reasons for Murphy's appointment over O'Brien are uncertain, but in many ways O'Brien used the railway to the advantage of some of his other enterprises; possibly Lawther had seen some conflicts of interest. Or perhaps O'Brien simply wanted

out from the confinement of the day-to-day job—for the past twenty years he had been self-employed, wheeling as he alone chose.

In preparation for another grim winter Murphy had eighty men working in early October, building one mile of snow fence in the vicinity of Soda Springs. Locomotive No. 2 was in the shops being readied for the onslaught. Intentions were to operate the line all winter, since the experience gained last winter would help in this year's running. However, on November 20th, orders came from London: shut down the railway for the winter! The directors of the company chose to close the road until April for a four-month period of hibernation. The last train ran to the summit and back on Saturday, November 23. Winter operations were ordered to cease because of difficulties keeping the line open during this period of little traffic—there has been but little traffic on the road for some time. Staff was laid off for the winter, except for Mr. Murphy who remained in charge of the office and properties.

Over the season the KMR had forty-four men on the payroll, composed of: two general officers, one office clerk, three station agents, three station men, one engineer, one fireman, one conductor, one brakeman, five section foremen, and twenty-seven trackmen. (An indication of the difficult conditions was that track maintenance men were almost 75 percent of the employees of the KMR.) Between 1908 and early 1912 the number of men was reduced to less than thirty per season, mainly through the reduction in numbers of trackmen. It should be noted that only one locomotive crew was on the payroll, since only one locomotive (almost exclusively No. 2) was used until the early part of the 1912 season.

Activities in 1907 ceased with a letter from McGiverin, Haydon & Greig, dated December 30, to the Department of the Interior, requesting approval for permanent use of the land at Old Inn station (mile 2.58), where the company's only wye near the Dawson end of the line was located. The railway company wished to lay additional track on this ground in the spring of 1908, and a letter explained the need for the land "to accommodate cars of machinery which are expected to require transportation". The company was anticipating the dredging of the wye-site which was within registered mining claims, and wished to nail down the surface rights for the railway.

The initial year of operation had been a shocking disappointment. Hawkins' prospectus of February, 1902, had envisioned an average annual passenger ridership of about 100,000, with an annual revenue of $220,000. To June 30, 1908, the Klondike Mines Railway had carried just 6528 passengers, for an income of $21,164. The prospectus also estimated freight revenue of $575,000 per year, but from October, 1906, until June 30, 1908, freight traffic actually generated only $62,053. Instead of a predicted surplus of $330,000 per year, the road operated at a loss of $60,923 to June 30, 1907, and a loss of $45,341 in the year to June 30, 1908. Only mixed trains had run for a total of 27,040 miles until June 30, 1908. The boom was over—the Klondike was already in a state of slow decline.

This late winter view was taken lower on the KMR line—possibly near Grand Forks where winter snows have already melted. This is the same train shown on page 60: engine No. 2, box car No. 122, and coach No. 202. Note the side-boards on the tender to hold what appears to be wood, possibly engine fuel. Visible on the front of the locomotive is a plow for clearing snow drifts encountered farther up the line.

MacBride Museum, 93-29 X901.3A.29

Chapter Ten

Retrenchment
1908 and 1909

In the new year, general manager Murphy attacked land problems, first disposing of excess frontage which had been leased at Klondike City and never used, and then demanding a refund. He challenged the lease fee, one dollar per foot per year, and succeeded in reducing this to a nominal one dollar for the whole of the railway's water frontage along the Yukon River, since a precedent had been set by the White Pass on similar water frontage at Whitehorse.

However, plans to secure the land at Old Inn station met no such gains. The railway's only north-end wye was located on creek claims which were owned by a mining company, and still in good standing. Wrangling over this land would continue until the end of the railway's life. Already on the land, known as Lot 265, were 32 buildings, primarily cabins of single men. Also included was The Old Inn House with a stable and gardens, the Bonanza Bakery with a garden, and several family homes. In mid-August a letter from the Department of the Interior to Commissioner Henderson, acting on behalf of Murphy, advised that "The Department cannot dispose of the surface rights of claim land in good standing without first giving opportunity to the Bonanza Basin Gold Mining Company to acquire the surface rights". This company owned creek claims 106, 107, and 107A Below on Bonanza.

Later that year, Murphy temporarily laid aside his bid to gain rights to Lot 265 and applied to Council for permission to build a wye in downtown Dawson. Murphy referred to a plan on file since September 5, 1905, which he said included provisions for a wye situated between Duke Street and Albert Street at the north end of Dawson. The 1905 plan did show a spur and rail yard branching off the Front Street main line, but not a wye—none would ever be built here.

In readying the line for the 1908 season, tracks had been cleared to the summit by the end of March. Murphy

himself made the inspection trip, telephoning to say that an engine had arrived there and would be leaving soon for Dawson. There was much hard-packed snow, and a large group of men had been required to clear cuts, switches, and depot yards; he hoped gales would not drift snow over the road once again. The first revenue train for the summit would leave Dawson on April 1. The schedule remained the same as in 1907—Train No. 1 southbound from Dawson in the morning to return by afternoon as Train No. 2 from Sulphur Springs.

But Klondike winters do not end this early in the year. April 2 saw the heaviest snowfall of the year, with strong gales which drifted snow over the railway tracks. Four days later the storm was over, but the tracks were once more deep in snow, the work of a week earlier obliterated.

In early June, a new public time table was released, with a change. It read:;

> Train leaves Dawson 9 a.m. DAILY except Sunday, connecting at Sulphur Springs with our own stages for Sulphur Creek and Dominion Creek points. Daily stage leaves Granville 7 a.m. connecting with train at Sulphur Springs. Daily stage leaves 33 Below Dominion at 8 a.m. connecting with train at Sulphur Springs. Independent stage from Quartz Creek meets trains daily.

The railway now operated its own stages, but did not hold a monopoly on passenger service. Orr and Turkey Stage Lines had been operating since the early days, and in competition with the railway ran all summer long from 1907 to 1909. Orr and Turkey's franchise included all of the railway's way points in addition to stops on Hunker and Gold Run Creeks; moreover the stage line operated twelve months a year.

As a public relations effort Murphy offered a midnight excursion trip, Saturday evening, June 20, "Dawson to King Dome". See the ad on page 68. "Three large cars comfortably arranged carried a large party to the Dome

Klondike Mines Ry. Co.

MIDNIGHT SUN

EXCURSION

Saturday Evening. June 20

DAWSON

..TO..

KING DOME.

Train will leave Dawson at 8 p. m., arriving at Sulphur Springs 11 p. m., where a stop of two hours will be made to allow excursionists to view the Midnight Sun.

There is a good trail from depot to summit of King Dome, a distance of quarter of a mile.

This dome is the highest in the country, being 3,000 feet above Dawson.

One Fare for the Round Trip.

$5 Including a lunch at the Dome Roadhouse **$5**

Dawson Daily News, June 20, 1908

Saturday night. A very scenic trip, and a splendid luncheon was served by the railroad at the Dome, provided by congenial host Mr. Murphy". The train returned to Dawson at 4:45 a.m..

Transportation in the Klondike was fast changing—at least during summer months. A party of men from the Geological Survey of Canada visiting the goldfield during August, 1908, commented: "the district is well supplied with good roads, so that an automobile was used throughout"; the trip covered the lengths of all five creeks surrounding the Dome. It was a far cry from the chaos described by Ogilvie only nine years earlier. In addition to looking at placer operations, the Survey crew also examined a 900-foot "tunnel" being drifted under the Dome as a quartz-mining prospect—lode mining was still thought to have a future in the Klondike.

For two weeks in late September, Lawther revisited Dawson to redefine the railway's future. He toured the country to assess its potential and talked of a connection with an outside railway. Although pleased with what he saw, he knew prospects of development of quartz mining—crucial to the railway's long-term survival—were still uncertain. With marginal hopes he noted that the railway had lost money in its initial year of operation, and this year was not much improved.

Traffic was so light that no more than one locomotive at a time was operated. This meant a minimal train crew was on the payroll, and the fact was pointed out in a news story of October 23, 1908. The *Yukon World* reported;

There will be no train out this morning, as the Klondike Mines Railway is engaged in a lawsuit and the only engineer is a witness...a suit of Asam against the railway, where two years ago Asam was to abandon his stage line from Dawson to Dominion and work in conjunction with the road when it was completed.

The case was dismissed, the engineer went back to work next day, and trains were once more moving.

The summer of 1908: engine No. 2 is pulling out of Dawson City with one box car and one coach. This is a mate to the photos on pages 45 and 48.
The Bancroft Library, Berkeley, 1905.1709 6265

A heavy southbound mixed train in August, 1908, on Lower Bonanza Creek: behind engine No. 2 are five flat cars--one loaded with lumber, the others with cordwood, box cars 116 and 124, and coach 202. Two of the flat cars have no markings, indicating they are recently-converted box cars. Yukon Gold Company dredge No. 1 was built in 1906, and is seen here advancing up the bed of Bonanza Creek which has been cleared of brush and thawed by a cordwood-fired steam plant.

Glenbow Museum, NA1466-33

By early winter, with about one foot of snow in the hills, there was very little business on the line. The final ad of the season read:

Klondike Mines Railway Company

Will close operations for winter months on Oct. 31st and resume operations May 1st, 1909, with a through connection to Sulphur, Dominion and Quartz Creeks.

E. A. MURPHY, Gen. Mgr.

A week later the **Dawson Daily News** reported the Grand Trunk Railway might abandon its plans to cross the Rockies (at Yellowhead) instead running north to the headwaters of the Stewart or Dease Rivers, then making for the coast. The item continued, adding this rumour was probably the work of the president of the Klondike Mines Railway.

The first train of 1909 ran on April 19 "as No. 2 with Lyman Annable at the throttle came out fresh from the repair shop and ran as far as 70 Below." Next morning the plow-equipped engine left with a

May 10, 1909: a Klondike Mines Railway stage on Hunker Creek. Barely visible on the panel below the driver's seat is the lettering, "K M Ry". The company had just started up the stage service, and picked up a mail and express contract over the objections of other stage lines in the area.

National Archives of Canada, C 398

coach, twenty-five men, blankets, and grub, expecting that the line could be opened for business on Monday, April 26th. The engine was equipped with a portable phone and a lineman to make connections with headquarters via the company's private telephone line which was strung along the right-of-way. Having left the shops at 9:00 a.m., the train was in Grand Forks by noon, and was expected to reach Flannery, or possibly Soda, by afternoon. The year before, a crew of fifteen to twenty men worked for ten days clearing the line, but no problems were anticipated this spring.

However, just as in 1908, late storms would be troublesome. April 22 found the road still not clear, as conditions were found to be much more difficult than anticipated. Gales had dumped more snow on the track—wet and heavy at lower levels, dry on the ridges. Although six feet of dry snow here could be handled easier with the plow than one foot of wet snow along Bonanza, the big crew of men with shovels were still needed to clear the grade at Soda. By April 24 the government wagon roads leading down from the railway depot at Sulphur were

cleared for traffic to Gold Bottom, Dominion, Hunker, and Quartz Creeks, and by midnight of the 25th the rail line was cleared. Mr. Murphy found that after the line had been cleared there were several heaves in the line due to frost; since they were not too severe, they would be repaired later. Two days later the first train was dispatched, arriving at Sulphur at 12:15 p.m., to return to Dawson about 4:00 p.m..

While train service was initially the same as in 1908, with a single return run six days a week, stage service beyond here was reduced. The railway's stages now ran daily from Sulphur Springs connecting with Sulphur Creek and Quartz Creek, but offered service only three day per week

71

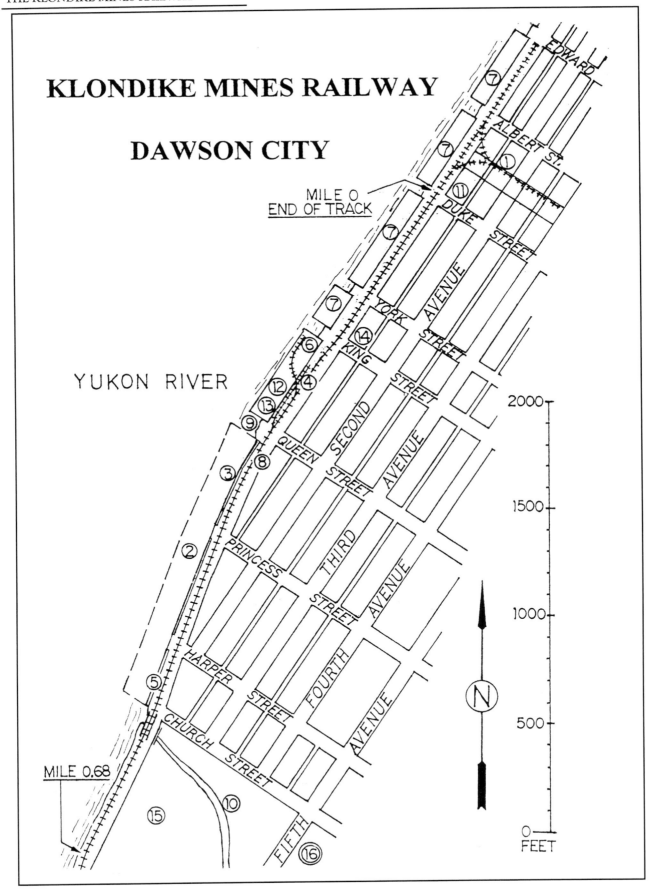

KLONDIKE MINES RAILWAY

DAWSON CITY

YUKON RIVER

MILE 0
END OF TRACK

MILE 0.68

KLONDIKE MINES RAILWAY COMPANY
REDUCED RATES
EFFECTIVE MONDAY, MAY 24TH

Dawson to Granville..................... **$ 8.00**
Round Trip........ .... **15.00**

Reduction also made in local fares. Train now leaves from end of Government bridge. All express matter and light freight received as usual at Dawson depot.

to points on Dominion Creek. "Bill McAdam, an old White Pass driver, will have charge of the Sulphur line. A daily stage also runs on Quartz as far as Stollards." Staff this year included agent A.J. Dewar and auditor H.B. Iseman; no station would be maintained at Grand Forks, but P.D. Bushe would still be in charge at Sulphur. The closure of the Grand Forks station was the direct result of rapidly changing mining operations on Bonanza Creek and Eldorado Creek, and the completion of more dredges by the Yukon Gold Company. In early May, Murphy offered a reduction in passenger fares, Dawson to Granville $8, round trip $15.

With snow gone and ground thawing, re-ballasting on the railway grade between Dawson and the Forks began on

May 8, 1909. "Peggy" (engine No. 1) was again brought into use, and handled the work train in order that there be no delays in scheduled traffic. A spur had been run off the main line at 104 Below and a bridge built across Bonanza Creek to reach a tailings dump, for use as ballast, at Guggieville, which was the camp of the Yukon Gold Company. This spur may have been also used by the railway to ship freight directly onto the company's property. Ballast for the grade between Grand Forks and Sulphur was taken from a hydraulic dump at 18 Above. At Carmack Fork some ties had sunk so deep into muskeg that other ties had to be placed right on top of them in order to level the track. Twelve men under foreman McLean worked well into summer to get the grade in shape.

Work on the main line had hardly started when more trouble developed. On May 10, ice on the Klondike River took out the southern approach to the railway's bridge leading to Dawson; like a saw, slabs of ice had cut off twelve pilings supporting two piers. Just when it was thought the crisis was over, the centre section of the steel bridge was struck by ice, causing it to swing, forcing the tracks six feet out of alignment. A temporary station,

Opposite:

Early Features (now gone)
1) KMR terminal yard and wye (planned, but never built)
2) Proposed KMR rail yard (flooded at high water); no sidings were ever built, but the area was used for storage of timber and cordwood, sawn on the site, which was loaded directly onto flat cars on the main line
3) KMR Dawson City station, formerly Boyle's Wharf, originally the Seattle-Yukon Transportation Company wharf
4) KMR line change in July 1912: track was removed north from mid-block (between Queen and King Streets) and a spur (no switch) was run through the White Pass warehouse onto the White Pass dock, to become the north end of the KMR line
5) Track north of Church Street was removed in September 1913
6) White Pass & Yukon Route wharf and warehouse
7) Wharves and warehouses
8) Ferry tower (Pulled down in 1945)
9) Ferry landing
10) Slough (now filled)

Existing Features
11) Yukon Saw Mill (restored)
12) Steamer **Keno**
13) Canadian Bank of Commerce (original)
14) Tourist Information Centre
15) Government Reserve
16) Dawson City Museum

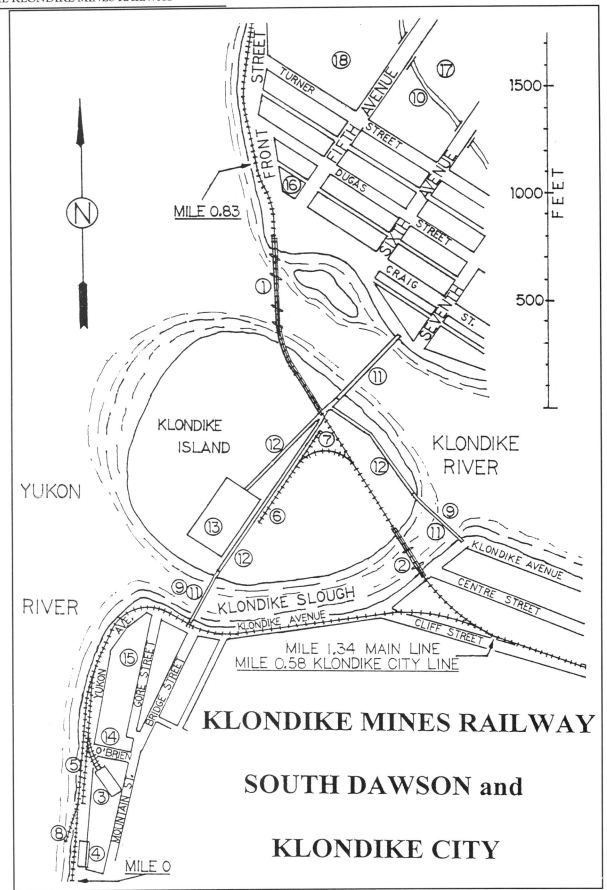

KLONDIKE MINES RAILWAY

SOUTH DAWSON and

KLONDIKE CITY

station, with a wide space for teams to turn around, was built on the south bank of the Klondike River. Passengers were notified that trains could be boarded at the south foot of the government bridge, and coaches provided service between Dawson and there. All express and light freight would still be received as usual, and was forwarded to Old Inn for loading onto box cars or flat cars. The railway bridge would not be repaired until the 1911 season.

Reports for the year ending June 30, 1909, submitted by the railway to the federal government disclosed a list of the ten largest shareholders of voting securities; they and the number of shares—all common stock—held were:

Dawson, Grand Forks, and Stewart River Railway Company, London, U.K.	10,580
Thomas W. O'Brien, Dawson, Yukon	670
William H. Parsons (one-time merchant in Dawson, now of Fairbanks)	603
Lawther and Latta, London, U.K.	603
Jonathon H. Hughes, New York City	208
William White, once the solicitor for the KMR in Dawson, now of Vancouver	190
S.E. Adair, New York City	110
Kirkham Wright, San Francisco	100
Louis Sloss, co-owner of the Alaska Commercial Company, San Francisco	100
Harold D. Weeks, once passenger and freight agent of the KMR, now of Seattle	58

Shares were valued at $100, and in spite of all his efforts it is apparent that O'Brien, the only local shareholder, was getting little or no return from his investment. Of the original five charter members, only O'Brien still retained stock, although McGiverin, or rather his firm, remained the Canadian solicitor for the railway.

The railway was awarded the Post Office contract for handling mail on Hunker, Sulphur, and Dominion, effective July 1, 1909, for one year, distributed by stage as the previous contractor had done. The company was still losing money however, and Murphy appealed to Council for a five-year tax exemption because of the railway's slim income. The Territory was presently taxing the railway at the rate of $100 per mile of trackage. From November, 1906, to May, 1908, railway earnings were only $128,058 and expenses were $246,655 for a deficit of $121,596 which, Murphy stated, had been met and paid for by the English stockholders of the company. During this time the company employed an average of thirty-five men who were paid standard wages, and where possible everything the company used was bought in Dawson. Murphy's argument continued: the company hoped that quartz mines would be operating within two years, but until then operations would run at a loss. Unimpressed, councilman McAlpine countered;

> If the Stewart River country turns out well, it will be due to prospectors, not the railway. The railway was not built until the country was developed, and if the promoters showed such poor business

Opposite:

Early Features (now gone)
1) KMR Klondike River bridge, 320 feet in length
2) KMR Klondike Slough bridge, 80 feet in length
3) KMR engine house and shops
4) KMR coal bunkers
5) KMR Klondike City yard
6) KMR saw mill spur
7) KMR coach storage spur
8) KMR temporary riverside spur
9) Klondike Slough, now silted in
10) Slough, now filled
11) Public bridges
12) Public roads
13) Klondike Mill
14) Klondike Brewery
15) Red light district

Existing Features
16) Power house
17) Minto Park
18) Government Reserve

The Klondike Mines Railway bridge in its original configuration over the Klondike River. It is spring as ice and debris pile up against the bridge piers; just beyond the bridge is the Yukon River, also at springtime high levels. Note the flat car over the southernmost bridge pier, weighed down with iron to help resist the force of the mass of ice and water. Ice like this damaged the bridge on May 10, 1909.

National Archives of Canada, C 18660

foresight as to build a road when traffic was on the decrease, they should not ask council to help. The railway has driven teamsters from the field, ruining the business, and still have high freight rates, while service is still incomplete. The company got the mail contract without a single investment earlier this year. The road hauls freight to the Dome, and then dumps it there—and no freighting in the winter.

It was a scathing but accurate assessment, nevertheless Council did allow the railway a two-year exemption from taxation.

Shop men at the railway's engine house found an unusual job in early September. A Shay locomotive arrived, knocked-down and without instructions, at Klondike City in early September, and was assembled at the Klondike Mines Railway engine house for use on the Coal Creek railway. Earlier in the year the Northern Light, Power

and Coal Company, Limited, had been granted a charter to operate in Canada, and by mid-summer had bought the properties of the Coal Creek Coal Company (and the Sourdough Coal Company), the Yukon Telephone Syndicate, the Dawson Electric Light and Power Company, and the Dawson City Water and Power Company. Included in the deal was the steamer *Lightning*, and the railway of the Coal Creek Coal Company, which included two 0-6-0 Porter locomotives. Already on the way from England, whence financing for the new company had come, was some 2,500 tons of equipment for building a 6000-kilowatt, coal-fired, power station near the old coal mine on Coal Creek, twelve miles up from the Yukon River. The tonnage to be hauled for construction of the plant could not have been handled by the dinky Porters, so a Shay locomotive, construction number 2190, built by the Lima Locomotive Works, was purchased on behalf of the Dawson Electric Light and Power Company.

The Shay was a type of geared locomotive, designed for slow-speed and power on steep, winding, railways such as found in mining and logging country. The most common of three types of geared locomotives, the Shay had its two-cylinder or three-cylinder, vertically-mounted, engine placed on the right side of the boiler, which was located offset to the left of the locomotive center line. The crankshaft of the engine was directly coupled to drive shafts leading to the front and rear trucks, with universal joints on the drive shafts for flexibility. All wheels were relatively small, of the same diameter, and driven through bevel-cut pinion and ring gears, with a drive reduction of 3.07:1, sacrificing speed for power. This was in contrast to a "mainline" locomotive, designed for speed, whose cylinders were coupled directly to large diameter driving wheels. Some Shays had a separate tender, also with wheels driven by a third drive shaft, but the smaller models, such as the Dawson Electric Light and Power model, had fuel and water stored on the rear of the engine. Climax and Heisler were two other popular types of geared locomotives manufactured in the United States.

This was the only Shay ever to have reached the Yukon. The machine was described as a wood-burner—obviously an error. The locomotive was, of course, 36-inch gauge, with 26-inch wheels and two-8x10-inch cylinders. The Shay would be used from 1909 until possibly as late as 1912, and was subsequently used in construction of the Salmon Creek hydroelectric dam, developed by the Alaska-Gastineau Mining Company at Juneau, Alaska. In 1921 the Shay was bought by the Biles-Coleman Lumber Company operating near Omak, Washington.

After a relatively uneventful season, management announced that Klondike Mines Railway service in 1909 would cease on October 30, to resume business in May, 1910. At the same time another notice reminded customers that the railway was now operating a winter stage service, departing the Dawson depot Mondays, Wednesdays, and Fridays for Granville, and returning the following days. In charge of the office, at the depot, for winter stages was auditor Harry B. Iseman.

Eugene Murphy noted, in late 1909, that the Klondike River bridge was still out of service—"...it may be repaired this winter." In the spring of 1909 Murphy had applied to Council for permission to build a wye at the north end of Dawson, but only a few days later the bridge across the Klondike River was knocked askew. With a pathetic balance sheet the railway made no attempt to repair the bridge, instead picking up passengers at the foot of the government bridge on the Klondike City side of the river, and picking up freight either at the Klondike City docks or at the Ogilvie Bridge. This practice continued during the 1909 and 1910 seasons.

Murphy once again attempted to sway officials into granting title to the ground at the railway's Old Inn wye site. In October he wrote; "we may at any time be obliged to move our wye, which we have always considered our terminal, from the present location and if we should find this necessary we would simply have no place in which to turn our engines as we have no turn tables nor have we another wye." On November 1, 1909, Gosselin, Crown Timber and Land Agent, asked if Murphy had requested a release from the mining company for the surface rights. Murphy responded that he was unable to get a release, and was therefore making an amended application to cover only Creek Placer Claims 106 and the upper and lower halves of 107. Pursuing this attack into January and April of 1910, Murphy gained not an inch. The Department of the Interior reiterated, "the land has recently been made available for mining and therefore is not open to the railroad". No further communications dealt with this difficulty, and the wye site was destroyed by dredges in 1913.

In the period June 30, 1908, to June 30, 1910, when freight trains were introduced in addition to mixed-train service, 7306 passengers had been carried for revenue of $25,036—up somewhat from the previous two years. Freight revenue in these two years was $72,733—also up slightly. Total train mileage was 19,806—down about 25 percent from the previous two-year period. Efficiency had improved though: while an operating deficit of $4912 had been seen in the twelve months prior to June 30, 1909, a profit of $965 was shown in the twelve-month

period to June 30, 1910. In the first years of service the railway listed "merchandise" as the main freight business, but by 1909 a new listing, "other forest products", not lumber, began to dominate tonnage hauled; this commodity was in fact cordwood, hauled up Bonanza Creek from wood yards at Klondike City and Dawson to be dumped off cars at several Yukon Gold Company dredge sites, and used for steam thawing of frozen ground in front of the advancing dredges. When operations began in 1906, the railway had ten flat cars and thirteen box cars, but the anticipated high class freight never materialized, and by 1910 seven of the box cars had been stripped down and added to the fleet of flat cars, used chiefly for cordwood-hauling.

At about 80 Below on Bonanza Creek, a southbound freight, pulling seven flat cars loaded with large diameter steel pipe, steams upgrade. The pipe is destined for a hydraulic mining operation, possible south of Sulphur Springs. Note the wooden flume of a bench-mining operation in the foreground. About 1909, the bed of Bonanza Creek here has not yet begun to be worked by dredges, but it shows the efforts of numerous small underground/placer operations.
Yukon Archives, Chisholm Coll'n, 5630

CHAPTER ELEVEN

STRUGGLE, AND DEFEAT
1910 TO 1913

Over the winter the railway bridge across the Klondike River was dismantled; the three steel spans were pulled off the piers and were now resting alongside the trestle forming the bridge approaches at the south end. The work of putting in new, permanent, piers was deferred—no bridge work was done that summer. The railway began operations on May 2, 1910, and instead of six passenger (mixed) trains per week, service was now reduced to three trains weekly, Mondays, Wednesdays, and Fridays with stage connections at Sulphur Springs for Quartz, Sulphur, and Dominion Creeks. The railway now also ran a stage to Hunker Creek, leaving the depot at 2:00 p.m. also on Mondays, Wednesdays, and Fridays.

Business settled into a routine and the newspapers found

This photo was probably taken in October, judging from the light and uniformly-deep layer of snow, of what could be any year from 1907 to 1911. Southbound engine No. 2 with combination coach (combo) No. 200 awaits as the photographer captures the scene on the trestle over Homestake Gulch at mile 15. There were 400-foot long trestles on each of Gauvin, Homestake, and McKay Gulches, but the one over Homestake Gulch was the highest at 65 feet. Trestles were built totally of timber; no concrete was used for footings of the trestle bents. Plow-equipped No. 2 has already bucked some snow on the grade down line.

Vancouver Public Library, 16958

79

The community of Grand Forks, at the junction of Bonanza Creek and Eldorado Creek died slowly. In its heyday it was a thriving village in the midst of the richest claims in the Klondike goldfield. In those boom days, it took a large labour force to mine and sluice pay dirt, but as individual claims were sold to syndicates, mining became more mechanized, and less labour was required. With the arrival of dredges, manpower demands were further reduced, and Grand Forks withered. Then fires took their toll. March 2, 1910: "...one-half of Grand Forks was destroyed by fire this morning". On July 11, more of Grand Forks burned. As dredges worked their way up Bonanza Creek, many of the miner's log cabins were used to feed boilers for steam-thawing. By the early 1920s when dredges finally ate their way through what had been downtown Grand Forks, only a few hillside homes, and some old-timers, remained.

The date is August 9, 1911, as Yukon Gold Company's dredge No. 8 takes shape near downtown Grand Forks, also known as Bonanza. On the hillside to the left is the KMR rail grade and the company's Grand Forks station, a wagon road leading up to it. Note how carloads of cordwood have been simply dumped off the grade, below which a steam-thawing plant will soon be working. Grand Forks is dying, having been incrementally reduced by fires, and with business diminished by the onslaught of mechanized mining and the associated reduction in manpower. Upper Bonanza Creek falls through the valley at right of centre, while Eldorado Creek joins Bonanza Creek just out of the picture to the near right.

National Archives of Canada, PA 96365

In April or May of any year from 1907 to 1911, possibly on Lower Bonanza, the railway has just re-opened the line for service. The KMR did not have a rotary snow plow, and so had to depend on a wedge plow and a gang of men with shovels. Engine No. 2 with combination coach No. 200 in tow is in front of a station house--note the company's telephone/telegraph lines.

Dawson City Museum, 984R-148-1

few railway activities to report until early August, 1910. Visiting Shriners from the Gizeh Temple of Victoria wound up their five-day visit to Dawson with a chartered excursion to Sulphur Springs and King Solomon Dome. The train left Dawson at 10:00 a.m. with the coaches and two "open-air coaches", and there was little space left—the group included fourteen local Shriners;

> The visitors were afforded a splendid view of Bonanza Creek as the train whirled along past dredges, hydraulic plants, electrical elevators, and individual workings. The train arrived at the Dome at 1:15 and 'Dad' Hartman had a mammoth spread of everything good under the sun to eat and drink, and the visitors were kept busy consuming supplies in relays of 30s.

With little snow on the ground the railway announced its closure for the season, the last train running on October 14, 1910. The final advertisement appeared on October 4 reminding patrons that after the 14th the railway's stage service would resume, from Dawson to Gold Bottom, Dominion, and Sulphur Creeks. But a week later the company changed plans, announcing the Klondike Mines

Railway was getting out of the stage business; "Commencing Monday, October 17th, stage business will be turned over to R.B. Robertson, who will operate from the Minto Hotel". It would appear the mail contract, awarded to the railway only on July 1, 1909, would also be relinquished.

March 25, 1911, found Council granting the Klondike Mines Railway a further two-year exemption from the track mileage tax—the company had asked for a five-year exemption. Murphy had in the previous November also petitioned Council to endorse the federal government-approved policy regarding reinstallation of the steel bridge over the Klondike River as a joint railway and traffic bridge. The bridge, which had been out of service since mid-May, 1909, was now being repaired. Commissioner Henderson had earlier announced the railway company would do the work of re-installation with the government contributing a maximum of $16,000. In exchange the Yukon Territory would have permanent use of the bridge for all traffic, even though the railway might eventually sell out.

Freight train on the Klondike Mines Railway

Although printed from a damaged glass plate negative, this photo is nevertheless superb. In this only known photo showing KMR engine No. 3 in action, details abound. Probably taken in 1910 (Government bridge, visible left centre, was demolished in April, 1911) when freight business was on the up-swing, No. 3, sans headlamp, was finally put to work (in the first years of operation engine No. 2 was used for almost all trains).

The crew can be seen on the locomotive, and perched on the tender and farther back are at least six labourers, who will pitch the cordwood off the flat cars at some steam-thawing plant up Bonanza Creek. The ten flat cars, led by Nos. 105, 111, and 101, each carry about nine cords of green spruce wood weighing 18,000 lb. Although the cars were rated for a 15-ton capacity, they had to be loaded by hand from grade level, hence the limited height of loading.

At the extreme left is the railway bridge leading from Klondike Island to Dawson in the distance. The Klondike River is in the middle of the photo, with the houses of South Dawson beyond. A public road follows the bank of the Klondike River, and crosses Klondike Slough on a low bridge.

The tail end of the train is on the railway bridge over Klondike Slough while the engine is in a sub-division of Klondike City. Specifically the fifth flat car straddles Klondike Avenue near Center Street, while the engine is nearing Cliff Street where the main line merges with the Klondike City line. The "streets" of Klondike City were little more than foot paths or cart paths.

National Archives of Canada, C 4887

By April 20 the work of rebuilding the railway bridge had been completed, and it was soon in use by the railway, horse teams, and pedestrian traffic. However, the bridge now had a different look. Two of the three steel spans had exchanged positions; where originally the spans were, from north to south, 100, 140, and 80 feet in length, the longest span was now at the north end, the 100 foot span in the middle, while the shortest was, as before, at the south end. A new pier was built to support the two longest spans. The pier, fifty-one feet long—in line with the current of the river—was twelve feet wide, and twenty-one feet high; piles were driven into the gravel river bed. A long piling and timber trestle made up the bridge approach from the south, while a much shorter timber trestle led up to the bridge from the Dawson side; both were part of the original work. Horse and wagon traffic reached the bridge by way of short, steep, planked inclines built right at the piers supporting the steel-work. The bridge roadway was nine feet wide, with the railway tracks along the center. A footwalk was laid on the east side, three feet wide, with handrails on both sides. The other side was planked for teams, and at mid-bridge was an extra wide portion where teams could pass. The old wooden suspension bridge upstream, purchased by the city years ago from O'Brien and company, and known as the government bridge, was dismantled.

A Klondike Mines Railway work train crossed the steel bridge on April 20, the first train into Dawson in two years. From along Bonanza Creek it had hauled rock for use as rip-rap to strengthen the cribwork of the new bridge piers. Three days before scheduled service began, the company opened the line to Sulphur. Three- to twelve-foot drifts of snow were met en route, thirty men were shovelling, and with a plow on the engine Sulphur was reached late in the day. General manager Murphy now had Herbert Brown, formerly of the White Pass, as the Dawson agent, while P.D. Bushe was back at Sulphur.

On Front Street in Dawson, two blocks north of the ferry tower, are the stores and warehouses of the Northern Commercial Company (on the corner of Front and King Streets). The rails have been planked in to permit safe crossing by horse and wagon, and they are joined by a planked runway for loading rail cars by handcarts. Two tram lines cross the tracks, a boiler awaits delivery, and beef and mutton on the hoof await the butcher.
Yukon Archives, MacBride Museum Coll'n, 3824

In the early spring of 1911, the Klondike River bridge was repaired, and use by public traffic was permitted. But the bridge now had a different look: the 140-foot span (formerly the center span) became the northernmost span and the 100-foot span was positioned at center, rails were re-positioned off-centre, and planking was laid down for horse, wagon, and pedestrian traffic. This photo clearly shows the angle at which the bridge was built. There were ramps leading to roadways built off the steel-work at each end of the bridge. This photo showing a stylish couple and their fine team and rig was probably taken in the summer of 1911.

Dawson City Museum, 984R-218-15

Service resumed on May 1, 1911:

KLONDIKE MINES RAILWAY CO.

Will Resume Service Monday, May 1st, 1911

Trains will leave from foot of Queen Street Mondays, Wednesdays and Fridays at 9 a. m. for Sulphur Springs. Stage connection made at Sulphur Springs for Quartz, Sulphur and Dominion Creeks and Granville.

TELEPHONE 14.

Buda No. 14 Section Motor Car

(Patents Pending)

Copied from the Buda Foundry and Manufacturing Company catalogue, this illustration of the "Section Motor Car" is the standard gauge version with wheels outboard of the frame rails. The KMR's narrow gauge version had the wheels inside the frame. Sometime after 1944, the wheels were taken from the KMR car at Klondike City, and in 1994 the remains of the machine were placed in the Dawson Museum's locomotive shed for safekeeping.

Previous schedules had designated train numbers, either northbound or southbound, but July, 1911, schedules spoke of trains as eastbound to Sulphur Springs and westbound to Dawson.

A temporary disruption of the schedule took place on May 26 when a cylinder head on a locomotive blew out, and the railway's Buda motor car was instead sent out with mail. Probably acquired in 1906, the Buda was described by the builder as a "section motor car." Powered by a 10-horsepower, two-cylinder, air-cooled gas engine, it was an open car with seating for about six people. The remains of the car are presently in the Dawson Museum locomotive shed.

Until now the railway had run only mixed trains, often consisting of no more than one coach and one box car, but freight, express, and passenger traffic was changing with declining population on the creeks, and the advent of dredges. On July 14, the railway announced another reduction in passenger coach service; trains would leave the depot only on Mondays and Fridays, with a "motor car" running on Wednesdays, "carrying a limited number of passengers, mail, and express." (See the advertisement below.) It is not certain if this "motor car" was the railway's Buda motor car or an automobile running over the public roads. Trains would still run more than twice a week though, as freight-only trains began to rack up mileage.

Dawson Daily News, July 14, 1911

Activity on Front Street in Dawson City has declined considerably from the glory days. In 1908, this scene includes the KMR tracks, poorly-ballasted, with grass growing between the ties which are sawn from local spruce, slabbed on two sides only. The building behind the second telephone pole is the Klondike Mines Railway's "**Grand Central Depot**"; the most northerly railway station, ever, in Canada.

Below the tracks, on the edge of the river, is the railway's Dawson City yard. Tied up at the docks is the steamer **Prospector** (which was scrapped in 1912); at river's edge are a variety of barges. Beneath the ferry tower, which straddles Front Street, are two box cars on a siding at the Aurora Docks warehouse. Although the Yukon River is not very wide here, the extreme height of the tower was necessary to give the main ferry cable, anchored in solid rock on the west bank of the river, clearance well above the smoke stacks of passing steamboats. The tower, which was 125 feet tall, was built in 1901 and survived until March 23, 1945, when it was demolished; with the main cable gone, the legs of the tower were sawn partly-through, and a YCGC bulldozer out on the ice of the Yukon River hauled the tower down with a long tow line. A motorized ferry operated on the river thereafter.

In the summer of 1908, Frank H. Nowell, who was the official photographer for the Alaska, Yukon, Pacific-Seattle Exposition, toured the north and captured this and several other fine views of Klondike Mines Railway activity.
 Univ. of Alaska Archives, Fairbanks, Erskine, 70-28-195N

In August the Klondike Mines Railway became a coal hauler for a short time as the Yukon Gold Company began testing the use of bituminous coal from the Tantalus mines and lignite from the Coal Creek mine for firing the boilers of its thawing plants. The heavy black smoke in the valley, instead of the pleasant-smelling, white, wood smoke was noted with distaste. The mining company soon resumed using cordwood. Although coal produces two to three times as much heat per weight compared to wood, handling and storage alone must have created some problems.

On September 29, 1911, the last train of the year ran. At less than five months this would be the railway's shortest operating season. It was also the last year in which coach No. 202 and combination coach No. 200 would be used; they would be parked on a spur on Klondike Island, from which they would never again move. Starting October 1, Granville Stage Line, operated by Greenfield and Pickering, assumed all passenger, express, and mail once carried by the railway.

A news item dated October 13, 1911, noted that two new dredges of the Yukon Gold Company, on No. 6 Above on

The only known photo showing the Klondike Mines Railway's "roundhouse"—the long sheet-metal covered building on the right—in Klondike City. 30x80 feet, the building could house four locomotives, and it served as the company's shop. It appears that steam was piped from O'Brien's brewery to the engine house. On the Yukon River are rafts of wood which will be hauled up the "jack ladder", rising out of the water onto shore, where a saw will cut the timber into four-foot lengths. As soon as the wood is cut, it will be piled onto the empty flat cars in the distance, parked just opposite O'Brien's brewery (with the tall smoke stack). Four loaded flat cars, each carrying about eleven cords of wood, are parked on the main track in the left foreground. On the track leading to the coal bunkers is engine No. 1, and parked at the entrance to the engine house are engines No. 2 and No. 3. Compare with the photo on page 10, which was taken prior to the coming of the railway.
Dawson City Museum, 994.279.60, John Gould Collection

Bonanza and on No. 7 on Eldorado, had been running a few days;

> They are steel-hulled with buckets of 7-1/5 yard capacities. Each dredge will handle 4000 to 4500 cubic yards in twenty-four hours. The machinery was supplied by Bucyrus-Erie while the hulls were built by a contractor in San Francisco. One is eating up the townsite of Grand Forks while the other is devouring one of the most famous of early Eldorado claims. They are supplied with power from Treadgold's North Fork hydro-electric plant.

The days of small operators on Bonanza and Eldorado Creeks, at least during this era, were over.

Before the 1912 season opened, the *Seattle Post Intelligencer* of Wednesday, April 10, 1912, carried a sombre news item;

> Yesterday in New York City, E.C. Hawkins died in hospital following an operation. He was born on September 8, 1860, in South Haven, Suffolk County, New York. His home was in Seattle and he is survived by his wife, three sons, and two daughters.

General Manager E.A. Murphy returned to Dawson in March, and announced that the railway had bought a new locomotive which would arrive on one of the first boats—the company would have a large quantity of fuel to haul this season, from Klondike City to points on Bonanza Creek. The railway started operations for the season on May 1. Murphy put a number of men to work, first hauling ties and other materials for repair of the roadbed, although the first revenue train to the Dome was not expected to run until about May 20. It was anticipated that this year's business would be hauling a significantly greater tonnage of coal and other fuel for the several dredges on Bonanza, and it was freight-only in 1912—not even express. In that year not a single advertisement was published by the company since passenger service was no longer available. Carrying on

the passenger, express, and light freight business assumed last October was Greenfield and Pickering's Granville Stage Line. Reflecting the railway's new mode of operation was a new Table of Tariffs, listing freight classification only, published in the May 2, 1912, issue of the *Canada Gazette*. (See Appendix B)

Still with dreams of getting an outside rail connection, the *Dawson Daily News*, May 12, headlined "the White Pass may come to Dawson and Fairbanks".

The railway bridge which had been re-installed only a year ago was once again damaged by ice that spring, but temporary repairs were quickly made. On May 30, 1912, it was reported that the rebuilding of the bridge was successfully carried out by the railway company, under contract with the government, at a cost of $17,735.16.

An application dated June 5, from E.A. Murphy to George Black, Commissioner of the Yukon Territory, proposed the construction of a spur track leading from the railway's main line on Front Street, at a point opposite the Aurora Dock, onto the waterfront property now held by the White Pass and Yukon Route. This trackage was urgently needed to handle an unusually large amount of freight and machinery due that summer—loading would be done directly from barges. Arrangements had been made with the White Pass, but permission from Council was still needed. The request was heard, but some complaints were expressed by the fire department, which wanted no switches which might block or interfere with fire engines—the fire hall was located opposite the proposed spur switch. The solution agreed on was to extend the main line, curving through the White Pass warehouse, and onto the White Pass docks, with no switch to be installed. The Front Street line northward would be abandoned, and the White Pass docks would thus become the north end of the line. Permission was granted on July 11.

Opposite Top: Seen here at the Baldwin Locomotive Works in Philadelphia is c/n 37564 which was built to order in March of 1912 as No. 4 for the Klondike Mines Railway. Baldwin specification sheets state No. 4 and its tender were painted olive green and aluminum. From 1955 until 1985 ex-KMR No. 4 passed through several central U.S. states, working on tourist railways, and is presently in El Reno, Oklahoma.
> *Railroad Museum of Pennsylvania, Strasburg, PA, 3842*

Opposite Bottom: In this busy scene on August 2, 1912, construction is under way on the barges which will support Canadian Klondyke Mining Company dredges No. 3 and No. 4. On the temporary spurs built from the Klondike Mines Railway main line can be seen all four of the ex-DYMCo Porter locomotives and the two steam shovels brought in by that same company in 1904. At mid-distance is the KMR's wye and Old Inn station—a fair settlement has grown here. To the left is the original Ogilvie Bridge over the Klondike River, and farther away—the large buildings—is Guggieville, the camp of the Yukon Gold Company. Bonanza Creek sweeps down the right of this scene, and across the foreground.
> *Yukon Archives, MacBride Museum Coll'n, 3835*

The C.K.M.Co. Construction
Camp Bonanza Basin

Photo By J. Doody

On July 2, 1912, the steamer *Whitehorse* left Whitehorse, shoving a barge on which was a new locomotive destined for the Klondike Mines Railway. Arriving at Klondike City on the 4th, the railway's first new locomotive, a Baldwin 2-6-2, lettered No. 4, had been built to order for the company in March—cost reported to be $10,883. It was put to work alongside engines No. 2 and No. 3—the latter had finally been rolled out of the engine house at Klondike City after several years of idleness there. The company had doubled operating staff, which now included four engineers, three firemen, and six brakemen; only one train crew had been utilized in 1911. With longer consists, trains working twenty-four hours per day were delivering enormous amounts of cordwood to Yukon Gold Company dredging sites. Additionally, machinery and construction material was being hauled from the Dawson docks to a site 2½-miles up-line, adjacent to the tracks, where two new giant dredges were being built by Joe Boyle's Canadian Klondyke Mining Company.

Before construction of the dredges began, two deeps pits near the Ogilvie Bridge had to be dug to make ponds in which the barges supporting the dredge machinery could be floated. Spur lines were built from the Klondike Mines Railway line just west of the company's wye, and on July 12 the *Dawson Daily News* reported, "108 men are at work...four locomotives...are hauling gravel up an incline from the pits...loaded by steam shovels...". The mining company's four Porter saddle-tank locomotives and a pair of Marion steam shovels, brought to the Klondike in 1904 by predecessor Detroit Yukon Mining Company, were being put to use here.

The only fatality ever related to the Klondike Mines Railway's operation happened in the early morning of August 12, 1912. A drunk labourer, James Kelly, was sitting beside the railway tracks at 23 Below on Bonanza at about 3 a.m. when the northbound train cut off his legs. Taken to hospital, he later died from loss of blood.

Neither the engineer, conductor, nor crew had seen him until too late. Until 1911 trains had run only during daytime, but beginning in 1912 crews worked twenty-fours a day to deliver unusually large volumes of freight, mostly cordwood.

Passenger service had been terminated in the fall of 1911, and day shift-only operations then ceased. During the 1912 and 1913 seasons it was only freight traffic, with 24-hour operation. No longer with the need to run passengers into Dawson City on a guaranteed schedule, locomotives always turned on the Old Inn wye when northbound, to back all trains into Dawson City and into Klondike City. Although uncertain, it appears the railway may have had to utilize the spur, rebuilt into a wye, at 104 Below on Bonanza (about one-quarter mile past Old Inn) on which to turn trains after a dredge had cut through the Old Inn wye in mid-June of 1913.

During the previous summer the railway had hauled coal to the Yukon Gold Company's steam-thawing plants on Bonanza Creek, and now the mining company was looking at another alternative to wood for fuel in firing boilers. In late July the Klondike Mines Railway delivered 1200 barrels of fuel oil to the steam generating plants for further experiments, but after all was done, neither coal nor oil would supplant cordwood for fuel which would be used until dredging operations ceased some fifty years later. Wood was the major fuel consumed in the Klondike. Initially, the local hills supplied all the wood needed for mining operations and domestic use, but by 1899 wood-cutters had to go far afield. When the number of dredges in the Klondike rose, so did the number of associated steam-thawing plants with their enormous appetites for wood fuel. In a very short time the cutting and hauling of cordwood had developed into a major, little-publicized, industry. The October 23, 1912, issue of the *Dawson Daily News* gave a detailed description of the cordwood industry in

---

Opposite Top: At the center of this 1912 photo are the buildings of the old Magnet Roadhouse at about 25 Below on Bonanza Creek. The bench claims across the valley have been extensively worked by hydraulic mining, and the creek bottom has been "high-graded" by sluicing operations. Now Yukon Gold Company's dredge No. 5, which arrived here in 1910, is working its way upstream, extracting gold from the lower-paying gravels. Freight trains of the KMR have dumped off cordwood just above the boiler house where steam is being generated to thaw the permafrost in advance of dredging; the main steam line can be seen leading off to the left.
Yukon Archives, Schellinger Coll'n, 5952

Opposite Bottom: Taken within a few hundred feet of the photographer's viewpoint of the upper photo, this view is looking upstream past the steam plant. It shows the grid of steam points driven into the creek bed with the boiler house at lower centre. Farther upstream are mounds of gravel, once high grade, mined from shafts sunk into the permafrost, that has already been sluiced for gold. The public wagon road to Grand Forks crossed the railway grade at several points.
Yukon Archives, Schellinger Coll'n, 5953

KLONDYKE MINES R.R.

This only known photo showing KMR engine No. 4 in action was taken about October, 1912, on Front Street in Dawson City. No. 4, brand new when delivered to Klondike City in July, is backing a string of flat cars on the re-configured Dawson City trackage, through the warehouse (note the large opening in the wall) belonging to the WP&YR, and out onto the docks belonging to that company.

Earlier that summer, track four blocks northward from here was torn up, and the new spur onto the White Pass docks became the north end of the line. A large shipment of machinery for construction of two dredges for the Canadian Klondyke Mining Company had arrived late in the shipping season, and the KMR was hustling to wrap up the season.
Univ. of Alaska Archives, Fairbanks, Bassoc, 64-92-129

the area. Summarized, the article (quoted in Appendix C) related how about 50,000 cords of wood had been cut in the 1912 season alone. One cord of wood is a pile four feet high by four feet wide, by eight feet long, thus the one-year cut, if laid in a single pile four feet high by four feet wide, would stretch out for seventy-five miles! The industry involved hundreds of men, felling trees from as far away as 150 miles up the Yukon River, and was an annual half-million dollar business. The timber, mostly spruce, with some pine and aspen, from three to 12 inches in diameter, was floated down-river in rafts and sawn into four-foot lengths at wood yards in Klondike City and Dawson City to sell for $9 to $10 per cord. Of the total cut, about 35,000 cords were delivered to Yukon Gold Company dredge sites, all brought there by the Klondike Mines Railway. Charges for delivery to the dredge sites, however, boosted the cost of wood to $13 per cord. However, the steam-thawing plants were far from being the only consumer of cordwood. In addition to the

demand for local heating in Dawson, steamboats plying the Yukon River (and some of the side streams) had equally-insatiable appetites for fuel. Contractors situated at regularly-spaced points along the full length of the Yukon River felled timber, bucked it into cordwood lengths, and piled it at the river's edge for convenient "wooding up" by steamboats. The cordwood industry was sustained long after the demand for fuel at steam-thawing plants had diminished.

Although the shutdown of the railway that year went by unreported, general manager Murphy left Dawson October 28 on the first stage of the winter. Railway operation had probably ended about October 20, 1912.

At a meeting of the Yukon Labour Council in early April, 1913, auditor Harry B. Iseman of the Klondike Mines Railway pleaded for taxation relief saying, in part;

We have to hire one extra engineer; since we cannot get one here, Mr. Murphy is bringing one in. We pay the engineers 77 cents per hour, but if they work only one hour, they are paid for ten; if they work over 10 hours they are paid 77 cents [sic]. Last year we borrowed men from the White Pass, and cheques in summer ran up to $300 to $400 per month because of overtime. We intended to promote a fireman here to engineer this year, but he left us for a year-round job.

Although not mentioned, Iseman also appealed for a further two-year exemption from the track mileage tax; in 1909 and 1911 similar breaks had been granted. The appeal was granted, and in 1915 a three-year exemption would also be approved.

On Monday, April 21, 1913, the railway came to life again when a work train made a run up Bonanza from Dawson to a point two miles above Grand Forks. The

"Ground Thawing for Dredge Operation, Lower Bonanza near Lovett Gulch" *about 1913. Two men with sledges on tall ladders drive "steam points" into the permafrost of the valley bottom, and two other men are assisting. The points were arranged in a grid, and were fed with live steam from a cordwood-fired boiler not far away. First driven only a few feet into the ground, the points were driven progressively deeper as thawing took place—a back-breaking job—a job done for some time by one Frank (Francis) Berton, father of Pierre Berton. Beyond the site is a dredge working through ground only recently thawed. A cow munches grass on this side of the dredge, but as the dredge advanced up the valley, it became a barren moonscape not capable of supporting vegetation for years to come.*
Yukon Archives, Martha Black Coll'n, 3299

railway had recently secured a large order of "fine spruce ties," which would be hauled from Dawson to points along the line for track improvement. During this season the company would have considerable work on the line between Dawson and the Forks, most of it hauling wood for the Yukon Gold Company's thawing plants. With trains preparing to work night and day, the company now had six engineers on the payroll.

Eugene A. Murphy, general manager, had already returned to Dawson after spending the winter Outside and resumed charge of the railway. Mrs. Murphy and sons Gene and Jack remained home in Portland that summer, schooling a priority. Murphy had visited London, England, where he had conferred with the directors of the company regarding the railway's future. He talked with Lawther, director, and Treadgold of the Yukon Gold Company, but few plans were revealed to the public.

They did however decide to continue business as last year, and to operate only between Dawson and Homestake Gulch, three miles above Grand Forks, where the Yukon Gold Company had a thawing plant in need of wood. However, the last trains of the 1913 season would run the full length of the line in delivering freight to Sulphur Springs. "There would be heavy shipments of wood for the seasons ahead for the dredges." Revenue trains would begin operating on May 1, although work trains had been busy for some time. Having totally abandoned passenger service in 1912 the railway found it unnecessary (as in 1912) to publish time tables in 1913.

Construction of Canadian Klondyke Mining Company's dredge No. 3 and dredge No. 4, just west of the railway's wye, was winding down. By May 12, dredge No. 3 was already working its way westward, down the Klondike River valley. Finished soon after, No. 4 moved up-valley

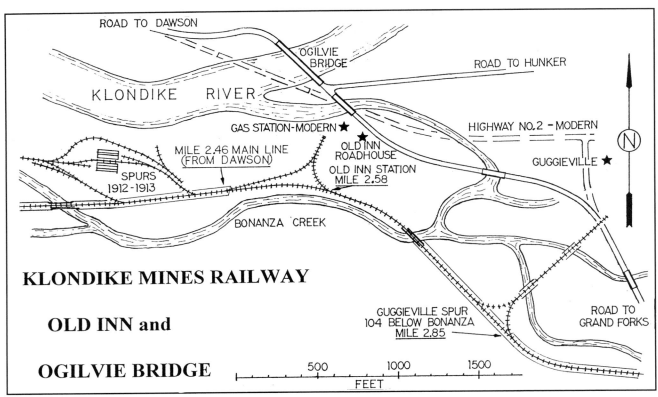

KLONDIKE MINES RAILWAY

OLD INN and

OGILVIE BRIDGE

Few of the features shown remain today. The entire area south of the Klondike River was dredged; prior to dredging, Bonanza Creek split into many channels just above its junction with the Klondike River. Today Bonanza Creek is a single channel approximately following the line of the rail grade.

Station 104 Below on Bonanza was a spur built in 1909 to reach a ballast supply (dredge tailings) at Guggieville; it is believed additional track was added in mid-June, 1913, to convert the spur into a wye.

The spurs at the west end were built in 1912 to service the dredge construction, as shown in the photo on page 89

Pity the poor fireman's helper! Mountains of cordwood were consumed by the boilers on the creeks of the Klondike, thawing ground in advance of the dredges. This man has about one-half cord of spruce wood on the car, and now must push it to the boiler house, some distance away, over a poorly-laid tramway. He has set aside some pieces of wood which are too big to feed into the firebox—they will have to be split with a wedge and maul. Today a deadly overhang of the woodpile such as this would soon have union men and workers compensation inspectors shutting the operation down—promptly! Note the hillside in the background, stripped of trees.
Yukon Archives, Schellinger Coll'n, 6003

and a short time later was munching away at the west leg of the Old Inn wye. No reports describe this event, but photos indicate the wye would be gone by mid-June, as the dredge moved eastward, chewing away right to the margins of the rail grade. By late June, dredge No. 4 was about to work its way through the Old Inn Road House when, at the last minute, it was found this ground was the property of the Yukon Gold Company. The railway probably converted the Guggieville spur (104 Below on Bonanza) into a wye for use during the final months of 1913. It would have been extremely difficult to operate without a north end wye.

As a follow-up to the October, 1912, description of the wood-cutting industry in the Klondike, the ***Dawson Daily News*** provided an up-date on May 13;

> Frank Neil, woodcutter, has 14,500 cords of wood cut and ready to ship on the banks of the Stewart

and the Yukon Rivers. This will be towed down river by the steamer ***Argonaut*** to Klondike City where it will be cut into four-foot lengths for transport by the railroad to the dredges on Bonanza Creek. It is understood that the Yukon Gold Company will bring in enough wood to Bonanza for all the remaining thawing needed there, and it is estimated that the thawing and dredging on the creek will be done by the end of 1915.

This last statement sealed the fate of the railway's operation—by the end of 1913 Yukon Gold would have enough fuel on hand for two more mining seasons. As in 1912 the railway worked 24 hours a day, delivering wood to stockpiles along Bonanza Creek. With no other freight of significance, temporary or permanent shutdown was imminent. Although Murphy had told the press that the railway's future was uncertain, it was now apparent a well-conceived plan was actually under way.

KLONDIKE MINES RAILWAY

The Transportation Line

——— OF THE ———

Klonkike Mining District

E. A. MURPHY, Gen. Mgr.   HARRY B. ISEMAN, Auditor

P. D. BUSHE, Agent

DAWSON, YUKON TERRITORY

The full-page advertisement from the **Dawson Daily News**, *Special Edition of August 17, 1913. Ironically, in another ten weeks,* **"The Transportation Line"** *would transport no more. Note the typographical error.*

Compare this view with the photo on page 89, in which Canadian Klondyke Mining Company's dredge No. 4 is under construction. In this photo of mid-June, 1913, dredge No. 4 is working up the Klondike River valley, and has already severed the west leg of the Klondike Mines Railway's north end wye—rail as far as the tail of the wye has been pulled up. All of the settlement in the foreground, known as Old Inn, would be plowed under by 1915. Note that no steam-thawing plants are installed here since ground beneath, and adjacent to, the Klondike River valley was not underlain by permafrost.
Yukon Archives, Henderson Family Coll'n., 82/204 1A

O'Brien had not been in the news for some time, but in mid-August an advertisement read, "Tom O'Brien has a new store and hotel at the mouth of Donjek on the White River". The O'Brien Brewing and Malting Company had in past years continually run advertisements, listing a variety of brews, soft drinks, and cigars. On August 17, 1913, Discovery Day, Tom's brewery ran a rig in the parade, "with a high and fancy platform laden with bottled beer, and with four steeds drawing the load".

A special Discovery Day edition of the *Dawson Daily News*, now the only newspaper in Dawson, included a full page ad placed by the Klondike Mines Railway, subtitled "**The Transportation Line**". (See opposite.)

A letter, dated September 5, from E.A. Murphy to Commissioner Black requested permission to take up enough rail and fastenings from the main line between Queen Street and the steel bridge in order to lay a spur track from the main line at 69 Below. The company was presently short of rail and fastenings, and promised to relay the Dawson tracks in the spring of 1914. The new spur was urgently required in October to move 1000 tons of freight from 65 Below to Sulphur Springs—dredge move for the Yukon Gold Company. Commissioner George Black gave verbal permission to Murphy. The change in Dawson City trackage was to create some hostility, expressed by Black who wrote Murphy on October 23;

> ...referring to our authority to move part of your track to Bonanza Creek...it was not contemplated that you would thereupon convert Front Street, in front of Government Reserve, into freight yards, which has been done since removal of the tracks referred to, and is now being done.

Murphy immediately responded;

> ...we are using this section to load wood and machinery here where there is the only grade low enough for easy, economical work. The railroad will move although it will be more difficult for workmen who are having a difficult time as it is, and more costly for the railroad too...but I will comply. There will be no more car spotting on the Dawson side of the Klondike River.

Black's response was even quicker as he upheld his compassion for the plight of the working men, although his order still held—uptown Dawson "in front of Government Reserve" would not become a distasteful rail yard.

By November 1, all of the Yukon Gold Company's dredges on Bonanza had shut down for the season. In the November 4 and 5, 1913, issues of the *Dawson Daily News*, the railway's last, ever, advertisement ran. It read;

NOTICE

—

All bills against the Klondike Mines Railway should be presented before November 6th, as our accounts will close on November 10th.

E. A. MURPHY,

General Manager.

On the 6th, the season's story was told. The Klondike Mines Railway had shut down after a successful season. The *Dawson Daily News* wrote: "The locomotives are in the winter quarters and will not move a wheel until spring." During the final 27 days of the season the railway had hauled from lower Bonanza to the Dome (Sulphur Springs) one of the Yukon Gold dredges weighing 1000 tons. The dredge was knocked down into manageable sections and a spur, at 69 Below, built right to the edge of the old pond where the parts were loaded onto flat cars with a crane. With its tremendous pulling power, KMR engine No. 3 (the Vauclain compound) was apparently used for this final big job, for when it went into storage at shutdown it was parked at the doors to the engine house, in front of No. 4. All material set out at Sulphur Springs was hauled by horses and sleighs to No. 12 claim on Gold Run Creek later in the winter. The pit on No. 12 had already been dug in the fall of 1913. During the 1913 season the railway had hauled approximately 35,000 cords of wood from the mouth of Bonanza Creek and the mouth of the Klondike River to points along Bonanza, from 95 Below to 36 Above—all dumped off at Yukon Gold steam generating plants.

In the spring of 1911 the railway had begun running freight-only trains, and by fall had discontinued mixed train service. From June 30, 1910, to the end of 1911, the railway had carried only 2297 passengers for revenue of $9377. In the next accounting year, with no official passenger service, the company listed two passengers carried for $4 revenue. The increasing volumes of cordwood hauled to supply thawing plants at new dredge sites steadily boosted annual freight tonnage. To June 30 (previous twelve months) in the years 1911, 1912, and 1913, freight revenue rose from $38,794, to $57,564, to $110,180; in the final half of 1913 (in fact only four months) a whopping $112,176 was realized. Profits rose accordingly in these four periods, from $2793 to $8506, to $38,212, to $60,057—but still far short of the annual $330,000 surplus hypothesized in Hawkins' prospectus of 1902. (See Appendix A.)

Directly reflected in the rise in profits in the final year were wages of enginemen and trainmen—up about 300 percent, and locomotive fuel—up thirty percent and more. At least three of the four locomotives had run with full crews, often operating overtime. However, instructions had come from London; trains stockpiled cordwood at points along Bonanza Creek for use several years ahead in anticipation of shutdown of the railway. The amount of cordwood hauled jumped from 21,231 tons in the twelve month period prior to June 30, 1912, to 39,833 tons in the next twelve months, to 41,606 tons in the final four months of 1913; annual consumption of cordwood by the dredges on Bonanza Creek at that time was probably about 20,000 cords (one cord of spruce wood weighs about one ton).

Passenger service had been eliminated, express was handled by others, and business had swung fully to bulk haulage; by 1911 only two box cars remained, and by 1912 these were also converted for a total of twenty-three flat cars on the equipment roster. In the final two financial reporting periods train mileages had doubled from about 7000 to 14,000 miles per season.

The Klondike Mines Railway's existence had been less varied and colourful than first visualized, and far less profitable. The proposed extensions—and connections with other railways—never materialized, lode mining prospects which might have provided business were never developed, no vital communities were located on-line, and passenger traffic in the end was non-existent. In the eight years of operation, Klondike Mines Railway locomotives had racked up a total of 90,579 revenue miles, the greater portion credited to engine No. 2. In total, only 158,800 tons of freight was hauled in eight seasons; a modern class 1 railway can carry this tonnage in about sixteen 100-car freights.

Initially the railway carried many passengers, mostly working men from the camps south of the divide serving large mining companies. Although trains averaged about 10 mph between Dawson and Sulphur Springs, it was more convenient to take horse-drawn stages from the camps on Dominion, Sulphur, and Quartz Creeks directly to Dawson, and back—besides, trains did not run during winter months. Thus the railway gradually lost all passenger traffic and declined, from mixed train service with a fair proportion of express and high class freight, into a common cordwood hauler. Until 1911, the railway provided days of excitement and pleasure to Dawson residents, and visiting tourists and conventioneers, in special excursions. The lower Bonanza valley provided a panorama of what was keeping Dawson alive—the dredging camps of the Yukon Gold Company, and from the Forks to Sulphur some of the most beautiful vistas and scenery in the Klondike could be relished. In retrospect however, the passenger business done by the Klondike Mines Railway never met expectations; only 16,131 were carried in six seasons of service.

The railway's home base was in Klondike City, a collection of homes, farms, and small businesses: the brewery, Joe Gatt's Klondike Hotel (sometimes in trouble over liquor violations), the Klondike Mill, and many tidy two-room cabins belonging to prostitutes who had been banished from Dawson by the local elite several years earlier. Wood-yards provided most of the business originating at Klondike City, when the line to Dawson City was out of order. Located at Dawson City were the White Pass docks where most high class freight arrived by steamer.

In the beginning freight was delivered to stations on lower Bonanza Creek, but in the end, cordwood was simply dumped off the railway grade above thawing and dredging plants. Once-booming Grand Forks died by degrees with fires and the arrival of manpower-efficient dredges—no agent was stationed there after the 1908 season. There were no settlements whatsoever on the southern eighteen miles of track—stations there were no more than service stops or flag stops. Nowhere on the line were there rough-and-ready roadhouses, gambling joints, or music halls—as one might expect in such a fabulously rich gold district. Although the railway handled gold shipments, not a single robbery was ever staged.

The end of the line, Sulphur Springs, was located on the windy divide between Gold Bottom Creek and Sulphur Creek. A transfer point for freight and express for creek camps to the north and south, it was a lonesome spot until the arrival of a batch of tourists. Sulphur was also the site of Cook's Roadhouse, a few hundred feet north of the railway station, which catered to travelers and those on holiday excursions. The Roadhouse was a complex of stables, out-buildings, and the main lodge which was a two-story log structure. It was several steps in class above the dingy roadhouses described in Laura Berton's book, *I Married the Klondike*, on her passage one winter, up Gold Bottom and across the divide to Granville. Over the years, Cook's Roadhouse hosted numerous visitors who came simply for the train ride and the sights, or for those watching the sunset on the longest day of the year, or for others interested in a short jaunt up to King Solomon Dome, the highest point in the Klondike goldfield.

General manager E.A. Murphy left Dawson on November 14 of 1913 "for his winter home in Portland", Oregon, where Mrs. Murphy and their two sons lived. In reporting the final events, newspapermen seemed blithely ignorant of facts they had earlier published themselves. Murphy would never return and it would not be six months, but 41 years, before locomotives No. 1, 2, and 3 would "turn a wheel".

No passenger service had operated to the Dome since 1911. In late October of the 1913 season, the last freight train of the year had steamed homeward leaving Sulphur Springs—forever—it was the last, ever, KMR train to operate. It was a gloomy, anti-climactic, event compared to the jubilant, optimistic, opening of the whole line to traffic almost exactly seven years earlier.

South Dawson, the Klondike River valley, and Klondike Island as they looked in the winter of about 1916. A Canadian Klondyke Mining company dredge has recently eaten up the river bottom and stacked the barren tailing in distinctive "worm burrows"; dredges No. 3 and No. 4 had been built in 1912/13 about a mile upstream. The Klondike Mines Railway has been shut down for several years, and although the rail bridge to Dawson is still intact, it is now used by wagon traffic and maintained by the Yukon government. Of interest is the string of flat cars just visible at the base of the hillside on the Klondike City line; the cars would be soon moved to the main line adjacent to the left of the square plot of farm land on the island. It is believed the mining companies used the Klondike City line to haul supplies directly from the Yukon River to dredge sites, utilizing one of the ex-Detroit Yukon Mining Company Porter locomotives and dump cars chassis.

Yukon Archives, Schellinger Coll'n, 5930

CHAPTER TWELVE

AFTERMATH
1914 TO 1928

The Klondike Mines Railway was shut down after having delivered several years' supply of cordwood to the Yukon Gold Company. In the spring of 1914 the Yukon Gold Company was once more mining with dredges at 17 on Eldorado, 18 Above on Bonanza, 90 Below on Bonanza, 60 Below on Bonanza, 52 Below on Bonanza, and 12 Below on Bonanza, all with huge stockpiles of cordwood to fire their thawing plants for some time to come. Although the Klondike Mines Railway stored all equipment with thoughts of re-opening in a few years, business prospects continued to decline. In the next ten years dredge activity diminished, and what cordwood was needed was delivered by local contractors. By 1920 a new technique of ground thawing, known as cold-water thawing, was developed. This by no means displaced the use of cordwood-fired boilers for steam generation, but it did cause a significant reduction in cordwood demand—eliminating any immediate hope for the railway.

On May 29, 1914, six weeks after the railway would normally have been back in operation, word from Ottawa announced the appointment of Harry B. Iseman to succeed Eugene Murphy as general manager for the coming year. Finally, in early June, 1914, Iseman arrived on the steamer *Casca*. Back from London, he had conferred with the heads of the company, and on the way he had stopped in Ottawa at the railway's head office. While in the London, Iseman spoke to men associated with the Yukon Gold Company: Treadgold, Newhouse, Bredenburg, and Dolan. Lawther and Latta still hoped future operation of the railway would be possible, but in the meanwhile the road and equipment would be maintained as is—the locomotives would remain locked in the engine house at Klondike City. Eugene Murphy, who had been general manager for the last seven years, was no longer connected with the Klondike Mines Railway, but was still with Lawther and Latta in another capacity. Iseman would now represent the company—in

reality only a property manager. He had come to the Klondike in the early days, involved in mining promotion until 1907 when among other jobs, he became auditor with the railway, a position he held until 1913.

Little more than three weeks later, Iseman commenced legal action on behalf of the railway against the Yukon Gold Company for general damages and an order to stop the company from dumping tailings at the mouth of Lovett Gulch and Fox Gulch. Iseman contended that the tailings from bench claims would eventually cover the railway tracks.

Discovery Day, August 17, 1914, was celebrated as usual, and the Klondike Brewery's (legally, the O'Brien Brewing and Malting Company) *Dawson Daily News* advertisement extolled "Klondike Beer" and soft drinks, informing all that the brewery was "the sole agent for Lovera Cigars". O'Brien's advertisement featured a photo of the brewery (next door to the railway engine house), a team of horses hitched to a beer wagon, and behind the wagon was O'Brien himself. The photo was taken before 1914, since the locomotives had been locked in the engine house since the fall of 1913.

On April 9, 1915, the railway once more petitioned Council for exemption from rail mileage taxation for five years. General manager Iseman appeared on behalf of the railway, stating that the road had been shut down for several seasons (in fact, one and one-half years) because of a lack of business, thus it was only fair to forego the tax. He also claimed that should the road start up, a heavy outlay would be necessary before it could be ready for business. A week later the railway was granted exemption from the mileage tax of $100/mile/annum by the Yukon Council, but only for a period of three years. The railway would continue to pay the municipal tax on all properties.

This photo shows two of Tom O'Brien's loves in the Yukon: his brewery and his railway. The scene was used in an advertisement for the Klondike Brewery in the August 17, 1914, issue of the **Dawson Daily News** but was actually taken in the summer of 1913 or earlier. O'Brien's store and warehouse were in 1904 transformed and added to, to house the new Klondike Brewery. The portly, white-haired, gentleman behind the wagon is Tom himself. The two young men behind and beside the wagon might be Tom's sons Henry and James, who at that time were listed as "bottlers" in the brewery. The beer wagon survives today, on display at Guggieville. Because Tom had played a leading role in developing the Klondike Mines Railway, he included engines No. 2 and No. 3 in this view. Note the flat cars loaded with cordwood, and the stub switch—a type of switch commonly used on narrow gauge railways until recent times.

National Archives of Canada, C 16904

An arrangement had been made with the railway, where a part of the tracks from the Klondike River bridge, around the Klondike Bluffs, as far as the wye site was graveled "to make it serviceable for rigs". The work was in preparation for the advance of a Yukon Gold Company dredge, which by mid-August was eating up the road approach on the south end of the Ogilvie Bridge. Taking several weeks in all, the dredge worked past the bridge, temporarily diverting traffic over the railway bridge and the graveled railway tracks. Maintenance of this temporary road was the responsibility of the mining company.

Lawther and Latta's Dawson, Grand Forks and Stewart River Railway Corporation, which in 1904 had been chartered for the purpose of construction of the railway, declared voluntary liquidation on February 25, 1916— gold production in the Klondike had fallen to new lows, and prospects for extending the railway line appeared non-existent. However, during World War I, John Latta's ocean shipping firm would make huge profits transporting nitrates, a product essential in the manufacture of explosives, from South America to Europe. For his service to the country in the war effort he was created a baronet, becoming Sir John Latta in 1920. Robert Lawther had withdrawn from the shipping enterprise in 1911.

Discovery Day was celebrated on August 17, 1915, and O'Brien's Klondike Brewery advertised;

The Beer that Made Klondike Famous and Made Milwaukee Jealous.

However, O'Brien's health was failing, and in late summer the brewery was being managed by one of his past partners, Joseph Segbers. Prohibition came to the Yukon in 1917, but the brewery sold other bottled products until 1919 when it was shut down. The brewery equipment remained unused until 1933 when it was shipped to Fairbanks, Alaska.

On the evening of August 24, 1916, Thomas William O'Brien, one of the most noted of pioneer Yukoners, passed away at St. Mary's Hospital in Dawson City. He had succumbed to liver troubles. O'Brien's funeral on August 28 was;

> one of the largest and most representative ever held in the Yukon. Dawson suspended business this morning in the solemn hour while Yukon laid to rest all that is mortal of one of her most notable pioneers and empire builders. In compliance with his request he was buried in the Pioneer Cemetery in Dawson, in the land to which he had devoted the greater part of his energetic life.

Although unpopular with miners at times during the early days, O'Brien was probably the most respected man in Dawson. He was one of the charter members of the Yukon Order of Pioneers, a man who had made his fortune in the Yukon, and he stayed here, calling this place his home. Paying last respects were miners, judges, tradesmen, civil servants, the Territorial Commissioner, merchants, and labourers; he was survived by his wife Anna, a daughter, and three sons.

Although the company which had financed construction of the Klondike Mines Railway had declared voluntary liquidation, the operating company was still attempting to hold on to property. In early 1918, representative Iseman was informed that the fees on leased water frontage in Klondike City were much in arrears. Iseman pleaded that the company wished to retain the leases but remittances from London were slow in coming due to the war. He asked for a deferment of the fees.

It was mid-summer of 1917 and the dredging companies in the Klondike were in financial difficulties. The war, a shortage of manpower, and disintegration of management had resulted in a steady decline in gold production. The Granville Mining Company and the North West Corporation went into receivership, and Boyle's Canadian Klondyke Mining Company would follow in 1918. The mining operations struggled on, on a hand-to-mouth basis for a time. Managing the North West Corporation was F.P. Burrall, who in trying to get Canadian dredge No. 1 back in operation "estimated that some four miles of railway track would be needed. Possibly this could be obtained from the Klondike Mines Railway". It appears that John Latta may have had an interest in the Granville Mining Company, and its reorganization was in the offing. The Yukon Gold Company operating along Bonanza Creek was not in much better condition.

The Tanana Valley Railroad may have been interested in Klondike Mines Railway engine No. 4 at this time. Dated October 15, 1917, on letterhead of the Alaskan Engineering Commission, Ship Creek, Alaska, is a report describing a narrow-gauge, Prairie-type, Baldwin locomotive "in the Anchorage yards". Although axle spacings given do not correspond with those of Klondike Mines Railway engine No. 4, an attached sketch refers to "Locomotive No. 4 Dawson", which certainly was never in the Anchorage yards. The memo has puzzled historians of Alaskan railways for some time, since no other similar locomotive in the North is known.

The year 1919 found Iseman still representing the railway and its property. A letter from the Crown Timber and Land Agent noted that the Klondike Mines Railway had not been operating in years, and that the local represen-tative had no funds; "During the past summer the City of Dawson purchased from the agent of the company certain timbers which were in stock, and paid the rentals on the water frontage".

A mining company wanted rails, the City of Dawson had taken lumber in lieu of lease fees, and now the Department of Works wanted a piece of the railway bed for a roadway. A section of road leading up Bonanza Creek had been washed out as a result of mining action by the Yukon Gold Company, which had made offers to pay some of the damages. Although Iseman was the Dawson representative, he had insufficient authority to speak for the directors in England. A letter from the Dawson Department of Public Works to Ottawa got a reply on August 30, 1919, from one-time railway

executive Andrew Haydon. He could not give an answer to the question of removing rails since he no longer had an interest in the company. Since its operations "appeared to have been abandoned by parties formerly interested", he had no instructions of any kind at all. Discussions dragged out without any contact with the owners. In October the Gold Commissioner, in Dawson, wrote the government in Ottawa stating his case, saying rails had been practically abandoned for years and there was no likelihood of the track ever being used again. In responding, the Minister of Justice, Canada, cautioned him not to remove rails before contacting the owners.

By the spring of 1920 the road problem was becoming more critical. Dawson Council was informed that 800 tons of equipment to be hauled from the Forks had to be taken by freight rig down to Dawson on the old rail

Probably in the early 1920s, this view shows the Klondike Mines Railway bridge still intact, but modified for use by horse and wagon—note the off-ramp. Rails are gone from Dawson City, but are still in place on Klondike Island in the foreground. At the lower right is a string of flat cars which would stay there until 1942, when bought from the YCGC by the White Pass. At lower center the Klondike Mill spur curves away from the main line, and on a stub track are the KMR's two coaches which were parked there in the fall of 1911. The coaches were destroyed by fire in the late 1940s, but the trucks are there today, in a stand of cottonwood trees.
British Columbia Archives and Records Service, HP 72511

Klondike City in 1922: in the foreground is the track of the Klondike Mines Railway, poorly ballasted and overgrown with weeds. O'Brien's brewery (with the tall stack) is boarded up, the plant moved to Alaska. Also boarded up is O'Brien and Moran's store. Only a handful of people lived in Klondike City at the time of this photo; the cabin on the left appears to be occupied. The railway's engine house is out of sight behind the brewery, and the railway's 1500-ton coal bunker—in the distant right—was still intact at that time.
National Archives of Canada, PA 100463

grade. Gold Commissioner McKenzie then made a formal move. Writing to John Latta in London, he asked for use of the railway bed from the Forks to Brown's Hill, a distance of about two miles. McKenzie quoted Iseman who had informed him that the only reason for wishing the rails kept along this stretch in question was in the event the railway might re-open. In a fit of brashness McKenzie then made the mistake of bluffing; "A legal advisor says the railroad is practically abandoned. If judicial proceedings were instituted the government would undoubtedly secure the rights through the Courts to utilize the road bed. If objection to rail being pulled up, additional material could be placed on the road bed. Please telegram collect". The telegraphed reply dated June 23, 1920, addressed from Latta to McKenzie, was not the humble response the Commissioner had expected; it read: "Letter May 10 received. Surely you cannot countenance confiscation our rights. Guggenheims are responsible. Willing assist by leasing road bed fair yearly rental providing Yukon Territory Government guarantees prompt replacement if we require". Signed Latta.

A letter, also dated June 23, 1920, followed detailing the telegraphed reply. Latta stated that he wanted to keep the railway as a whole entity, and that it could not be legally taken away just because there was no business on the line. He added that there had been many offers to break up the road, all refused. He also implied that the railway could possibly be moved as a unit to other locales in the Yukon Territory. Deviating from this business, Latta then questioned conditions in the Yukon, mentioning that he and Lawther had associated themselves with the North West Corporation, and, with other financial organizations, was looking ahead to development in the Yukon; this would appear to be part of Treadgold's plan to return to the Klondike for a final, almighty, amalgamation of mining properties. In closing however, Latta took shots at what he thought was widespread maladministration by all government departments of the country. Obviously still smarting from the sorry demise of his Klondike Mines Railway, he considered civil servants, like McKenzie, to be partly responsible. Latta's bitter reaction must have cowed McKenzie. He made one more timid attempt to gain right to the roadbed, saying he thought Latta unreasonable to ask a fee. There was no further correspondence on the subject until summer, 1925.

An application was made to Parliament of Canada in January, 1921, by Robert B. Young for incorporation of the Mayo Valley Railway Limited, but watchdog Iseman, speaking for the Klondike Mines Railway, telegraphed Ottawa objecting to the proposal. The Klondike Mines Railway Company, located in Dawson, Yukon Territory, had ample equipment, material, and strong financial backing. When sufficient business would develop, the railway intended to extend from Dawson to silver camps of Mayo, or by an alternate route from Mayo to the mines. The latter route was practically the same as Young had proposed. Gold Commissioner McKenzie backed Iseman's objection, saying that if another charter were granted it might block bona fide investors—such as Lawther and Latta.

That summer the assets of the Canadian Klondyke Mining Company were taken over by Burrall and Baird, Limited. While large foreign concerns dominated the Klondike, mining great blocks of claims, there were still many sourdoughs in the Klondike working individual,

It is early summer, possibly in the 1920s, and this view over Klondike City shows many changes from what is seen in the photo on page 28. Most of the buildings are vacant, boarded up or doorless. Gone are some boardwalks, other are crumbling, and several buildings have been razed to make room for small garden patches. On the far right, at the corner of Bridge Street and Yukon Avenue, is a two-story building with two wings, a bay-window, balcony and porch complete with railings, and ornate gable trim. This building is believed to be Joe Gatt's Klondike City Hotel—"The Best Wines, Liquors and Cigars Always on Hand. Open Day and Night. Cafe in Connection". The hotel catered to a less select crowd, and of course to the nearby prostitutes and their customers. Joe Gatt, a member of the YOOP, had been brewmaster of O'Brien's brewery until its shutdown. He then turned to farming in Klondike City until his death in late 1947. Today none of these Klondike City structures remain, having been moved elsewhere, or destroyed by fires.
Provincial Archives of Alberta, P.7171

less accessible, claims. The **Dawson Daily News** of March, 1922, commented that a number of hand miners had stockpiled big dumps, using windlass and bucket over the past winter, for spring sluicing.

Dawson was no longer the metropolis it once had seemed to be. After a six-year absence from the Klondike, Laura Berton and husband Frank returned to Dawson in 1922. It was a melancholic sight; homes and businesses vacant everywhere, in Klondike City the sawmill had shut down, the brewery was shut down also, the rails up Bonanza Creek rusting and unused, and the homes of prostitutes empty—Klondike City was nearly abandoned, and the population of Dawson had sunk to 800.

The 1923 Public Works report shows that a government work crew had made additional repairs to the piers of the Klondike Mines Railway bridge over the Klondike River. Photos indicate that at some time after the railway had shut down in 1913 a fourth span, shorter and lower in profile than the others and probably of wooden

construction, had been added at the Klondike City end of the bridge. River channels were changing and flood waters were now cutting away at the margins of Klondike Island. At that time the bridge was still maintained since access was needed to a few small but productive farms on the south side of the river. While the bridge was safe for a while, a big ice jam on the Yukon River cut away the outside pilings from the Klondike Mines Railway's terminal station on Front Street in May, 1924. Shearing pilings like straws, the ice also took out platforms and a portion of the structure of the old railway office and warehouse on the river's edge. In 1925 the building was sold at an auction by the city and moved. Since almost none of the Klondike Mines Railway's business records have survived, it can be assumed they were lost forever with the demise of the depot.

During the third week of August, 1923, which was hot and very dry, bush fires from the valleys below King Solomon Dome swept up the mountainsides at Sulphur Spring, totally destroying all of the Klondike Mines

Another disastrous flood on the Klondike River once more takes out a pier of the KMR bridge—it is the spring of 1922. This time the pier at the south end is destroyed, but it would be repaired. Although trains had not crossed the bridge since 1913, it was for a time maintained by the government for the few residents of Klondike City.
Arthur E. Knutson, Eddie Boyce Coll'n, Kirkland, WA

The KMR passenger coaches were showing marked deterioration in 1922. They have been parked on a stub track near the Klondike Mill since 1911. Both cars were built in the 1880s, although their exact origins are not known. Both were bought in 1898/99 by the White Pass, and were numbered as WP&YR 208 and 202; in 1905 they were refurbished and sold to the KMR as No. 202 and 200. A grass fire in the late 1940s destroyed all the wooden parts of the cars, but the trucks and hardware are still there today, resting on rails which are buried by half a foot of forest debris.

O.S. Finnie, National Archives of Canada, PA 100395

Railway's southern terminal buildings and Hartman's (Cook's) Roadhouse; "...once alive with activity, now nothing but ashes".

Several big mining companies in the Klondike had been in financial difficulties for some time, some of them in receivership, and now the strongest, the Yukon Gold Company, was winding down. Back in England, Treadgold, although still personally bankrupt, began to take control of operating companies in preparation for his long dreamed-of monopoly of the Klondike goldfield. The Yukon Consolidated Gold Corporation had been chartered in 1923 with the intention of securing all Klondike creeks claims which were held by various mining companies. The Canadian Klondyke Mining Company had been taken over by Burrall and Baird, which in turn came under Treadgold's rule in 1925, as did the New North West Corporation. The Yukon Gold Company operated through 1925, but by 1926 had become part of the giant Yukon Consolidated Gold Corporation, under the management of Treadgold.

Of course Treadgold could not have gained so much power by himself. Many of the Klondike's first heavy investors had been English capitalists well aware of Treadgold's promotional abilities. He knew the goldfield and he was a dynamic organizer. Among his many London acquaintances were shipping magnates Sir John Latta and Robert Lawther. Treadgold had organized the Yukon Gold Company in 1906, and as early as 1911 Lawther and Latta had discussed consolidation schemes with Treadgold. But Treadgold's unwilling departure, and World War I, had delayed any action. About 1924 Lawther and Latta bought into a newly-formed concern, the E.Y. (English Yukon) Syndicate, which would in one year control a substantial block of shares in the Yukon Consolidated Gold Corporation. Lawther personally liked Treadgold, and when troubles arose he made many attempts to bridge differences between Treadgold and his critics. Latta likewise supported Treadgold. In 1925 Treadgold became the YCGC's first president, a position he would hold until 1932, while both Lawther and Latta would in time serve as directors of the corporation.

A minor, though interesting, character in the history of the consolidation of the mining properties was Harry B. Iseman. Following shutdown of the railway in 1913 auditor Iseman began acting as general manager, in fact only a property manager, of the company. When World War I ended British capitalists once more looked to the Klondike for exploitation, and about this time Iseman became something of a double, or triple, agent. Founder of the Yukon Consolidated Gold Corporation, Major Francis Cunynghame, revealed some of the clandestine tactics in his book, "*The Lost Trail - The Story of Klondike Gold and the Man who Fought for Control*;" the "Man" was, of course, Treadgold. Cunynghames's comments reveal a bit of the intrigue in these early stages in the consolidation of mining properties, and of Iseman's small part in it.

During the time when the North West Corporation and Burrall and Baird were being reorganized, Treadgold had retained Iseman to report progress. In fact, Treadgold held interests in both companies. Iseman may also have been in the employ of both of the mining companies, but he continued to send Treadgold detailed reports, criticizing and finding fault with everything being done by the managers and engineers of the companies. Later, the E.Y. Syndicate also paid Iseman for similar information. Once dissension had started between the E.Y. Syndicate and Treadgold, and when Treadgold was away in the Klondike managing the field situation, Iseman then sent reports to the E.Y. Syndicate, criticizing Treadgold and his actions. However, the E.Y. Syndicate suddenly and tragically lost its correspondent.

Harry B. Iseman had come to the Klondike in 1901, interested in mining. Born in Pennsylvania, he was a chartered accountant and worked for a number of concerns in Dawson, including the Klondike Mines Railway. After the war he had been employed off and on by Burrall and Baird, the Yukon Gold Company, and others, but he also dabbled in mining ventures. In early August, 1925, Iseman hired five men to assist him in prospecting a gold find up the McMillan River, a tributary of the Pelly, 150 miles south of Dawson. While relaying launches through swift water the canoe carrying the men capsized and all but Iseman made it to shore—he had been wearing hip-waders which were believed to have prevented him from swimming ashore. Iseman owned a fast motor launch, enjoyed hunting, and was a capable outdoorsman. He was fifty years old.

It can safely be said that by 1925 the property of the Klondike Mines Railway, owned by Lawther and Latta,

who also controlled the E.Y. Syndicate, became part of the pool of properties held by the Yukon Consolidated Gold Corporation. Thus the railway (whose construction had almost been stopped by Treadgold), the Yukon Gold Company (which Latta had partly blamed for the railway's demise), and Treadgold were now all part of one big co-operative. And Treadgold did indeed "own" the Klondike Mines Railway, for in a letter dated December 15, 1925, the Department of Works and Buildings asked Treadgold for use of a certain piece of rail grade for a roadway—the same piece of rail roadbed which Commissioner McKenzie had attempted to get from Latta five years earlier. The Department noted that no progress has been made since first requesting permission to use this portion of the road bed in 1919, and that met "only with resentment". The request added that the tracks presently terminated at Adams Gulch, and that only the portion of the grade from Adams Gulch to Bonanza (Grand Forks) was needed.

Treadgold apparently did not respond to this request, because on July 30, 1928, Gold Commissioner McLean wrote Treadgold asking for permission to remove rails and ties, so that the rail grade could be used as a public road. McLean noted; "you have acquired sole proprietary right in the Klondike Mines Railway". A month later Treadgold's hand-written letter approved the use. It read;

> 6 Sep. 1928 This authorises you to take and use for a Public Road the Right of way of the Klondike Mines Railway from 6 below Discovery on Bonanza Creek up to the Forks. I rely on your putting aside in secure position, accessible to our people, the rails in the section mentioned above. yours faithfully, A.N.C. Treadgold, President of the Yukon Consolidated Gold Corporation Ltd.

Treadgold had done a magnificent job of getting all mining properties under one roof, but he was a difficult man for the directors to control. While most knew him as a brilliant organizer, he was also unorthodox, managing operations in his own unapproved ways. A few "conspirators" plotted Treadgold's overthrow and in 1932 found evidence enough to have his ownership of shares in the Yukon Consolidated Gold Corporation cancelled because of failure to disclose his interest as a promoter in dealings with the company. Treadgold was once again banished from the Klondike, never to return. Through the courts he would try again and again to have his shares reinstated, without success, and in 1951 he died in London, bankrupt, at age eighty-seven. Although both Lawther and Latta were good friends of Treadgold and had supported him, they were businessmen first, and as such wanted the company run in a business-like manner. With order restored, YCGC dredges would continue to eat up the creek bottoms of the Klondike for years to come.

In May, 1928, the historic Klondike Mines Railway bridge over the Klondike River was again severely damaged by ice. The **Dawson Daily News** reported;

> One of the finest structures of its kind in the Yukon, the railway bridge at the end of 5th Street, may have to be dismantled as a result of damage to piers, making it unsafe. ...ice so undermined one of the piers on the south side, so that a partial collapse now exists. Repairs would cost much, and there is little traffic, so work is not justified. It has been condemned, and probably will be removed by the owners.

Photos taken in 1933 show only the two northern spans in place, and the 80 foot southern span with the shorter, later, addition completely gone. By 1938 no bridge spans or piers remained.

The Klondike Mines Railway, and its property, were forgotten for the next fourteen years—absent from both government reports and newspaper accounts.

Again the Klondike River threatens the KMR bridge with extinction, this time on May 14, 1925. The approach from the Dawson City side will be repaired when the waters subside; note there are no longer any rails on the bridge. The bridge had been extensively rebuilt in the spring of 1923 when the south end was damaged. New pier pilings were sunk at the far end of the steel work, and a new, lower and shorter, span of wooden construction was added there—it can be seen in this photo. The channel of the Klondike River was changing, cutting away at Klondike Island. In the 1930s the river would once more knock down the southernmost span—it was not repaired and the remaining bridge spans were later removed.

Yukon Archives, Claude Tidd Coll'n, 7640

CHAPTER THIRTEEN

FORSAKEN, AND REMEMBERED

Following the turmoil of consolidation, the Yukon Consolidated Gold Corporation methodically and routinely mined and shipped gold from the Klondike for years, finally shutting down in 1966. Well-organized and well-financed, the YCGC became a small empire in itself, operating almost independently of Dawson and the Territorial Government. The property of the Klondike Mines Railway—rolling stock and track—remained unused and tightly controlled by the mining company almost to the end.

In mid-summer 1933, Professor Harold Adams Innis, Canadian historian, travelled through the north country gathering material for his treatise, *"Settlement and the Mining Frontier"*. He and a companion boated down the Yukon River, and camped for one week at Klondike City, and of the degeneration of the Klondike he wrote; "...empty houses in Dawson, engines formerly on the Klondike Mines Railway and now locked in the roundhouse, abandoned saw-mills...these are indications that the economic cyclone has spent its force".

Steamboats of the White Pass and Yukon Route continued to ply the Yukon River during the summer months, as they had since the early days of the boom. Hauling in supplies for the community, and bringing in tourists, a half-dozen sternwheelers made Dawson a regular stop. In late August, 1940, Arthur Knutson from the crew of the White Pass steamer Yukon spent a day taking in the sights of Klondike City. One of the old-

timers took Art and friends by rowboat across the Klondike River where a good number of buildings were still standing, but abandoned. Among them were the prostitute's huts, a saloon, the brewery, and the engine house with four locomotives still inside.

The *Dawson News*, Thursday July 9, 1942, wrote, "The steamer *Whitehorse* arrived here Tuesday evening with freight, and left yesterday afternoon, but stopped at Klondike City. Today it is still loading railroad equipment, including a locomotive, several tenders, and freight car trucks destined for the South end". Two days later the newspaper added, "The steamer *Whitehorse* that left Dawson Wednesday cleared Klondike City the following afternoon with an engine from the long gone Klondike Mines Railway".

The railway of the White Pass and Yukon Route had been leased by the U.S. Army and was moving tremendous volumes of freight over the line in connection with the Alaska Highway project. A number of 36-inch gauge locomotives had been brought from the south, but still more were needed. Remembering that the Klondike Mines Railway's engine No. 4 had seen only two years of use, the White Pass acquired it, along with its tender and the tender from engine No. 3, from the Yukon Consolidated Gold Corporation. The absence of couplers and air compressors on the three remaining locomotives today suggests that the WP&YR may have acquired these components at the same time. All had been stored in the

About 1937, Premier "Duff" Pattullo of British Columbia actively promoted the annexation of the Yukon Territory by the province of British Columbia in conjunction with construction of a highway north to the Yukon and Alaska, and the plan very nearly succeeded. Having begun his career in Dawson City in the early boom days, Pattullo held an affinity for the Klondike. His proposed road had support from the U.S. government, but little from the federal government; the Japanese attack on Pearl Harbor in December, 1941, eventually mobilized construction along a route different from what Pattullo had visualized, and the Alaska Highway was pushed through by contractors in 1943. The Alaska Highway would have profound effects on the future of the Yukon Territory.

engine house at the southern end of Klondike City. Although No. 4 had not moved since 1913, the old Baldwin was rebuilt as WP&YR No. 4, and since it was a lightweight engine it was to put work as a yard goat at Skagway. However, J.D. True, a WP&YR fireman at the time, recalled one occasion when No. 4 was put into service on the main line as a work train, running as far north as Glacier.

All of the mechanical parts of the Klondike Mines Railway flat cars at Klondike City were also taken—the wooden frames and decks were so deteriorated since last used in 1913 as to need complete replacement. Records indicate only twenty-two cars were taken although the railway had twenty-three cars at shutdown in 1913. Photos show that the string of flat cars was first stored on the Klondike City line, just west of its junction with the main line, and that they were later moved to the main line, between the bridge on Klondike Slough and the Klondike Mill spur. This move would appear to have been a consequence of some freighting being done after the demise of the Klondike Mines Railway, utilizing the Klondike City line from the Klondike City docks directly to dredge sites. Motive power at that time was almost certainly one of the little Porter locomotives, towing the stripped-down dump cars brought to the Klondike with the Porter locomotives in 1904. The chassis of two of the dump cars were, until 1994, on the bank of the Yukon River in Klondike City, resting on rails of the old Klondike City line.

In June, 1944, a White Pass riverboat man, Ron Willis, visited Klondike City with fellow crewmen and photographed the scenes. The two derelict coaches, on the spur where they had been parked since 1911, were within a hundred yards of the old cable ferry landing, and a quarter mile away was the site of the railway's engine house. There were still three locomotives here, fully exposed to the weather.

In the late 1940s a hay field fire set by farmer John Buss got away, destroying the woodwork of the coaches parked on Klondike Island. The trucks and other scorched and rusting hardware are still there today.

Most of the rail from Klondike City to Sulphur was still in place as late as 1928. Some was soon pulled up for use by the Yukon Consolidated Gold Corporation. The YCGC, referred to as the "wyceegeecee", was lord and master of all property, including the Klondike Mines Railway's assets, in the district. One could not so much as take a length of pipe without the company's authorization. Almost 5000 feet of rail was used as reinforcing and surfacing in the concrete floor of YCGC's Bear Creek heavy equipment shop. The shop survives today, as part of a Parks Canada visitor's attraction.

During World War II, miles of power lines leading to the YCGC's dredges fell into disrepair because of a manpower shortage. In total the YCGC had over fifty miles of power lines, much running along waterlogged valley bottoms. Permafrost, in which power poles had

Part of the remains of Klondike Mines Railway coach No. 202 which was destroyed in a grass fire in the late 1940s.
  Eric L. Johnson, Vancouver, B.C.

On June 16, 1944, Ron Willis and seven other dissatisfied shipmates, "mutinied" from the White Pass steamer **Whitehorse** when it landed at Dawson. With a few days to tour, Ron visited Klondike City and the site of the KMR's "roundhouse". When the White Pass bought KMR engine No. 4 and its tender in 1942, the engine house was pulled down to get at the locomotive, which since 1913 had been parked behind No. 3—in addition the White Pass also took the tender from No. 3. At the near left is the KMR's Buda narrow gauge "Section Motor Car", at the centre is engine No. 3, and to the right is engine No. 2, minus its smoke box number plate. Partly hidden behind No. 2 is engine No. 1. In the foreground are a pair of doors from the engine house—the rest of the corrugated sheet metal building has been salvaged.

Ron WIllis is seen in the fireman's seat of No. 2. Ron's Klondike sojourn was short-lived as he was soon back on the White Pass, no longer on the Yukon River boats, but on the Carcross/ Taku run for the balance of the season.

Both photos Ronald W. Willis, Vancouver, B.C.

been set to a shallow depth, thawed and poles tilted in all directions and some toppled over. As a remedial measure lengths of rail, pulled up from the KMR line, were driven deep into the ground alongside the wooden poles which were strapped to the rail to provide more permanent support. Among the dozens of men hired by the YCGC for postwar rehabilitation of the mining plant was Don Macintyre, who spent the whole summer of 1946 repairing power lines between the North Fork power plant and Bonanza. In the bogs and spruce swamps thick with black flies, Don and a partner hauled fifteen-foot lengths of rail into place, climbed onto a stack of oil drums set up next to the wooden power poles, and with sledges drove the rails into the ground to shore up the

power poles. Their handiwork can still be seen along the Klondike River and many of the creeks today.

Most of the Klondike Mines Railway's track remained in place until the 1960s. The White Pass was not interested in buying the rail, which was of 45-lb and 52-lb weight, since it was too light for operations of the postwar years. It is believed that much salvaging of rail took place after 1966 when the YCGC finally shut down operations. It seems likely that Ernie Striker, a contractor who salvaged most of the YCGC's equipment from the Bear Creek camp between 1966 and 1970, also pulled up what remained of the rails for sale as scrap. However, many lengths of rail can still be found in the hills today, piled

Klondike Mines Railway engine No. 1 as seen in Minto Park, Dawson City, in the early 1960s, a long way from its first home on the Kansas Central. This Brooks locomotive initially ran in track construction duty on the KMR, and later saw limited use on work trains.

Carl E. Mulvihill, Skagway, AK 1356/3

White Pass' second No. 4, ex-KMR No. 4, is seen here being loaded onto a ship at Skagway in 1955, bound for Wisconsin and a new career on amusement park railways.
Dedman's Photo Shop, Skagway, AK

here and there. Near Flannery, where there were four trestles, several dozen lengths of rail are scattered across the ravines, a result of the collapse of the wooded trestles. Noticeably absent are the fish-plates which joined the rails end to end; these were found by miners to be ideally suited for use as riffles in sluice boxes. Very few of the switches, frogs, and other hardware along the line remain today, suggesting their removal by Striker rather than the YCGC which would have had no use for the track fixtures. While rail had been completely removed from Dawson not long after shutdown of the railway, some sections of track in Klondike City line never were removed. Deep in forest litter several hundred feet of rail remain today; beneath the trucks from the pair of coaches, along Yukon Avenue, and leading to the site of the engine house. A recent mining operation rooted out a number of lengths of rail along Klondike Avenue.

In 1950 the village of Whitehorse was incorporated as a city, and in March, 1951, the seat of government in the Yukon Territory was transferred from Dawson to Whitehorse. In 1955 a highway connection between Dawson and Whitehorse was made when a spur from Stewart Crossing to Dawson was completed, and in that year the Yukon River steamers ceased operating. In the 1950s the Klondike Visitor's Association was organized to promote interest in the Klondike, and by the late 1960s had federal government support in preservation of the district as the "*Klondike National Historic Site*".

The Dawson City Museum and Historical Society had planned to move the three remaining Klondike Mines Railway locomotives (donated by the YCGC) from Klondike City to Dawson during the winter of 1959-60, but a mild winter and thin ice on the Klondike River postponed the move. In mid-February, 1961, Dick Gillespie, Don Neff, and Harry McDonnell hauled the first locomotive and its tender to the present museum site. Brush and snow had been packed over the ice of the Klondike River to strengthen it, and using equipment provided by Mr. Gillespie the remaining two locomotives followed. On seeing the locomotives for the first time in almost fifty years, long-time residents of Dawson, Mrs. (Harry) McDonnell and Mrs. Elizabeth Vifquain recalled the first excursion; "The coaches were named after popular dancehall girls and were decorated with bunting and streamers...it was a breathtaking experience peering down over trestles spanning deep gulches". DYMCo locomotive No. 4, stored for years at the Bear Creek camp, was also donated by the YCGC to the museum at that time. All four locomotives sat in the open on the museum site until 1987, when a fine new locomotive shelter was completed.

When the locomotives were brought to Minto Park in 1961, the wooden cabs of all three were intact, but in the intervening years much of the woodwork deteriorated. The cab of No. 3 has disintegrated, that of No. 2 has fallen away, and pilot beams have rotted, as have the stringers beneath the tenders—the museum quite simply did not have the money for preservation of the locomotives and tenders. Protected from the weather today, the locomotives are in stable, but rough, condition. Many parts of the locomotives are missing, including bells, whistles, headlamps, smoke box number plates—most taken years ago by souvenir hunters. Other missing parts were probably stripped for use in 1942 by the WP&YR, and still others may have been taken for local use. Noticeably absent are air pumps (air compressors—the

mounting brackets are on the left side of the boiler just ahead of the cab) and the air reservoirs (cylindrical tanks which were suspended beneath the cabs) on No. 2 and No. 3. This was original equipment on No. 3, and likely non-original on No. 2. No. 1 was not originally "air-equipped", and it is uncertain where its pump was later placed, but the air reservoir still remains, mounted on the rear of the tender. All of the air equipment, usable where any steam plant was available, may have been taken for some Klondike machine shop or mining operation.

Automatic (knuckle) couplers linked locomotives No. 2 and No. 3 with their tenders, and all KMR freight and passenger cars were similarly equipped. The automatic couplers are now missing, probably acquired by the WP&YR in July of 1942. Up front, however, both locomotives had link and pin drawbars, and pilots ("cow-catchers"). The link and pin drawbars and No. 3's pilot are still in place today—the pilot from No. 2 was removed not long ago. Although it is thought locomotive No. 1 might have been tied to its tender with an automatic coupler, a link and pin drawbar is in place at the rear of the tender. Additionally No. 1 was not fitted with a pilot, only a step-board. These fixtures indicate No. 1 was used only on work trains or for switching duties—it was not well suited for main line service anyway.

All three locomotives were built with the less sophisticated Stephenson valve gear; note the absence (actually, out of sight) of complex valve operating mechanisms as seen on more modern locomotives. All three locomotives were also fitted with flangeless tires on the middle drivers —necessary on track with the sharpest curves allowed.

This small Porter, saddle tank, locomotive, Detroit Yukon Mining Company (DYMCo) No. 4, was one of four brought to the Klondike in 1904 to work placer claims at the mouth of Bear Creek. DYMCo No. 4 actually rode KMR rails for a short time, and is the only one of the four still remaining in the area. It was donated to the Dawson Museum (where it is parked today) in 1961, and was placed alongside KMR engines No. 1, 2, and 3; because of the sequential numberings (engines 1, 2, 3, and 4) many visitors have naturally assumed that No. 4 was part of the KMR's roster—not so.
Eric L. Johnson, Vancouver, B.C.

KMR No. 1 is appealing for its "vintage" spark arrester (diamond stack) and remarkable for the relatively good, original, condition of its cab. The locomotive is more than 115 years old! The 2-6-0 wheel arrangement was designated a Mogul type, typical of hundreds of locomotives seen on both narrow gauge and standard gauge railways of North America in the mid/late 1800s. Of the three locomotives in the shed, No. 1 is the best preserved.

Both No. 2 and No. 3 have a 2-8-0 wheel arrangement which is designated a Consolidation type. This was a type typically seen on railways at the turn of the century. Of the pair, No. 2 is in the poorest condition with its stack knocked off, and pilot and cab completely gone. It was the most-used locomotive on the KMR.

KMR No. 3 was the biggest locomotive on the railway's roster, and in fact has the most massive appearance, due to two features: its outside frame, and huge cylinders. It is a "Vauclain compound" locomotive. Designed and developed by Samuel Vauclain, and first built by the Baldwin Locomotive Works in 1889, this famous (or infamous) four-cylinder compound system (double-expansion) gave Vauclain locomotives "improved thermal efficiency, through reduced fuel and water consumption", and "better dynamic characteristics which resulted in a smoother impact upon the track, and correspondingly less track pounding and wear". At a given speed, it was not claimed a compound locomotive could haul a heavier train better than could a single-expansion (two-cylinder) locomotive of similar weight and class—adhesion limits being equal. However, it was claimed Vauclain compounds could keep a train moving at very low speeds, or on heavy grades, where single-expansion locomotives would slip and stall. This was credited to the Vauclain's more uniform application of power throughout the stroke.

Of the 901 locomotives built by Baldwin in 1899, 241 were Vauclain compounds. The WP&YR acquired their No. 6 and No. 7 (re-numbered 56 and 57 in 1900), new, in 1899. The sale of No. 57, one of the newest and most powerful locomotives on the WP&YR's roster, to the Klondike Mines Railway in 1906 was not as magnanimous as it might first have appeared. It was found that reliability problems outweighed the advantages, and most Vauclain compounds were soon "simpled", that is they were rebuilt into single-expansion locomotives. WP&YR No. 56 was simpled in 1907, and remained on the roster until 1938 when it was scrapped. KMR No. 3 was little used until the final two or three years of the railway's

operation, and today is the only extant Vauclain compound in Canada outfitted with the original system.

Outside-framed narrow gauge locomotives were not uncommon, and a number still exist today. Exposed to view are all of the suspension parts, and almost hidden inside the frame are the wheels. The seemingly-complex array of parts combined with cylinders, main rod, and side rods hung so far outside the track, gives outside-framed Vauclain compound locomotives a rather brutish appearance.

In contrast was KMR No. 4 with a 2-6-2 wheel arrangement, designated a Prairie type, almost delicate in appearance, and again, not an uncommon type on North American railways. KMR's No. 4, which had left the Klondike for Skagway in 1942, was continuing its travels. After serving as a yard engine for the White Pass at Skagway, it was sold in 1955 for use on a "theme park" railway at Oakwood, Wisconsin. The Oak Creek Central Railroad never materialized, and in 1960 No. 4 was moved fifteen miles away to Waterford, Wisconsin, where it did operate on the Peppermint and Northwestern Railroad until 1964. Continuing its summer only, theme park, railway career, the engine went to the Petticoat Junction Railroad at Sevierville, Tennessee. This operation, not to be confused with the railway seen on the TV series of the same name, folded after only three days of operation in early July, 1965. By 1969 engine No. 4 had been moved to Osage Beach, Missouri. Here it worked on the Gold Nugget Junction Railroad until 1979 when, in need of a major overhaul, it was shut down. After laying idle for five years No. 4 was moved to El Reno, Oklahoma, where today it is in storage.

Except for the locomotives, there is nothing in Dawson today to indicate that trains once ran the length of Front Street. Nothing remains of the bridge and piers over the Klondike River, and station, tracks, and grade have long disappeared. But in Klondike City a number of features can easily be found. To explore and document what remains of the railway, the Dawson City Museum and Historical Society commissioned a research project, which was completed in 1992 by Barbara Hogan and Greg Skuce. Hiking almost every foot of the 31-mile right-of-way, the team reported the complete survey in photographs and notes.

Since Klondike City was the home base of the railway, a number of relics can still be seen there. Original survey maps imply a neat grid of streets, dividing the "city" into orderly subdivisions, but in fact only a minimum of rough roads existed and buildings and cabins were scattered randomly. At its peak Klondike City was cleared of brush, and, located on higher ground than either South Dawson or Klondike Island, it was settled with homes, businesses, and farms. With the abandonment of properties, some buildings were moved to Dawson and even to Mayo. After destruction of the remaining

buildings by fires, nature reclaimed the land which today, except for a few clearings, is once more thickly overgrown with aspen, cottonwood, and willow.

On Klondike Island, directly across the Klondike River from the foot of Seventh Street in Dawson, 200 feet from the river's edge, are the trucks, truss rods, and other hardware of the railway's two passenger cars. Since the

LAKE OF THE OZARKS

On the opposite page are three incarnations of Klondike Mines Railway No. 4:

Top: It was photographed in July, 1956, by W.H.N. Rossiter "just north of Kenosha, Wisconsin." The locomotive was purchased from the White Pass in 1955 by Mike Molitor for a theme park railway at Oak Creek, Wisconsin; the grade there was built, and some track laid, but the "Oak Creek Central" never became operational. No. 4 was moved to Waterford, Wisconsin, in the early 1960s, and it was operated there for a short time.
W.H.N. Rossiter photo, M.D. McCarter Collection, N-11190, Campe Verde, AZ

Middle: Steam fan and photographer William J. Husa, Jr., visited the Peppermint and Northwestern Railroad at Waterford, Wisconsin on September 29, 1962, and got this photo of ex-KMR No. 4 pulling two home-built coaches in passenger (tourist) service, service it had never had provided while on the KMR or with the WP&YR. Owner Mike Molitor added a fake spark arrestor to No. 4 for character. Although the tender is fully lettered for the P&NW, the cab sports a "NorthWestern" herald not unlike that of the Chicago & NorthWestern.
William J. Husa, Jr., Cochran, GA

Bottom: Yes, this is the **Hooterville Cannonball** *of the Petticoat Junction Railroad. The date is July 5, 1965, the location is south of Sevierville, Tennessee, and the narrow gauge engine is ex-Klondike Mines Railway No. 4. But it is not the* **Hooterville Cannonball** *which was seen on the popular TV series,* **Petticoat Junction**. *Railway action sequences of the 148 episodes of the TV series were first filmed in 1963 on the standard gauge Sierra Railroad in California. The Sevierville, Tennessee, operation was somewhat less successful, operating for only three days—July 3, 4, and 5 of 1965.* **Cannonball** *fireman Thomas Lawson, Jr., now of Birmingham, Alabama, took this picture on the last day of operation.*
Thomas Lawson, Jr., Birmingham, AL

bodies and even the main frameworks of the cars were of wood construction, there is little here to tell anyone except railway enthusiasts that these cars were in fact passenger cars. Six inches below the surface of a deep bed of leaves and forest debris can be found the rails on which the trucks still rest. Surrounded by tall cottonwoods, the rusting remains are not very accessible during high water in the months of May and June. A few hundred yards west are the remains of the Klondike Mill, and immediately to the south is a disaster zone which for some years had been a tidy garden patch. A recent attempt at placer mining there left a dismal mess—rails and relics rooted around, dirt piled high, deep and broad pits filled with water; done in 1991 the "mining" seems to have been a failure. But Klondike Island is no longer an island. Klondike Slough, which was once a channel of the Klondike River separating Klondike City from the island, is now a boggy depression, silted in years ago. The single span railway bridge which crossed Klondike Slough is long gone.

A quarter-mile south, at the southern tip of Klondike City proper, is a private cabin built where the railway's coal bunkers once stood, and a few hundred feet north in a stand of tall trees, are a few tons of junk at the site of the engine house. A heap of wheels and axles, a decaying wood and steel snowplow, rail, sheet metal, and the caved-in service trenches which lay between the rails show this once was an active maintenance shop. A hundred feet northeast is a mound of quart bottles—beer bottles from O'Brien's brewery next door to the engine house. Klondike City is a National Historic Site, and as such is protected; the removal of any relics is prohibited.

Much of the abandoned road leading from Klondike City to the Ogilvie Bridge follows the railway grade, and the odd piece of rail can be found there. Just behind the present day Shell gas station was the railway's only north-end wye, at mile 2.8, but it and the Old Inn road-house were obliterated when dredges plowed through prior to 1920. The wye had been of an unusual layout to permit northbound engines to turn around in order to back trains into Dawson, two and one-half miles distant. Where the east leg of the wye curved directly onto the main line, the west leg extended in a tangent for several hundred feet before joining the main line; this formed a sort of siding where a locomotive could run around even the longest train. The beer wagon of the O'Brien Brewing and Malting Company still exists, and is on display at Guggieville, up the road from the Shell gas station.

Along the Klondike Bluffs is the grade of the Klondike Mines Railway, blasted out in early 1905, but now a public road leading to the site of Klondike City. A length of pipe with a wooden cross-arm supported wires of a telegraph and telephone system first strung and operated by the railway.

Eric L. Johnson, Vancouver, B.C.

120

From the junction of Bonanza Creek with the Klondike River to well above Grand Forks, the railway grade has been thoroughly fragmented, or obliterated, by dredging and hydraulicking operations over the years. A short section of grade here, a rock cut, a length of rail there, and traces of wooden trestles are all that can be found.

Except for a couple of decrepit cabins on the hillside, there is nothing at the junction of Bonanza and Eldorado Creeks to indicate the bustling town of Grand Forks, population 10,000, once existed here. Survey maps of 1900 show a neat layout of streets and avenues spreading far up the hillside, away from the creeks, but in fact nothing more than a wagon road and a few trails left the creek bottom. Business development was concentrated along First Avenue, and with the exception of a church, only scattered log cabins were located above Second Avenue. Hawkins' first plans for the railway would have had the line running into town at creek level, but when plans were changed in 1904, the grade was surveyed to pass well above the townsite. The road leading to Upper Bonanza and the Dome today lies on the old rail grade, overlooking the townsite, but except for some lengths of rail no other traces of the rail yard or the Grand Forks station can be found.

Between Dawson and Grand Forks the grade is at most 1%. However, from Grand Forks to Soda, where the grade rises steeply from valley bottom to the ridge separating the valleys of the Klondike River and Bonanza Creek, the grade averages about 2.5%, but the ruling grade, near Flannery, is about 3.48%. Between Soda and Sulphur the grade rises by, on average, a mere 0.5%. Three deep ravines east of Grand Forks, about one, two, and three miles distant, called for tightly curving track on trestles which were each 400 feet in length. The trestle on Homestake Gulch was said to be the highest at sixty-five feet, and is the site depicted in several photos. The first two ravines, Gauvin and Homestake Gulches, have been mined extensively, while McKay Gulch at about mile sixteen has hardly been worked at all. Few remains of the ravine crossings exist today. Some of the earth abutments can be seen, and at McKay Gulch, some traces of trestle timber can still be found.

Beyond McKay Gulch, the grade of the Klondike Mines Railway line is practically undisturbed, although overgrown with brush. In fact the flat bench provided by the grade at higher elevations has actually promoted heavier growth than is seen on the adjacent slopes— spruce trees on the railway bed stand thick and tall compared to the ground birch and shrubbery on the slopes above and below the grade. Sulphur Springs and Grand Forks had communication with Dawson by both telegraph and telephone, owned by the railway, while Flannery and Soda had only telephone connection; in the Upper Bonanza region, tangled lengths of phone or telegraph wire can still be found in many places.

At Flannery station, mile 20, and well below the ridge, four trestles have collapsed, and the station buildings have all crumbled. The water tank which once stood there has keeled over, and only the filler spout lying below the grade identifies what the structure once was. The earth abutments for the trestles are clearly identifiable, with lengths of rail jutting out where the trestles once stood. In the ravines between the abutments can be seen a few trestle bents, and lengths of rail where they fell when the trestles collapsed. Flannery derived its name from James Flannery's Halfway House, built in 1899 on the old Ridge Road above the head of Carmack Fork. Beyond Flannery the railway grade rises steeply to reach the crest of the hills, and swings into the Hunker Creek watershed in wending its way south-easterly. The railway grade can be traced on Government air photos, although recent bulldozer roads do confuse interpretation.

En route to Sulphur, one reaches the site of Soda station at mile 27—where a most interesting feature can be found—one of the two remaining pieces of the Klondike Mines Railway's box cars. When the company began converting box cars to flat cars in 1907, the superstructure from one was moved to Soda where it was set up next to the Soda siding, probably to serve as a station building. Amazingly, after nearly ninety years and numerous bush fires in the area, the building has survived and is in remarkably good condition today. Of Douglas-fir construction, the thirty-foot box car was built by the White Pass to a standard design, and exhibits professional workmanship. The floor has suffered some from visiting campers and slight decay, but walls and roof are sound, and the original catwalk is still in place along the roof ridge. The sliding doors of the box car were replaced by narrow doors, and two small windows were cut into the southeast, track-facing, side. The switch stand and a frog are still in place at the south end of what was an eight-car siding, but only a few rails remain. Klondike residents have referred to this area for eighty or more years simply as Boxcar. Only recently the Yukon Government began moves to make Boxcar and Sulphur Springs "historical reserves".

The remains of the second box car extant is located in the Upper Bonanza Creek area. In a stand of trees, leaves and damp conditions have contributed to a more rapid rate of decay—it is not in as good condition as the car at Soda. Unmodified, with sliding doors and most of the original hardware yet, this box car is still remarkably preserved considering its ninety years there in the hills.

Beyond Soda the modern road leading to King Solomon Dome crosses the rail line where the old grade once more swings back into the Bonanza Creek watershed, then into the watersheds of Quartz Creek and Sulphur Creek, to reach the end of the line. At mile thirty-one, this is "Sulphur". One mile west of King Solomon Dome just below the site of Cook's Roadhouse, the modern road drops downward at a tight bend in crossing the location of the south switch of the Sulphur Springs siding. The roadhouse was built in October, 1898, by Joe Cook and Frank Cleveland, and was known as "Cook and Cleveland's Dome Road House"; it later became simply Cook's Roadhouse. It was most conveniently located for business, only a few hundred feet uphill from the railway's Sulphur Station. A few feet west of the modern road/railway grade crossing were the station buildings, and to the east of the crossing was the wye. Rusting cans, broken bottles, track switch fixtures, clinkers from the locomotive fireboxes all testify to the once-present railway terminal buildings, and the odd length of rail, two shallow rock cuts, a built-up grade, and a broad cut on the Gold Bottom side of the ridge define the wye and probably the location of the engine house. In August, 1923, bush fires destroyed all of the buildings of the Klondike Mines Railway and Cook's Roadhouse at Sulphur Spring.

Final survey maps of the railway's Grand Forks/Sulphur Springs section show the southern terminus and yards, but no wye, one-half mile east of where construction actually ended. There on the slope of King Solomon Dome and at the very head of Sulphur Creek was the "real" Sulphur Springs, but Hogan and Skuce found no evidence that the grade had ever been advanced this far— construction of a wye here would have been impossible for lack of flat ground. It is likely that, in the late fall of

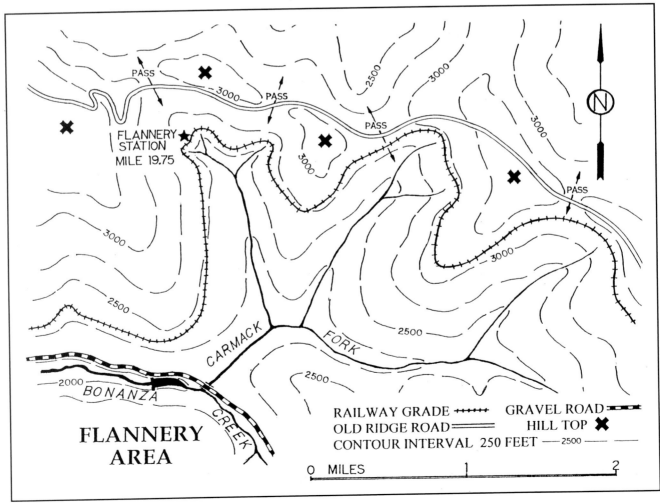

FLANNERY
STATION
MILE 19.75

FLANNERY
AREA

RAILWAY GRADE ++++++ GRAVEL ROAD ▪▪▪▪
OLD RIDGE ROAD ═══ HILL TOP ✖
CONTOUR INTERVAL 250 FEET ─2500─

0 MILES 1 2

The Klondike Mines Railway maintained three water tanks on its 31-mile line: one at Klondike City, and others at 37 Below on Bonanza (mile 9.6) and at Flannery (mile 19.75). This photo, taken June 8, 1995, shows the author with a water spout just below the grade at Flannery; parts from the wood stave tank, which collapsed long ago, can still be found there also.

Greg Skuce, Dawson, Yukon

June 8, 1995; Greg Skuce points out lengths of 45-lb rail which had once been laid on one of four trestles at Flannery. Some timber from the collapsed trestle bents—about thirty feet high at this gully—can still be found there. Seen here are a pair of rails resting in the crotch of a birch tree which somehow has resisted their weight.

Eric L. Johnson, Vancouver, B.C.

This superstructure of a box car which had been converted to a flat car in about 1907 became the Soda station building. In remarkably good condition ninety years later, the box car and surroundings are now slated for government protection as a heritage reserve.
                                        Eric L. Johnson, Vancouver, B.C.

At the site of the 8-car Soda siding (Boxcar), Mac Swackhammer and Greg Skuce examine a switch frog and some rails.
                                        Eric L. Johnson, Vancouver, B.C.

1906, the urgency of completing a south end terminal dictated an interim location—after all, plans called for extension of the road to the Stewart River in the next season. But, the extension never materialized, and Sulphur Springs remained the southernmost point on the railway, and as close as the Klondike Mines Railway would ever get to the Outside.

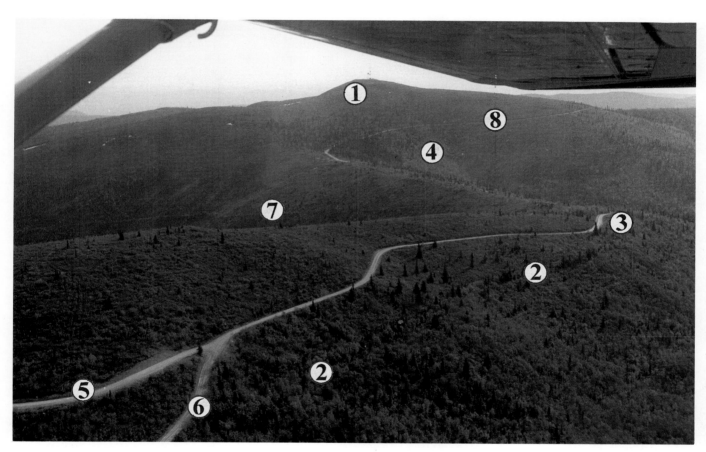

1) King Solomon Dome
2) Grade of the Klondike Mines Railway
3) Sulphur Springs - end of steel
4) Site first surveyed for Sulphur Springs Terminus
5) Road from Dawson
6) Quartz Creek Road
7) Gold Bottom Road
8) Sulphur/Dominion/Hunker Creeks Road

June 14, 1992: an aerial view easterly towards King Solomon Dome, the highest point in the Klondike goldfield. The modern Ridge Road and the Quartz Creek road are well-used today, but the Gold Bottom Road has been abandoned for years. Below the Ridge Road in the foreground can be seen a string of spruce trees, grown up on the old rail grade which, where it converges on the public road, reaches the site of the Sulphur Springs terminus.

Eric L. Johnson, Vancouver, B.C.

In June, 1995, Dawson Museum director Mac Swackhammer and Klondike researcher Greg Skuce survey one of two remaining ex-KMR box cars, this one located on Upper Bonanza Creek. However, resting in a stand of trees, collecting dead leaves, and suffering from decay, this car body has deteriorated more than the one at Soda.

Eric L. Johnson, Vancouver, B.C.

EPILOGUE

Financed by capitalists who had believed the Klondike Mines Railway would eventually become a part in the exploitation of Canada's Northern Frontier, the railway never met a fraction of the goals forecast in its promotional prospectus. In fact, the Yukon Territory in general was never developed to the extent of early hopes and prophesies. Had the railway begun operating soon after being chartered, there is little doubt that it could have made huge profits in the labour-intensive days of 1900 to 1905. In 1906, when the railway began operating, economic conditions and development had changed drastically from the boom days, and over the eight years the railway operated, total income practically balanced total expenses. The railway had been doomed to failure by over-optimism, and factors unforeseen even as late as 1904.

In development of the Klondike goldfield, the railway was of not much economic importance. With the railway's arrival, much of the summer work of teamsters was eliminated. But, the railway was no more than a trunk line, although about one-half of the business was initially done along Lower Bonanza, and in summer teamsters provided all the branch lines. When the railway ceased winter operations in the fall of 1907, teamsters once more resumed full service until spring. Although the railway hauled 158,800 tons of freight in all of its working years, this could have been easily handled by teamsters, which had sufficed before the railway, and continued to do so after its demise. However, in the very active summer months the railway did provide low-cost and very efficient service, particularly to the Yukon Gold Company which controlled most of the gold properties along Bonanza Creek.

The railway also provided glamour and excitement for entertainment-hungry Dawson. Excursions to the Dome on the summer's shortest night, and on St. Patrick's Day, Dominion Day, and Discovery Day were all zealously patronized. The good citizens also enjoyed excursions by Yukon River steamers, but the railway tour reminded all of what provided their livelihood. Lower Bonanza gave vacationers a splendid spectacle of the goldfield at work, while the ridge line with its Sulphur destination offered a magnificent, 360-degree, panorama. Although Lawther and Latta probably cursed the day they had become involved with the Klondike Mines Railway, Klondike history is richer for its existence.

July of 1914: the KMR did not reopen that spring, and this piece of poorly graded, poorly ballasted, track near Klondike Bluffs is already being overcome by grass.

National Archives of Canada, PA 103849

APPENDIX A

THE KLONDIKE MINES RAILWAY PROSPECTUS

No copies of Hawkins' Klondike Mine Railway prospectus have survived, but the following story which appeared in the February 17, 1902, *Klondike Daily Nugget,* commented fully on the text*:

Prospectus Reaches Dawson
- Passenger Fare to be $2 to Grand Forks
- Freight Charges in Proportion
- Will be Completed 12 Miles by July 1.

One of the most interesting documents that has reached Dawson this winter is the prospectus for the Klondike Mines Railway Company issued by Mr. E. C. Hawkins to prospective investors, a copy of which a gentleman recently returned from the outside has kindly placed in the hands of a Nugget representative. The booklet is most comprehensive, the information being set out placed before the readers in a brief, concise form and without the usual verboseness one is accustomed to observe in such documents. Facts and figures are given as to traffic which may be expected, operating expenses and cost of construction which, while doubtless true, is positively startling, and if the intentions of the company are fully carried out mining in the Klondike will receive an impetus, the like of which has never been known before.

The deal of which the Klondike Mines Railway Company is the outcome was made last fall when on September 25 a memorandum of agreement was entered into between the provisional directors, consisting of Thos. O'Brien, J. A. Seybold, W. D. Ross, Llewellyn N. Bate and H. B. McGiverin, and E. C. Hawkins, having in view the early construction and operation of a railway between Dawson and the Forks. The directors agreed for the consideration of $18,000 cash and 2,200 shares of the capital stock of the company of the par value of $222,000, to furnish the right of way,

terminal grounds, etc., and subsequently to hold a meeting in Ottawa for the purpose of transferring to Mr. Hawkins the shares, stock and all rights, title and interest of the charter possessed by them, to elect new officers and pass a bylaw changing the head office of the company from Ottawa to Dawson.

The charter acquired by Mr. Hawkins, which is known as the O'Brien charter, is a very liberal one, and under condition of the railway being completed to the Forks, at the junction of Bonanza and Eldorado creeks, before July, 1903, is given the right of way, terminal grounds at Klondike City, 600 feet of water frontage on the Yukon River, station grounds at the Forks, and also the right to own and operate telegraph and telephone lines, water power, electric plants, etc. The route described in the charter allows construction up Bonanza, Eldorado, Dominion, down Hunker and the Klondike river, constituting a belt line covering the entire Klondike district. In consideration of the transfer to Mr. Hawkins of the rights and title acquired under the charter, he has agreed to construct, and equip and have in operation the first section of the road running from Dawson to the Forks before September 1, 1902, and in compliance with the terms of the agreement has secured subscribers of 2,500 shares of stock and deposited in the Canadian Bank of Commerce in Ottawa $25,000.

The agreement entered into September 25 was supplemented by a formal contract approved by the board of directors January 10, 1902, in accordance with which a construction company was incorporated and a contract entered into for the building of the road, furnishing the necessary buildings, equipment and all appurtenances, the construction company to accept shares of the company's stock in payment therefore. This stock of the par value of $100 a share is offered to investors at $80 a share and the belief is ventured that when the road has reached the Forks the stock will be above par. The capital for the first section of the road is $1,000,000,

---

*The newspaper article used lower case for "river" and "creek in proper names, and they have been reproduced as in the original.

divided into 10,000 shares of $100 each, is fully paid up and non-assessable.

The statement is also made that arrangements have already been made for the early delivery of all necessary track material and equipment and it is believed the road to the Forks can be put in operation by the latter part of July and a profitable business made this year.

The railway, to use a common expression, will "fill a long felt want". Since the summer of '97 the greatest difficulty and expense in regard to mining in the Klondike has been the transportation of mining machinery and supplies from Dawson to the mines and the supplying of the numerous plants with fuel and timber. The difficulty was partially overcome last summer by the construction of wagon roads, but it is a well-known fact that wagon roads, even if maintained in good order, do not take the place of a thoroughly equipped railway. The larger portion of machinery and supplies shipped to Dawson go up Bonanza for distribution and a very important feature in regard to the railway is the fact that the business awaits its construction just as was the case with the White Pass road. The promoters propose to make such low rates for fuel and freight, as well as passengers, that all competition will be removed and the large number of teams now employed in hauling freight from Dawson will be employed to equal advantage in distributing merchandise and other freight from the end of the railway to the numerous creeks. Mr. Hawkins expresses the belief and hope that the first section of the road will be built by the sale of stock to men directly interested and without the issue of any bonded indebtedness though an act of parliament authorizes the issuing of bonds to the extent of $30,000 for each mile constructed should the shareholders prefer to do so and pay interest on the bonds.

As soon as the first section is begun it will be the policy of the company to immediately arrange for extensions from the Forks to an advantageous point on Dominion creek, a distance of 20 or 22 miles, which it is said can be much more cheaply built than the first section.

A splendid outlook for the road is given under the head of earnings and business prospects. One of the principal sources of revenue will be from passenger traffic, as a great part of those engaged in mining and other make frequent, and in many cases, almost daily trips between Dawson and the Forks. An actual count of the people traveling on foot only on Bonanza from May 2 to May 6, last year, inclusive from 6 in the morning to 9 in the evening, and at a time when the roads were in their worst condition, gave a daily average of 182 persons. It is a well-known fact too, that not only would the Bonanza, Eldorado and Dominion creek miners and business people travel over the railway, but those from upper Hunker, Quartz, Sulphur, and the Indian river country would do likewise. In preparing estimates of earnings only a daily average of 300 was considered which, with three trains running daily each way, would only give an average of 50 to the train. In addition to the regular passenger fares a large business will doubtless be done in arranging frequent excursions. The present stage fare to the Forks of $5 will be reduced to $2, which upon the basis of the estimate made will produce a yearly revenue from passengers of $220,000.

Next in importance to the passenger business comes the handling of fuel and mining timbers. The hillsides for miles in the vicinity of the creeks have been practically denuded of timber, and one of the greatest expenses and inconveniences of mining in the past year has been the procuring of fuel and timber at a cost which could be avoided. In hundreds of cases the excessive cost of cordwood consumes nearly all the profits of mining and there are many mines idle on account of this unavoidable expense. It has become absolutely necessary to provide cheaper fuel and timber for these extensive districts, the supply in the immediate vicinity being exhausted. Last year over 100,000 cords of fuel and timbers were consumed on Eldorado and Bonanza and their tributaries. The railway has placed a rate of $2 per cord on fuel and upon an estimate of 80,000 cords a revenue from this source of $160,000 would be had.

Lumber for sluice boxes, cabins and other structures is also an important consideration. The saw mills of Dawson it is said cut about 6 million feet in a season, about one-third of which is used on the creeks. Two million feet of lumber of all kinds at a rate of $8 per thousand will produce a revenue of $16,000.

In 1901 over 32,000 tons of merchandise were delivered in Dawson and as probably the great majority of that is consumed on the creeks the assumption is made that at least 13,000 tons would be handled by the railway yearly. Merchandise has been classified into two classes, one to be known as "general merchandise" which will bear a rate of $10 per ton, and the other designated as "first class", at

$12 per ton, the total revenue from which is estimated at $142,000. Further earnings anticipated from mail contracts, express freight, refrigerator freight, etc., is expected to amount to $37,000, bringing the total estimated yearly earnings up to $575,000.

No figures are in the estimates of earnings for the handling of any ore or gravel for the reason that up to the present very little has been accomplished in the way of developing quartz or other metalliferous mines. Due cognizance, however, is taken of the discoveries running from Victoria gulch to the Dome and over to Indian river, which it is believed will eventually prove very valuable. It is also believed that in addition to the ordinary quartz mining yet to be developed there will be in the near future large quantities of the decomposed quartz and schists of the old channels to be worked over by means of machinery which will of necessity be located at some convenient point along the railway. Extensive beds of conglomerates carrying gold values from $3 to $12 per ton have been discovered in the vicinity of Indian river and while but little at present is being done toward their development it is possible that with construction of the road to Indian river these beds of conglomerates will be found to be workable at a profit.

In regard to cost of operation and general expenses of the road due consideration has been given to the high standard of wages and salaries obtained here as well as the expensive fuel. One feature, however, in connection with the operation of a railroad in the far north is exactly the reverse of what would be considered by those unfamiliar with the climatic conditions. Other means of transportation from the outside world to the Klondike are possible or at least profitable for only a portion of the year, but this road can be operated in the winter as well as in the summer and will not be interfered with by the heavy snowfalls as is the case with the road over the White Pass. The snowfall in the vicinity of Dawson is even very much lighter than it is in Whitehorse and in the construction of the road no expensive snow sheds will be required, although a few sections of snow fencing may be necessary along some of the hillside cuts.

The total expense of operation, including general expenses, is estimated at $245,000, which deducted from the estimated earnings, leaves a surplus of $330,000 upon a capital stock of $1,000,000 and it is considered by Hawkins safer to assume that the road will pay an annual dividend of at least 25 percent".

APPENDIX B

TARIFFS AND SELECTED STATISTICS

The *Canada Gazette* published tariffs for freight and passenger traffic rates on the Klondike Mines Railway, and other common carriers.

Following are two excerpts from the *Canada Gazette*. The tariff in the November 24, 1906 issue shows the rates effective 19th November 1906, the KMR's first year of operation. It lists freight and passenger rates in only one column.

The March 2, 1912 issue of the *Canada Gazette* shows the tariff taking effect April 15, 1912, listing only freight rates. It occupies 3½ columns. Note that Klondike is misspelled at the top of the second column.

THE KLONDIKE MINES RAILWAY COMPANY.

NOTICE. — The following Standard Freight and Passenger Tariffs of the Klondike Mines Railway Company have been duly filed with the Board of Railway Commissioners of Canada, and have been approved of by the Board as required by Sections 261 and 264 respectively of The Railway Act, 1903.

—

C. R. C. No. 1.

STANDARD FREIGHT MILEAGE TARIFF No. 1.

Effective 17th December, 1906.

Naming rates on Freight between all Stations. Governed by Canadian Freight Classification.

MILEAGE.	Rates in cents per 100 lb. Classes.									
	1st.	2nd.	3rd.	4th.	5th.	6th.	7th.	8th.	9th.	10th.
Not exceeding 5 miles..........	30	26	24	22	20	20	15	15	15	12
Over 5 miles and not exceed. 10	40	36	32	29	26	26	20	22	23	18
" 10 " " " 15	50	44	40	36	33	33	26	28	30	24
" 15 " " " 20	60	54	48	44	40	40	32	34	36	30
" 20 " " " 25	70	64	58	52	46	46	38	40	40	36
" 25 " " " 30	80	74	67	60	53	53	44	46	45	42
" 30 " " " 35	90	84	76	68	60	60	50	52	50	48

Minimum charge for not over 15 miles.. $1.00
For over 15 but not over 35 miles....... 1.50

—

C. R. C. No. 1.

STANDARD PASSENGER TARIFF No. 1.

To be applied in the absence of tariffs quoting lower rates.

Effective 17th December, 1906.

DISTANCES.	RATES.
Not over 5 miles..	20 cents per mile ; Minimum charge 50 cents.
Over 5 and not over 10 miles,	17½ cents per mile ; Minimum charge 50 cents.
" 10 " 20 "	16 cents per mile ; Minimum charge 50 cents.
" 20 " 30 "	15 cents per mile ; Minimum charge 50 cents.

Rules and Conditions.

Children over 5 years and under 12 half fare.
100 lb. of baggage free on each whole ticket.
50 lb. of baggage free on each half ticket.
Excess baggage 60% of first fare per 100 lb. or fraction thereof.
Excess baggage minimum charge 50 cts.
Baggage will be checked only on presentation of passage ticket, and in no case beyond destination thereof. Baggage will not be checked short of destination of ticket.
This Company will not be responsible for unchecked baggage.

H. BLOOMFIELD SMITH, C. E. M. INST.,
General Manager.
H. D. WEEKS,
General Freight and Passenger Agent.
Issued 19th November, 1906. 23-2

THE KLONDIKE MINES RAILWAY COMPANY.

NOTICE.—The following Standard Freight Mileage Tariff for Carload Traffic, C.R.C. No. 5, of The Klondike Mines Railway Company, have been filed with the Board of Railway Commissioners of Canada, and have been approved of by the Board as required under the provisions of The Railway Act.

C.R.C. No. 5.
Cancelling C.R.C. No. 2.

G.F.O. No. 3.
Cancelling G.F.O. No. 2.

THE KLONDIKE MINES RAILWAY COMPANY.

STANDARD FREIGHT MILEAGE TARIFF FOR CARLOAD TRAFFIC.

Effective, April 15, 1912.

Governed by Canadian Freight Classification.

MILEAGE.	RATES IN CENTS PER 100 POUNDS. Classes.						
	4th	5th	6th	7th	8th	9th	10th
Not exceeding 4 miles	22	20	18	16	15	14	12
Over 4 miles and not exceeding 8 miles	32	30	28	26	24	22	20
Over 8 miles and not exceeding 12 "	42	40	38	35	32	28	25
Over 12 miles and not exceeding 16 "	52	50	46	43	40	34	30
Over 16 miles and not exceeding 20 "	60	58	54	50	47	40	35
Over 20 miles and not exceeding 25 "	68	66	62	56	54	46	40
Over 25 miles and not exceeding 30 "	76	74	67	62	60	52	45
Over 30 miles and not exceeding 35 "	84	81	76	68	65	57	50

The rates named herein are subject to the terms and conditions of the Company's Bill of Lading or Shipping Receipt.

When freight is loaded by shippers and at shippers' account, the carriers will not be responsible for damage resulting from improper loading, nor for any discrepancy in account.

Lumber, carloads, must be loaded by shippers and unloaded by consignees. Should the company be required to load or unload, or both, the actual expense thereof will be added to the freight charges and collected from the consignee.

A demurrage charge of $10 per day will be assessed against all carload shipments not unloaded within 24 hours after arrival at destination.

The company reserves the right to demand prepayment of charges on any article that may be of doubtful value.

Live stock handled by special arrangement only.

Articles of freight exceeding 30 feet in length, requiring two cars, will be carried by special arrangement.

The company reserves the right to refuse any freight that is liable to damage any other freight in cars.

Freight weighing 2,000 libs. or over, per piece, or package must be unloaded by owners, or, when handled by the company, the actual cost of handling will be collected by the consignee.

E. A. MURPHY,
General manager.

36–2

THE KLONDYKE MINES RAILWAY COMPANY.

NOTICE.—The following Standard Freight and Express Tariff C.R.C. No.6 for less than carload traffic, of The Klondike Mines Railway Company, have been filed with the Board of Railway Commissioners of Canada, and have been approved of by the Board as required under the provisions of The Railway Act.

C. R. C. No. 6. Cancelling C. R. C. No. 4.
G. F. O. No. 9. Cancels G. F. O. No. 8.

KLONDIKE MINES RAILWAY COMPANY.

STANDARD FREIGHT AND EXPRESS TARIFF FOR LESS THAN CARLOADS.

Naming Rates Between Dawson and Sulphur Springs and Intermediate Points, and Points on Dominion, Sulphur and Quartz Creeks.

Effective April 15th, 1912.

E. A. MURPHY,
General Manager.

FREIGHT RATES GENERAL MERCHANDISE BETWEEN DAWSON AND POINTS NAMED BELOW.

RATES IN DOLLARS AND CENTS PER TON OF 2,000 POUNDS.	Grand Forks.	Sulphur Springs.	2 Below Sulphur	50 Below Sulphur	Granville.	Caribou and 7 B.L. Dominion.	33 B.L. Dominion.	Quartz Creek.
	$ cts.	$ cts.	$ cts.	$ cts.	$ cts.	$ cts.	$ cts.	$ cts.
1. 100 to 500 pounds	10 00	18 00	40 00	40 00	40 00	40 00	40 00	38 00
2. Over 500 and under 4,000 pounds	9 00	16 00	40 00	40 00	40 00	30 00	40 00	30 00
3. Over 4,000 pounds	8 50	15 00	35 00	35 00	35 00	25 00	35 00	25 00
4. Lumber, C.I., per 1,000 feet	8 50	16 00	28 00	35 00	40 00	30 00	35 00	30 00
5. Lumber, L.C.I., per 1,000 feet	11 00	18 00	35 00	40 00	45 00	35 00	40 00	35 00
6. Furniture, glass, etc	20 00	35 00	70 00	80 00	80 00	60 00	80 00	60 00
7. Dogs, each	1 00	1 50	2 25	2 75	3 25			

1. Covers all Merchandise N. O. S. in lots of 100 to 500 pounds.

2. Covers all Merchandise N. O. S. in lots of over 500 and under 4000 pounds.

3. Covers all Merchandise N. O. S. in lots of 4000 pounds or over.

4. Lumber—Common, in carloads of 7000 feet and over, loaded and unloaded by shippers.

5. Lumber—Common, in less than carloads.

6. Furniture set up, wrapped, crated or boxed ; Yukon sleds, show cases, (glass), doors, windows, plate glass and all glass of every description ; stove pipe, saddles and harness, smokestacks, hydraulic pipe over 12 inches in diameter.

7. Dogs—Securely fastened in cars, strictly at owner's risk.

Tinware, household goods, personal effects, glass of all kinds, hydraulic pipe, and all light and bulky articles will be taken at double the rate as shown above in quantities over 500 and under 2000 pounds.

All single pieces weighing over 2000 pounds, carried by special contract.

Continued on next page

RULES AND CONDITIONS.

The Company reserves the right to demand prepayment of charges on any article that may be of doubtful value.

Live stock handled by special arrangement only.

Articles of freight exceeding 30 feet in length, requiring two cars, will be carried by special arrangement.

The Company reserves the right to refuse any freight which is liable to damage other freight in cars

Freight weighing 2000 pounds or over, per piece or package, must be loaded and unloaded by owners, or, when handled by the Company, agents will assess the actual cost of handling.

EXPRESS RATES between Dawson and points named below.

	Sulphur Springs.	Caribou and 33 Below Lower Dominion.	Sulphur Creek Points.	Granville.
1 to 15 pounds......	$ .50	$ .50	$ .50	$ .50
15 to 25 pounds.....	.75	.75	.75	.75
25 to 35 pounds......	.75	1.00	1.00	1.00
35 to 50 pounds.....	1.00	1.50	1.50	1.50
50 to 100 pounds......	1.00	2.00	2.00	2.00

Blankets, war bags, etc., between points named below.

Dawson to Grand Forks..............$1 00
Dawson to 60 above Bonanza......... 1 50
Dawson to Sulphur Springs.......... 1 50
Sulphur Springs to Forks........... 1 50

Gold Dust from all Creek Points to Dawson— 4 cents per ounce.

Gold Dust or Currency—Minimum, $1.00.

Gold Dust must be in sealed pokes or boxes, and receipts will be given only on shipper's weight, as Company will not be responsible for discrepancy in weight between that shown by shippers and consignees.

Currency—Dawson to Creek points or *vice versa*, other than C.O.D. returns, one-quarter of one per cent.

C. O. D. Returns—Two per cent, minimum 50 cents.

36–2

Opposite:

Gold Production - It has been estimated that prior to 1901 as much as 10% more gold than was officially recorded was mined and taken out illegally to avoid paying the federal royalty tax.

Population - Estimates of population vary widely for the years 1898 to 1900. Some report as many as 100,000 people set out for the Klondike, although only a fraction reached Dawson City, and of these many caught the next passage out. No official census figures were available until 1901, when the population count was 27,219.

Dredges - In 1902 the first dredge operating in the Klondike (at 42 Below on Bonanza) could handle 700 cubic yards of gravel per day. It was said the machine and its three operators represented the labour of 156 men working with pick and shovel. Dredges became increasingly larger, with those built in 1913 capable of handling more than 15,000 cubic yards per day. Of the twelve dredges in the Klondike in 1913, only seven (owned by the Yukon Gold Company) operating on Bonanza Creek and Eldorado Creek were served directly by the Klondike Mines Railway; another Yukon Gold Company dredge on Hunker Creek was served indirectly. The four dredges owned by the Canadian Klondyke Mining Company, operating in the valley of the Klondike River, gave the railway little steady business.

the KLONDIKE 1895 - 1917

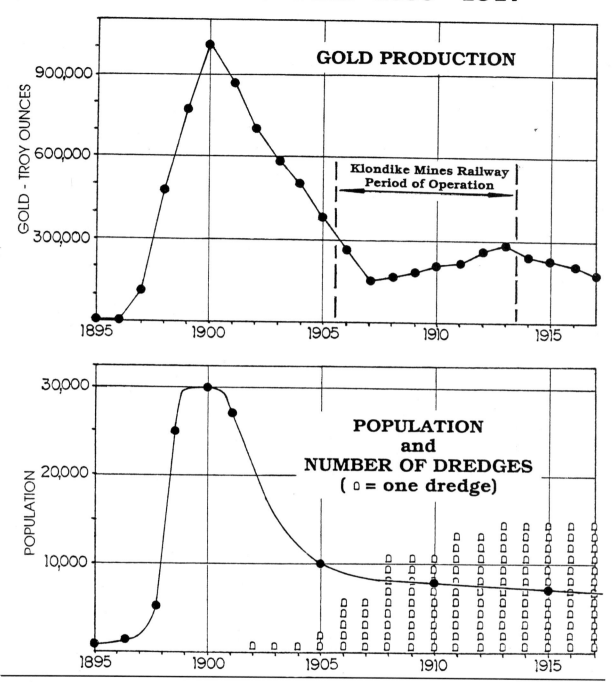

GOLD PRODUCTION

Klondike Mines Railway
Period of Operation

**POPULATION
and
NUMBER OF DREDGES**
(▫ = one dredge)

KLONDIKE MINES RAILWAY - MONTHS OF OPERATION

	Jan.	Feb.	March	April	May	June	July	August	Sept.	Oct.	Nov.	Dec.
1906							←—————					
1907	←———→											
1908				←——→								
1909					←——————————————————————————————————————→							
1910					←————————————————————————————————→							
1911					←————————————————————————————→							
1912					←————————————————————————————————————→							
1913					←——→							

SELECTED OPERATING STATISTICS

Figures cover the period July 1 of the previous year to June 30 of the year shown, except 1914, which covers the period July 1, 1913, to October 31, 1913.

TO JUNE 30 OF YEAR:	1907	1908	1909	1910	1911	1912	1913	1914
REVENUE ($)								
Passenger	8905	11259	13482	11554	7304	2069	4	0
Freight	26772	35281	30927	41806	38794	57564	110180	112176
Other	364	451	20	673	1204	401	6	0
Total	36041	46991	44429	54033	47302	60034	110190	112176
EXPENSES ($)								
Maintenance of Way	34393	29802	16239	17218	14073	17294	22956	11808
Maintenance of Equipment	9402	15139	2672	4565	1997	5196	4371	3396
Transportation	41655	30446	17449	20047	16010	17629	30855	25317
General	11514	16945	12981	11238	12429	11409	13794	11598
Total	96964	92332	49341	53068	44509	51528	71976	52119
BALANCE ($) Profit (+) Loss (-)	- 60923	- 45341	- 4912	+ 965	+ 2793	+ 8506	+ 38214	+ 60057
REVENUE DATA: PASSENGER								
Passengers Carried	2665	3863	4065	3241	1832	463	2	0
Passenger-Miles	59369	74887	91580	72277	43184	10730	26	0
Mixed Train Mileage	13640	13400	9920	9886	4526	1638	0	0
REVENUE DATA: FREIGHT								
Tons Carried	2314	6502	6093	14961	18044	23841	44400	42786
Ton-Miles	70452	92848	82764	150718	153418	245716	495594	444496
Freight Train Mileage	0	0	0	0	3136	6079	14186	14168
Total Train Mileage	13640	13400	9920	9886	7662	7717	14186	14168
FREIGHT BUSINESS (tons)								
Lumber	n.a.	0	119	311	105	393	1889	230
Other Forest Products	n.a.	0	4252	12867	17172	21231	39833	41606
Merchandise	n.a.	6502	1677	1275	642	431	60	169
Castings, Machinery	n.a.	0	0	508	0	1656	2051	0
Other Manufactures	n.a.	0	0	0	41	0	0	781
Other Products of Mines	n.a.	0	0	0	0	0	312	0
Bituminous Coal	n.a.	0	0	0	84	130	255	0
MAJOR EXPENSES ($)								
Roadwork	n.a.	19059	10766	8133	10277	11763	18087	9520
Ties, Rails, Bridges	n.a.	3646	2398	5926	2104	1500	7202	882
Snow Clearing	n.a.	5288	2768	2284	1106	264	363	0
Locomotive Repairs	n.a.	12647	2107	4044	1015	1481	2554	2569
Locomotive Fuel	n.a.	10643	7367	8647	7100	7152	10110	9826
Coach Repairs	n.a.	533	271	63	109	423	0	0
Freight Car Repairs	n.a.	3235	253	429	863	1937	1457	0
WAGES ($)								
General Office	n.a.	9562	7991	6900	6750	6600	9377	8055
Station Employees	n.a.	7426	2831	2825	2446	1938	5165	1596
Clerks, Attendants	n.a.	2659	2832	1641	2925	2785	2825	1450
Engine Men	n.a.	4611	2483	2503	2345	2373	5252	5063
Train Men	n.a	2645	2247	2968	2934	1955	6575	6011

APPENDIX C

THE CORDWOOD INDUSTRY IN THE YUKON

From the *Dawson Daily News* of October 23, 1912, came an excellent contemporary account of the wood-cutting industry in the Yukon:

WOOD MEN ARE WINDING UP BUSY SEASON
Thousands of Cords Brought Down the Yukon and the Klondike.
MUCH WORK THIS WINTER
Many Men Will be Engaged in Cutting and Hauling to Rivers.

Wood men on the Yukon and the Klondike have just ended an active season, and are preparing to handle big contracts next year.

Frank Neil, the wood contractor, who several days ago pulled out his steamer *Argonaut* at Stewart City, has just completed one of the busiest seasons of the many he has put in on the Yukon. He brought down the Yukon and delivered at Klondike City this year 12,500 cords of wood, all of which was taken up Bonanza by the Klondike Mines Railway and distributed at various places for the Yukon Gold Company's thawing plants. Neil sold the wood here for $9 a cord, or a total of $112,500. With contracts for poles and the like, Neil delivered this summer material which brought him a gross of $120,000. A large share of this he distributed among his many employees engaged in cutting the timber in the woods and rafting it to Dawson, but forest fire losses took most of Neil's profits. Most of this wood was from points along the Yukon and Stewart. It was rafted down the river in 16-foot lengths, and then cut with Joe Hamm's electric saw at Klondike City to four-foot lengths, the size in which it is hauled up the creek on the cars and in which it is used in firing the boilers which thaw the gravel for the dredges. One saw cut all this wood at Klondike City. It was necessary to run nights part of the time.

Some of the wood comes from up the Yukon as far as Selwyn, 150 miles above Dawson, and some from points up the Stewart as far as McQuesten River. It was cut, blazed, hauled and stacked on the river bank in the winter. Every stick of it was spruce. The wood which was delivered up Bonanza this season will be used in thawing next season. Hundreds of cords are thrown in huge piles, some places 50 feet or more in height, so that it will be as close as possible to the thawing plants. Mr. Neil gets an average of about 20 cords from an acre. Since this wood is used in mining, it is not subject to the stumpage or royalty of 50 cents a cord which the government taxes for all wood cut for other than mining purposes.

Mr. Neil has a contract to deliver 14,500 cords of wood to the Yukon Gold next year. He will be busy all winter superintending the hauling of the same to the river. He has camps at Moose Island, Calcite, Stewart City, White River and Thistle on the Yukon, and at Tenderfoot and Stewart Crossing on the Stewart, and one or two other points, making a total of twelve. He will have three teams engaged this winter. During the summer he always has 50 to 100 men at work.

The White Pass has contracted at all its old stations, about twenty between Dawson and Whitehorse, for wood for their boats. They are expected to use about 10,000 cords. About 20 separate contractors are getting out the wood. Each contractor is limited to one station.

Other heavy contractors on the Upper Yukon this year were: Mike Day, who brought down 4000 cords for the Yukon Gold, and John Sipkus, 1000 cords. Day is to bring 3000 next year.

It is understood the Yukon Gold also let a contract to Sam McCormack to deliver several thousand cords on Bonanza and Eldorado from Ainslie Creek, which flows into the Yukon below Indian, and over the divide westward from Eldorado. McCormack will haul the wood over the hills to Bonanza and Eldorado with horses and sleighs.

It is understood Charley Stone will deliver several thousand cords of wood on Hunker this winter from the hills for the Yukon Gold.

The N.A.T.&T., it is understood, is cutting 10,000 cords in four-foot lengths at the stump on the North Fork of the Klondike, to be sent down the river for the Yukon Gold.

A large quantity of wood was brought down the Klondike to Dawson this year. It is estimated Labbe, Chisholm and Hollenback landed 10,000 to 15,000 cords. The Chisholm boys brought down their wood for the Yukon Sawmill, and Hollenback brought his for the N.A.T.&T. It all went to the Yukon Gold.

Wood is said to be plentiful on the Dawson front for city purposes. Hundreds are piled up there, ready for sale in long lengths at $9 to $10 a cord. Hill wood held in Dawson since last winter is held a little higher. Those in touch say Dawson will not feel a wood shortage this winter. Sipkus will be the heaviest hauler this winter. He will bring from Moosehide, and probably land 3000 to 5000 cords.

Five or six years ago Dawson burned 17,000 cords a winter. In earlier days it burned 24,000 cords. Considerable coal, as well as wood, is now burned here every winter. Among the heaviest consumers in the area are the city and territorial governments and the police.

It is understood that Yukon Gold used about 35,000 cords of wood last year, and that its average cost laid down at the boilers on the creeks, ready to throw in the furnace is about $13 a cord. It is estimated the company spends $500,000 a year, in round numbers for fuel.

BIOGRAPHIES

Thomas William O'Brien

Thomas William O'Brien was born on March 8, 1862, on a farm three miles from the town of Barrie, Simcoe County, Ontario. He lived with his parents, attending school in the area, until 1876 when he left for Toronto. In the spring of 1879, which found O'Brien working as conductor and driver of street cars on the old King Street line, he went to Manitoba and for about a year worked on survey crews. At the time Manitoba was still a frontier territory, a small square of land along the U.S. border, not yet extending from the 49th to the 60th parallel.

Moving westward into the North West Territories, the part of which would later become the province of Saskatchewan, O'Brien spent another two years in the survey business. In 1881 he hired into the mail service in the Fort Qu'Appelle district and remained there for three years. By 1884 he had taken out a homestead near Fort Qu'Appelle. About this time the Riel Rebellion was gaining momentum, and O'Brien began plans to support scouting with freighting. Having by now acquired horses and wagons, he instead began freighting supplies for General Middleton's small army. With the termination of the rebellion in 1885, O'Brien wintered on his homestead and in the spring of 1886 he and a partner began work as railway contractors, first building grade for the Manitoba and North Western Railway, and then the Manitoba South Western Railway*. Moving back to Qu'Appelle in 1887, O'Brien sold his outfit and moved to the west coast, first to Vancouver and then to Seattle, where he learned details of the opportunities to be had along the Yukon River in the North West Territories and Alaska.

In July he and a partner were aboard the steamer *Olympia* sailing for Juneau. Outfitted there with over a ton of

goods they sailed for Dyea where they were joined by two other prospectors, and, with hired Chilkat packers, set out for the Yukon via the Chilkoot Pass. In a series of difficult hauls they eventually reached the head-waters of the Yukon River, and floated down-river on a raft to reach Fortymile in September, 1887. En route the company had met a number of Yukon old-timers who offered encouragement about the gold prospects in the Territory.

Several hundred men, mainly Americans, were now in the Yukon District working gold creeks with some success. For the next four years O'Brien and partners also prospected and worked creeks for gold, then in 1891 O'Brien went to work in McQuesten and Company's store at Fortymile. At that time the village was the largest in the Yukon District, and was in 1894 described by A.E.I. Sola as having the Alaska Commercial Company's store, barber shops, two bakeries, two restaurants, billiard parlours, distilleries, saloons, an opera house, and about eighty log cabins; "the chief amusements here were—in order—gambling, drinking, and dancing with squaws". O'Brien stayed at Fortymile until 1894 when he joined with William "Billie" Moran in opening up a store at Circle City, Alaska, under the name of O'Brien and Moran, a partnership which lasted for many years. In early 1896 the partners opened another store at Fortymile.

With the news of George Carmack's gold strike on Bonanza Creek in August of 1896, O'Brien and friends immediately made for the "Klondike" and staked claims on Bonanza Creek, and acquired other claims before winter set in. Early next year he and his partners bought a number of other claims, some of which, such as No. 1 Eldorado, were very profitable—he was reputed to have made $250,000 on this claim alone. With his profits he invested heavily in mercantile interests and property, most of which proved successes. By 1897, O'Brien and Moran established a new store on the bank of the Yukon River—some months before, this area had become known

---

* A newspaper biography listed these railways, but *Poor's Manual of Railroads* lists only the Manitoba and Northeastern Railway and the Manitoba Southwestern Colonization Railway.

as Klondike City. With an excellent river boat landing, Klondike City was also the foot of the trail leading to the rich goldfield.

In 1899 O'Brien backed an ill-fated tramway scheme originated by a Hill Henning. One of O'Brien's less popular, and less successful, ventures the road which ran up Bonanza Creek to Grand Forks, would be an embarrassment to him for years. Authority to go ahead in operating the line (officially the Pioneer Tramway Co. although also referred to as the Bonanza Tramway or the O'Brien Tramway) had been given without federal government sanction; the project was halted, and it would be seven years before O'Brien would be compensated in full for his investment loss. The responsibility was admitted, in 1902, by Yukon Council, which recommended indemnification of $35,000 he had invested.

In 1899 a charter was granted to the Klondike Mines Railway, with Thomas W. O'Brien heading the list of member applicants.

In 1900 O'Brien ran, unsuccessfully, as a candidate for Yukon councillor; two positions had just been created. In that year he was identified as the proprietor of the *Yukon Sun*, one of three major Klondike newspapers (the *Sun* was sold to F.T. Congdon in 1901), proprietor of the Dominion Hotel in Dawson, and partner in the Yukon Pioneer Trading Company in Klondike City.

In 1901 O'Brien was listed as one of three partners operating the Monte Carlo Saloon. In early June O'Brien and other associates bought the Klondike River bridge, formerly a toll bridge, and opened it—so the newspapers said—to free passage. However, reports of free passage on the bridge were incorrect, for in early 1902 "the O'Brien toll bridge has a number of people upset, a petition is circulating and the legality of the operation being doubted". Toll on the bridge was still being collected in 1904.

In November of 1901, O'Brien and four partners applied to Canada Parliament for a charter in the name of The Dawson White Horse Navigation Company (Limited), for the business of operating steamships and merchandising. Led by O'Brien's old friend from Fortymile, Edward "Black" Sullivan, the company bought three steamers, the *Tyrrell* to be used on the lower Yukon River, and the *J.P. Light* and the *Lightning* for the upper river (the *Tyrrell* was one of the few steel-hulled boats on the Yukon, and as such had a deep draft). However, this venture also proved less than profitable; the White Pass and Yukon

Route was quickly gaining a monopoly on freight out of Whitehorse, and on the lower river the North American Transportation and Trading Company and the Alaska Commercial Company both had large fleets of steamers—there was little room for independents. In 1903 the *Lightning* was sold to the Coal Creek Coal Company, while the *J.P. Light* and the *Tyrrell* picked up small freight contracts and ran Yukon River excursion cruises, but by late 1904 the Dawson White Horse Navigation Company was no longer in business.

O'Brien applied to Council for a franchise to operate a street car system in Dawson in July of 1902—nothing came of this.

On February 1, 1904, O'Brien and six other prominent Dawson businessmen incorporated the O'Brien Brewing and Malting Company (Limited), and with the chief place of business to be in Klondike City. Known also as the Klondike Brewery, the company was allowed business listed in twelve broad clauses which included brewing, malting, a variety of bottling works, and numerous associated credit, real estate, and promotional ventures. The owners included Dr. Alfred Thompson, prominent in the local Liberal Party.

The Klondike Brewery had a steady business, selling everything from Blue Label, Red Label Steam Beer, K.B. Special Brew, lager, porter, soft drinks, and cigars. The Dawson City Directory of 1910 listed two of O'Brien's sons, Henry and James O'Brien, as bottlers in the brewery. By 1916 O'Brien's youngest son Charles was added to the payroll as a bookkeeper.

In the spring of 1905 O'Brien was nominated as a candidate for Yukon Council. A bona fide sourdough, O'Brien was a popular man in spite of the odd business miscalculation. Where many developers took their money and ran, O'Brien called the Klondike home, spending his money here in developing local industry. Because of the beer-making process used in his brewery, O'Brien and his political friends were referred to as the "steam beers". Under attack in pre-election debate, largely because of the Pioneer Tramway debacle, O'Brien defended himself convincingly. The *Dawson Daily News* claimed O'Brien's speech was the best presented. The election was run on the 12th of April, and O'Brien won decisively, to become member of the Yukon Council representing South Dawson for a two-year term.

A charter member of the Yukon Order of Pioneers, O'Brien was president from 1905 to 1907.

The construction of the Klondike Mines Railway had begun in early 1905, but was halted by right-of-way injunctions in mid-summer, and the contractor quit that fall. Early in 1906 the contract for completion of the railway was awarded to O'Brien and MacKenzie, who by October had the line finished to Sulphur Springs. O'Brien carried on with the railway as interim general manager from March until July of 1907.

Over the winter of 1912-13 O'Brien and his wife lived in Seattle, where he owned property, and he organized Camp 2 of the Yukon Order of Pioneers in that city, chartered on January 9, 1913. He similarly organized lodges in the cities of Vancouver and Victoria, British Columbia.

The Klondike was now in decline, and several of O'Brien's businesses must have suffered, as implied in a newspaper item published after O'Brien's death: "Mr. O'Brien acquired an interest in No. 1 Eldorado, at the junction with Bonanza, from which he realized a quarter of a million dollars. He held extensive and varied properties, but hard luck overtook him for a time, and his poke was drained. He set together with characteristic energy, and by the untiring assistance of Mrs. O'Brien, built up a new fortune before he crossed the last divide to the last great camp".

The year 1913 witnessed another minor gold rush in which O'Brien once more took a business lead—possibly the financial recovery referred to above. A stampede to the White River found O'Brien building a new store and hostelry at the "mouth of the Donjek on the White River", offering all merchandise, with outfitting a specialty.

But O'Brien's health was failing. Planning to go to Seattle for treatment, he was instead admitted to St. Mary's Hospital in Dawson City, where on August 24, 1916, he died of liver trouble. He was survived by his wife Anna Josephine O'Brien, and four children; Charles and James who were at the time en route to the war in Europe, and Henry and Margaret who were in Seattle. The funeral was held four days later, and the *Dawson Daily News* reported;

> Dawson suspended business this morning in the solemn hour while Yukon laid to rest all that is mortal of one of her most notable pioneers and empire builders, Thomas W. O'Brien....In compliance with his request , he was buried in the Pioneer Cemetery in Dawson, in the land to which he had devoted the greater part of his energetic life.

O'Brien must have been married, or otherwise, while at Fortymile, because his oldest son, Colon Henry was born there about 1892, followed by James Jonathon on August 14, 1894, and Charles Thomas on October 6, 1896. It is believed O'Brien was married to a native woman, since the birthplace of the sons is listed as Fortymile, but no records of her name, the union, or of her death are known. In 1898 O'Brien married Anna Josephine Brazil, formerly of Denver, Colorado, and a daughter, Margaret, was born about a year later. Anna Brazil and her sisters Mary and Margaret (Mag) had in 1897 come to Dawson City with brother Robert—he was in the mining business. While Mag remained single, Mary Dwyer was a divorcee with a son named Maurice Francis Dwyer who was two years older than O'Brien's son Henry. O'Brien took a liking to Maurice, funding his medical school education, and by 1917 Dr. Maurice Dwyer was on his way to an outstanding career in radiology in Seattle, Washington.

O'Brien's sons, Charles and James, had enlisted in 1916 in the Canadian Army only a few weeks prior to O'Brien's death, and were not in Dawson for the funeral. After training, both arrived in England in February of 1917 as members of the Yukon Infantry Company, 231st Overseas Battalion. On June 19, 1917, O'Brien's oldest son Henry (Colon) died in Seattle, after an illness of two years—it seems likely that his poor health had prevented his enlistment. On August 10, 1918, O'Brien's youngest son, Sergeant Charles Thomas O'Brien, gun commander "C" Battery, was killed in France. With demobilization of the Army in 1919, James was discharged on May 20 and returned to Seattle, where for a short time he stayed with his stepmother. He returned to the Yukon Territory, and on April 14, 1931, died of pneumonia at Mayo. It is not known if James had any children.

James' half-sister Margaret and her mother Anna lived in Seattle for a time, but in 1919 Anna remarried becoming Mrs. Walter M. Richmond and moved to San Francisco-she had no children from this union. Daughter Margaret went on to attend the University of California at Berkeley, remained unmarried, and died in the San Francisco area in the 1930s. Anna (O'Brien) Richmond died in 1925, also in San Francisco, of pneumonia.

Harold Buchanan McGiverin

Born August 4, 1870, in Hamilton, Ontario, Harold Buchanan McGiverin was the son of Lieutenant-Colonel William McGiverin, M.P.. Educated in Eastern Canada, young McGiverin was called to the bar in 1893. He practiced his profession in Ottawa as a junior partner in the firm of MacCraken, Henderson and McGiverin until

1899 when he became the head of the law firm, McGiverin, Haydon and Greig. A Liberal, he became a very influential man and was council to a number of companies, including the Grand Trunk and other railways. He was the man who opened doors to legislators; both A.N.C. Treadgold and J.W. Boyle had used his power to gain mining concessions in the Klondike. A number of syndicates had applied to Ottawa for franchises to build railways in the Klondike, but only the Klondike Mines Railway, represented by McGiverin, et al, in 1899, was successful. McGiverin was in close touch with all phases of the Klondike Mines Railway's development, from land acquisition to final operations, and he served on the executive until the railway's demise. He also represented many other enterprises in the Klondike, including O'Brien's Dawson White Horse Navigation Company, pulling the necessary strings for approvals. In issue after issue of the **Canada Gazette** can be found a variety of newly-chartered businesses listing McGiverin as representative, or Ottawa agent; for instance the December 3, 1904, issue—notice in the name of "Northwest Telephone Company", H.B. McGiverin, solicitor, Ottawa; the April 5, 1905 issue—notices in the names of two companies, the "Vancouver, Victoria and Eastern Railway and Navigation Company", the other the "Kaslo and Lardo-Duncan Railway Company", both represented by solicitors McGiverin and Haydon.

McGiverin became Member of Parliament, representing Ottawa East, for the periods 1908 to 1911, and 1921 to 1925; during 1924-1925 he was a minister without portfolio in the Mackenzie King cabinet. He was also an excellent athlete, playing cricket and rugby. He died in Victoria, British Columbia, on February 3, 1931.

John Latta and Robert Allan Lawther

The Klondike Mines Railway was almost wholly owned by John Latta and Robert Allan Lawther.

John Latta was born on May 9, 1867, Ayrshire, Scotland. He was educated at Ayr Academy and started business life in Glasgow, but in 1888 left for London where he found employment as a chartering clerk. Here he came in contact with a number of shipping men, in particular Colonel J.T. North, the "Nitrate King", and Robert Allan Lawther with whom he formed the firms of Lawther, Latta and Company and the Nitrate Producer's Steamship Company Limited in 1892. At that time most trans-oceanic shipping companies were still using "tall ships",

i.e. sailing ships. In 1896 Latta married Mary Short, and in that way formed an alliance with the family of shipbuilders, Short Brothers, of Sunderland, who would build most of the large cargo carriers for the steamship company. Nitrate shipping from Chile became the company's major business and was of great importance in the early 1900s, but when nitrate sales collapsed after World War I Lawther, Latta and Company moved into the tramp ship-owning trade. The company would prosper until after World War II. Sir John Latta was created a baronet in 1920, mostly a result of his devotion, and the company's, to efforts during the Great War.

At the time of Latta's death, biographers wrote;
> Some called him old-fashioned; others said he was cold. Both were wrong. He had his own ideas how life should be lived and how business should be conducted, and if those ideas were different from those held by others, he agreed to differ. Essentially his was a character which was most at home in the surroundings of many years ago when ship-owners went their individual ways and carried out their own ideas of how business should be conducted without the aid of representative associations. Besides representing undiluted individualism, Sir John stands for extreme efficiency. None who has met the slim, dapper, youngish figure (in spite of advancing years) with the sparkling pince-nez, in his office could carry away a different impression. None who has read his annual speeches at the meetings could fail to recognize an independent, fearless, thinker and speaker.

Sir John Latta died on December 5, 1946, in London—he had never visited the Yukon Territory.

Robert Allan Lawther was born in 1866, the son of a well-established shipping fleet magnate, Samuel Lawther of Belfast, Ulster. Samuel had become an agent for shipping of Canadian timber, and was "the owner of a large number of iron and steel sailing ships". Robert Lawther apprenticed with the shipbuilding firm of Harland and Wolff, then following in his father's footsteps, became superintendent of the sailing fleet. With his father Samuel and his brother Henry Stanley, Robert became partner in world shipping and ship management firms. Although he ceased active business in London in 1911 he retained an interest in the London and Belfast businesses. His overseas enterprises included extensive Canadian interests and, along with Latta, the Klondike Mines Railway. He travelled twice to the Yukon Territory, in 1907 and in 1908, to assess personally the railway operation. Lawther also acquired an interest in mining claims in the Klondike at about this time. Following World War I, both he and Latta bought into what became the Yukon Consolidated Gold Corporation, and both in time would serve as directors. "Lawther was a very likeable Irishman, a great big fellow, who had plenty of money and lived well". Robert Lawther died on March 22, 1941, in Belfast.

Except for the Klondike Mines Railway, the business ventures of Lawther and Latta appear to have been unqualified successes.

Erastus Corning Hawkins

Erastus Corning Hawkins was born on September 8, 1860, in South Haven, Suffolk County, New York, U.S.A. In his late teens he acquired engineering skills, working on street and harbour projects in New York, and then moved west in 1883. Beginning in Colorado, he took on positions of increasingly greater responsibility as a civil engineer with railway and canal projects. Eventually he joined the construction forces in the building of the railway of the White Pass and Yukon Route. Coming to Skagway in early 1898, Hawkins began as chief engineer and following the road's completion in 1900, he stayed on as general manager.

In mid-July of 1901 Hawkins and Michael Heney, who had been the construction contractor of the White Pass, visited Dawson to spark rumors of their involvement in construction of the Klondike Mines Railway. In early September Hawkins resigned from the White Pass and immediately began promoting the Klondike Mines Railway. He formed the Hawkins Construction Company, and set about raising capital to finance the first section of the railway, from Klondike City to Grand Forks. The Seattle City Directory of 1902 lists Hawkins only as a civil engineer with an office at 41, Dexter Horton Bank Building, in Seattle; the 1903 and 1904 Directories list the Hawkins Construction Company at the same address.

However, Hawkins immediately ran into difficulties in finding backers for the Klondike Mines Railway. In late 1902 he did acquire an ancient Brooks locomotive from the White Pass, and rail enough to park it in Klondike City, but no more was done. The dealings dragged on, but finally in June of 1904 Lawther and Latta bailed Hawkins out. In Klondike City, O'Brien received a telegram from McGiverin, dated June 12, 1904, saying, "Have received several cables from Hawkins. Construction whole railway will assuredly be completed". On November 11, 1904, the Hawkins Construction

Company's contract with Klondike Mines Railway was terminated—probably to Hawkins' relief. The Seattle City Directories of 1905 and 1906 simply list Hawkins as a civil engineer, with an office still at the Dexter Horton Building. In fact he had been hired in 1906 by the Union Pacific Railroad and appointed chief engineer of Union Pacific lines in Washington. The 1907 Directory lists Hawkins as chief engineer of the Oregon and Washington Railway Company which was controlled by the Union Pacific. After 1906 Hawkins no longer had an office in Seattle, with only his residence, 1120 Jefferson, in Seattle, given.

In the meanwhile, Hawkins partner of old, Michael Heney, had begun promoting the Copper River and Northwestern Railway (CR&NW) in Alaska in 1905, and in 1906 began construction. In 1907 the team was re-united when Hawkins was appointed chief engineer. An even more difficult construction job than the White Pass had been, the CR&NW when completed had 195 miles of track between Cordova and Kennecott mine, and the last spike was driven by superintendent Murchison and Hawkins on March 29, 1911. From 1908 until 1911 Seattle City directories list Hawkins as vice president, chief engineer, and general manager of the Katalla Company, and chief engineer of the Copper River and Northwestern Railway Company

With the CR&NW completed, Hawkins left Alaska late in 1911. In late March of 1912 he went to New York City "in quest of health", as the New York Times wrote, but following a surgical operation he died in a hospital there on April 9, 1912. He was survived by his wife Emma A. Hawkins, three sons, and two daughters.

Eugene A. Murphy

Eugene A. Murphy was general manager of the Klondike Mines Railway from mid-August, 1907, until November, 1913, when the railway ceased operations. He had previously been with the Pacific Coast Steamship Company as the Skagway agent for several years. Prior to that he was with the White Pass, and he had first come to Skagway in 1900 from the Great Northern. He, his wife Maud, and two sons left for Portland, Oregon, in October, 1913, to be associated with other businesses controlled by Lawther and Latta.

John W. Astley

John W. Astley came to the Klondike in the early 1900s when he found work with O'Brien and the Klondike Mines Railway. Fifteen years earlier he may have had contact with O'Brien, for when the Riel Rebellion of 1885 began in force one John Astley, surveyor, was captured by Riel's men. In the subsequent trial of Riel, Astley proved to be a somewhat biased witness against the Métis leader.

In the Klondike, Astley laid out the route of the rail line as it was constructed from Klondike City to Sulphur Springs, and he also surveyed the extension from there to the Stewart River country. Final railway survey maps list J.W. Astley as field surveyor. He was also the Dawson agent for the company, at least during 1902 when progress on the railway stalled. In 1903 and 1904 "Jephson & Astley, Dominion Land Surveyors, Mining Engineers" operated out of Dawson City. With the resumption of construction of the Klondike Mines Railway in 1905, Astley was once more on the payroll, and on completion of the railway in October, 1906, he stayed on as chief engineer and general manager. In late March, 1907 Astley was replaced by Tom O'Brien as manager, and in mid-July Astley and his wife left Dawson for the new Hudson's Bay Railway, which hired him as a consulting engineer.

ROLLING STOCK
KLONDIKE MINES RAILWAY

Locomotives

KMR No.	Builder	Construction No.	Year Built	Wheel Arrangement	Boiler Pressure (psi)	Cylinder Bore x Stroke (inches)	Driver Size (inches)	Leading/ Trailing Wheel Size (inches)	Engine Weight (pounds)	Tender Weight loaded (pounds)	Tractive Effort (pounds)
1	Brooks	522	1881	2-6-0 Mogul	135	14 x 18	41	24	46,000	36,000	10,600
2	Baldwin	7597	1885	2-8-0 Consolidation	150	15 x 18	36.5	24	60,000	40,000	15,100
3	Baldwin	16456	1899	2-8-0 Consolidation	200	19 x 20 11 x 20	36	24	93,390	65,350	21,000
4	Baldwin	37564	1912	2-6-2 Prairie	160	15 x 20	37.5	24	77,000	38,000	16,000

Klondike Mines Railway No. 1:
a 2-6-0 (Mogul), built in 1881 by the Brooks Locomotive Works of Dunkirk, New York, construction number (c/n) 522, cylinders 14 x 18 inches (bore and stroke), drivers 41 inches (diameter), leading wheels 24 inches, weight: locomotive 46,000 lb. and loaded tender 36,000 lb., tractive effort (T.E.) 10,600 lb., boiler pressure 135 pounds per square inch (psi).

Brooks c/n 522, lettered the "Sidney Dillon", road number 7, was sold new to the Kansas Central Railway, a road which had been chartered in 1871, although controlled by the Union Pacific Railroad after 1879. The locomotive was named after Sidney Dillon who became president of the Union Pacific (UP) in 1880. By 1890, the peak year of the Kansas Central's 3-foot gauge life, the railway had 19 locomotives operating on 168 miles of track between Leavenworth and Miltonvale, Kansas; in that year the Kansas Central was standard-gauged.

The history of Brooks c/n 522 between 1881 and 1900 is uncertain, although several possible lineages have been suggested. One source claims that the locomotive became Union Pacific No. 102 in June of 1885, and in 1890 was sold to the Alberta Railway and Coal Company (AR&CCo) as their No. 9. The Brooks is then said to

have gone directly from the AR&CCo to the White Pass and Yukon Route (WP&YR) in 1900. The AR&CCo operated as a narrow gauge road from 1890 until 1904 when it was fully standard-gauged. A second source claims Brooks c/n 522 stayed with the AR&CCo, no road number given, only until 1895 when it was sold to the Trail Creek Tramway. This railway, in southern B.C., was reorganized in 1896 as the Columbia and Western Railway (C&W) which was bought in 1899 by the Canadian Pacific Railway (CPR). It is said the locomotive was never put into service on the C&W, and was sold to the WP&YR by the CPR in 1900. Other historians do not include either, or both, of the UP and AR&CCo in the lineage of the locomotive.

Brooks c/n 522 did arrive at Skagway in June of 1900, lettered WP&YR No. 63. No known photos of No. 63 in WP&YR service exist. In mid-1902 the WP&YR rebuilt No. 63 and sold it to the Klondike Mines Railway (KMR), re-lettered as KMR No. 1. It was loaded on the WP&YR steamer *Mary F. Graff* at Whitehorse on September 24 and arrived at Klondike City on September 27, 1902, and the tender arrived on September 28 on the steamer *Bonanza King*.

KMR No. 1 was parked at Klondike City, unused, until June of 1905 when construction of the KMR finally began. Records suggest the locomotive had not been paid for in 1902, and that it did not legally become KMR property until 1905. After completion of the KMR rail line in late 1906, locomotive No. 1 was not much used—only as a stand-in for locomotive No. 2, and for occasional work train service—and in later years was parked at the rear of the engine house in Klondike City. The railway was shut down permanently in October of 1913, and although the owners of the KMR, Lawther and Latta of England, thought the railway could possibly be moved as a unit to some other place in the Yukon Territory, such opportunities never arose. When a mining syndicate headed by Lawther and Latta was absorbed by the newly-chartered Yukon Consolidated Gold Corporation (YCGC), under which amalgamation of many properties took place about 1925, the assets of the KMR also came under ownership of the YCGC.

KMR No. 1 and its tender were moved to Minto Park in Dawson City in February, 1961, followed in May by locomotive No. 2, its tender, and locomotive No. 3, all donated by the YCGC to the Dawson City Museum which is the present owner. The three locomotives had been parked in Klondike City for almost 48 years, never once fired up.

Klondike Mines Railway No. 2:
a 2-8-0 (Consolidation), built in May of 1885 by the Baldwin Locomotive Works of Philadelphia, Pennsylvania, c/n 7597, cylinders 15 x 18 inches, drivers 36½ inches, leading wheels 24 inches, weight: locomotive 60,000 lb. and loaded tender 40,000 lb., T.E. 15,100 lb., boiler pressure 150 psi.

Baldwin c/n 7597 was sold new to the Columbia and Puget Sound Railroad (C&PS) as their No. 8. This railway had been originally chartered as the Seattle and Walla Walla Railroad (S&WW) in the early 1870s, with a proposed line to run between those two Washington cities. By 1880 22 miles of track had been laid by the S&WW in the Seattle area, and in that year the company was bought by the Oregon Railway and Navigation Company which re-incorporated the S&WW as the C&PS. The maximum number of locomotives owned by the C&PS was nine, in 1892; by 1893 the C&PS had a total of 54 miles of track southeasterly from Seattle, and by 1898 standard-gauging of the railway began. The trackage was eventually absorbed by the Northern Pacific Railroad.

C&PS No. 8 was sold to the WP&YR in 1898, and was re-lettered as their No. 5; in 1902 it was overhauled and re-numbered at Skagway as WP&YR No. 55. It served as both construction and revenue engine on the WP&YR.

WP&YR No. 55 was refurbished, re-lettered as KMR No. 2 and sold to that company, leaving Whitehorse in early August of 1905 on the barge *Pelly*, shoved by the steamer *Canadian*; No. 2 and its tender arrived at Klondike City on August 8.

When No. 2 arrived there, construction on the KMR had just been stalled by right-of-way injunctions, so the locomotive sat out the winter unused. In May of 1906 No. 2 went to work in construction service, and by fall was is revenue traffic. Until permanent shut-down of the KMR in October of 1913, No. 2 was the most-used locomotive on the company's roster. The history of No. 2 and its tender from here on is identical to that of No. 1: YCGC property about 1925, and Dawson City Museum property in May of 1961.

Klondike Mines Railway No. 3:
a Baldwin 2-8-0 (Consolidation), built in January of 1899, c/n 16456, a Vauclain compound with cylinder dimensions of 19 x 20 and 11 x 20 inches, drivers 36 inches, leading wheels 24 inches, weight: locomotive 93,390 lb. and loaded tender 65,350 lb., T.E. 21,000 lb., boiler pressure 200 psi.

Built new for the WP&YR, Baldwin c/n 16456 was originally lettered WP&YR No. 7. It was in 1900 re-numbered No. 57, and in 1906 sold to the KMR as their No. 3. It left Whitehorse on October 1, 1906, on a barge pushed by the steamer *Bonanza King*, arriving at Klondike City on October 4.

KMR No. 3 was little-used in the early years when projected freight levels were not attained. In about 1910 No. 3 was finally put to work hauling cordwood. Following shutdown of the KMR in 1913, No. 3 has had a history almost identical to that of locomotives No. 1 and No. 2: No. 3 became YCGC property about 1925, its tender was sold to the WP&YR in July of 1942, and No. 3 became property of the Dawson City Museum in May of 1961.

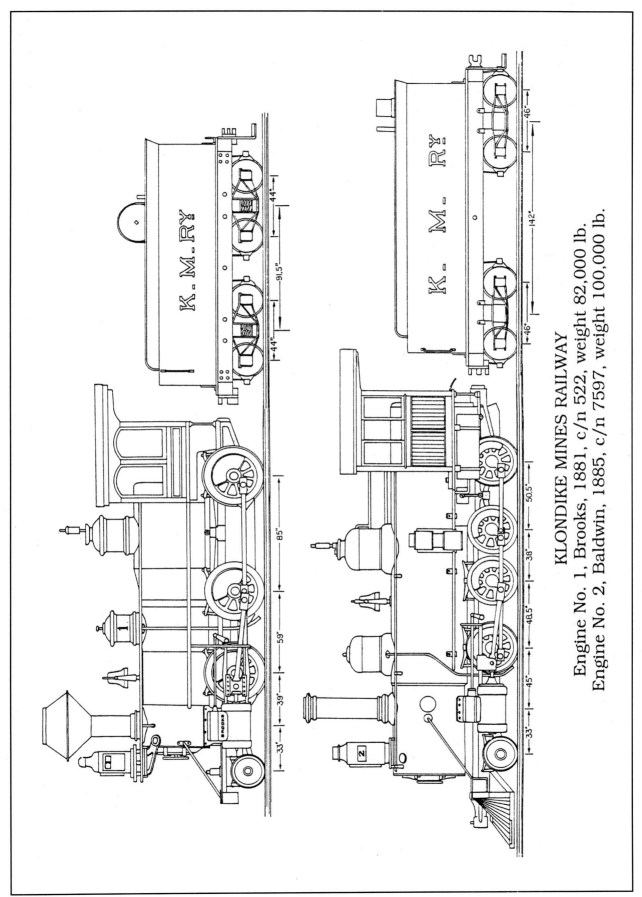

KLONDIKE MINES RAILWAY

Engine No. 1, Brooks, 1881, c/n 522, weight 82,000 lb.
Engine No. 2, Baldwin, 1885, c/n 7597, weight 100,000 lb.

Above: Of the three remaining KMR locomotives in the Klondike, No. 2 is in the poorest condition. Bell, whistle, headlamp, and number plate "disappeared" (as with No. 1 and No. 3) many years ago—taken as souvenirs. Note that the two middle drive wheels are fitted with flangeless tires—a requisite of long-wheelbase locomotives running on a rail line with many curves of minimal radii (an arc of radius 327 feet describes a 17½ degree curve, the sharpest used on the seven trestles on Upper Bonanza).

Below: Klondike Mines Railway locomotive No. 3, in 1991, now protected under a special shelter in Dawson. This Vauclain compound, outside-framed, locomotive is fully nine feet wide at the cylinders—riding on three-foot gauge rail! The Vauclain's compound cylinders, seen hanging well outside the width of the pilot, are built around a single casting which includes the small high-pressure cylinder below, the large diameter low-pressure cylinder above, and a cylindrical piston valve located out of sight, inboard.

Both photos Eric L. Johnson, Vancouver, B.C.

Klondike Mines Railway No. 4:
a Baldwin 2-6-2 (Prairie), built in March of 1912, c/n 37564, cylinders 15 x 20 inches, drivers 37½ inches, leading and trailing wheels 24 inches, weight: locomotive 77,000 lb. and loaded tender 38,000 lb., T.E. 16,000 lb., boiler pressure 160 psi.

Baldwin c/n 37564 was built for the KMR and it arrived with its tender at Klondike City on July 3, 1912, on a barge pushed by the steamer *Whitehorse* (the first *Whitehorse*). After only nine months of use during the 1912 and 1913 seasons, No. 4 went into storage at Klondike City. No. 4 became YCGC property about 1925, as did locomotives 1, 2, and 3.

In late June of 1942 the WP&YR began negotiations with the YCGC for purchase of idle KMR equipment, and on July 9, 1942, locomotive No. 4 with its tender, and the tender from KMR No. 3, left Klondike City for Whitehorse, on the steamer *Whitehorse* (the second WP&YR steamer so-named). Refurbished and re-lettered also as No. 4 for the WP&YR, the old Baldwin worked for a number of years at the Skagway yard, and was retired in 1952.

Overhauled by the WP&YR, No. 4 was sold to Mike Molitor of Oak Creek, Wisconsin, in 1955. It arrived in the Milwaukee, Wisconsin, area in September on board a Milwaukee Road flat car and was parked at the Oakwood Road station for unloading. Molitor had planned his Oak Creek Central Railroad as a tourist operation, located about one and one-half mile west and one mile south of the Milwaukee Road/Oakwood Road crossing (actually nearer the village of Caledonia). Here he installed the old Milwaukee Road's Oakwood depot building, some other structures, and began building a rail grade. However, it is believed the railway was never completed, having met with objections from residents in the area. It isn't known if the locomotive and tender were re-lettered for the Oak Creek Central.

After some delay Molitor in 1960 found another site fifteen miles west and south of the proposed Oak Creek Central. Here near Waterford, Wisconsin, at an amusement park called Peppermint Farms, he set up the Peppermint and Northwestern Railroad. Buildings in ¾-scale representing a frontier village were built, called Peppermint Junction, and a tight loop track was laid. Molitor had acquired some cars once used on the Rio Grande Southern, but these apparently did not make it to Wisconsin; instead some rather unattractive home-built coaches, based on flat cars, were put into service. Ex-

KMR No. 4, re-lettered as Peppermint and Northwestern No. 4 and fitted with a false diamond stack, began operating in 1962, wheels continually screeching on the tightly-curved track. It appears that Molitor funnelled off profits, ignoring bills, and creditors were granted injunctions that fall. Spring of 1963 found a new manager, who it seems was only a front for the Molitors, and after another very successful year (the operation was apparently very well patronized), Molitor declared bankruptcy. Since there was no record of profit or loss during the 1962 and 1963 seasons, courts could not ascertain if the company would be worth reorganizing, so instead the assets of the Peppermint and Northwestern Railroad were auctioned off, to satisfy creditors, at a Racine County sheriff's sale in September of 1964.

Purchaser of the railway assets was John Denton, a carnival operator based in Knoxville, Tennessee, who moved everything from the Peppermint and Northwestern to a site south of Sevierville, Tennessee. Here on the east side of Route 441 between Sevierville and Pigeon Forge he set up the Petticoat Junction Railroad, building a 1¼-mile loop track, no turnouts, switches, or sidings—the same trackage that had been used on the Peppermint and Northwestern. The locomotive was lettered as the *Hooterville Cannonball*, with no road number although it still had smoke box plate No. 4. The tender was lettered Petticoat Junction R. R., and rolling stock consisted of Molitor's three home-built "coaches" and a caboose. Denton was undoubtedly trying to cash in on the rising popularity of the television series, *Petticoat Junction,* whose rail action scenes were first filmed in 1963 on the standard gauge Sierra Railroad in California. Sierra's locomotive No. 3 was also lettered as the *Hooterville Cannonball*, but its tender was lettered as the fictitious C&FW Railroad, "operating" out of Petticoat Junction.

Just south of Sevierville, Denton had his railway ready to go by summer, 1965. Farther south, at Pigeon Forge, the Rebel Railroad had been organized in 1961, and equipped with ex-WP&YR locomotive No. 192 it was a successful theme park with many tourist attractions. The Rebel Railroad later became the Goldrush Junction Railroad, and still later, in 1968, Dollywood's Gatlinburg and Western Railroad. Denton figured he could "skim off" 10% of the tourist traffic heading south for Pigeon Forge, although his operation had nothing besides the train ride—no buildings, and no other entertainment whatsoever. But problems immediately arose in firing up the locomotive and in operating it, and after only three half-days of business—July 3, 4, and 5, 1965—Denton shut down the railway. Obviously unhappy, he paid off his staff, saying he would be moving the show to Branson, Missouri. However, legal complications kept the equipment on site during 1966, inactive. All was moved for storage to Knoxville, Tennessee, during 1967, and to Lebanon, Missouri, in 1968. Finally, in 1969, Denton moved everything from Lebanon to a newly-built railway just west of Osage Beach, Missouri.

Osage Beach, is located in the Lake of the Ozarks district, an extensive recreational area. On US Route 54, one mile west of Osage Beach, Denton set up the 1¼-mile track and began seasonally operating the Gold Nugget Junction Railroad. In 1972 Denton sold the operation to John Gallagan who set up an Old West theme park which he operated in conjunction with the railway. Gallagan continued operating ex-KMR No. 4 on the Gold Nugget Junction Railroad during the balance of the 1970s, but the old Baldwin was wearing out. In need of a new boiler, tubes, and cylinder rebuild, No. 4 was shut down in 1979. In 1980 Gallagan sold everything to Denny Hilton, a resident of Osage Beach who for a time ran an "opry" show called "Denny Hilton's Country Shindig". Hilton wanted to reopen the Gold Nugget Junction Railroad, but found the expense of rebuilding No. 4 too much. The locomotive, cars, and track remained idle until late 1984 when everything went up for auction.

The whole railway outfit was sold in September of 1984 to the Midwest Central Railroad of Mount Pleasant, Iowa; this tourist railway has been successfully operating for some twenty-odd years. The sale had hardly been completed when representative Stan Mathews of the Midwest Central was approached in October by another buyer. With "an offer he couldn't refuse" Mathews re-sold everything, still on site in Missouri, to Steve Wild of El Reno, Oklahoma.

Wild had previously owned a hunting lodge in Colorado, and after moving to Oklahoma he acquired several sections of land, setting up "Wild's", a fish and game park, complete with a herd of buffalo, near El Reno, Oklahoma. Running through the property was the grade of the long-abandoned Fort Smith and Western Railroad, and using part of this grade, new grade and trestles, the Wilds (father Steve and son David) planned as much as a ten mile loop railway as a tourist operation. With backing from a local banker they bought the assets of the Gold Nugget Junction Railroad, trucking all to El Reno. Soon after, the banker/partner moved to take over the operation, and after some litigation he left with the money he had put up, leaving the Wilds without the

resources needed to rebuild No. 4. They have had many offers to sell the locomotive but have refused, confident that one day No. 4 will again be hauling tourists. Ex-KMR No. 4 is presently stored on the Wild's game farm.

Passenger Cars

A combination coach/baggage car was bought by the WP&YR in 1899, origin unknown, and was re-lettered as WP&YR No. 202. In 1905 it was sold to the KMR, refurbished and re-lettered KMR No. 200, and shipped to Klondike City in September. Cast-in markings on the trucks, suggesting the builder, read "J. HAMMOND, SF, 1887".

A coach bought in 1900 by the WP&YR, origin also unknown, was re-lettered as WP&YR No. 208. In 1905 it was also rebuilt by the WP&YR, sold to the KMR as their No. 202, and shipped to Klondike City, arriving in September. Markings on the trucks of No. 202 read "BILLMEYER & SMALL CO, YORK, PA".

Both coaches were in service from 1906 until 1911, when they were stored on a spur on Klondike Island. Here the coaches, the property of YCGC after 1925, remained, deteriorating until the late 1940s, when the woodwork of both were destroyed in a hay field fire. The scorched and rusting trucks and hardware are still there today.

Freight Cars

In 1902 the WP&YR built six flat cars for the KMR—some may have been built from frames on hand since 1901, others of unknown origins. The new flat cars were lettered KMR and numbered 51, 53, 55, 57, 59 and 61. These were delivered to Klondike City in September, apparently unpaid for by the KMR, for after sitting there unused for more than two years, at least two were retrieved by the WP&YR and sold directly to the Tanana Mines Railroad in 1905; No. 51 and No. 53, were operated on the Tanana, still in KMR markings and numbers.

In early summer, 1905, the KMR ordered 23 more freight cars from the WP&YR. These were similarly built by the WP&YR using frames on hand since 1901, old gondolas and flats, and from other unknown sources. The four remaining flat cars from the 1902 order may have been included in this batch after being re-numbered in the 101

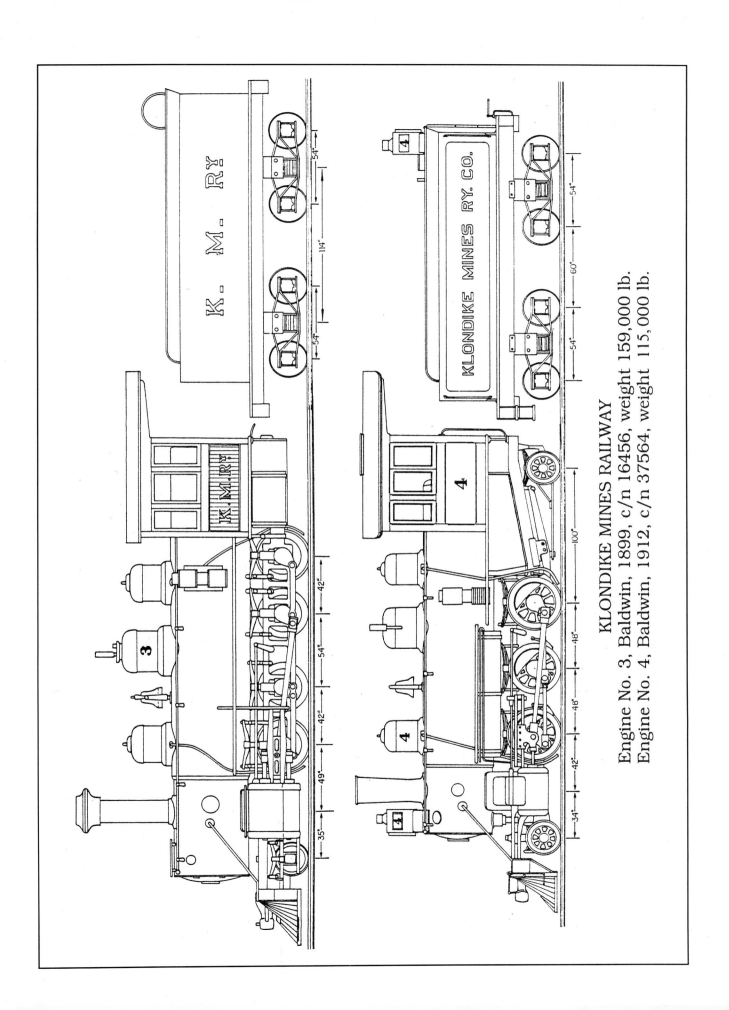

KLONDIKE MINES RAILWAY

Engine No. 3, Baldwin, 1899, c/n 16456, weight 159,000 lb.
Engine No. 4, Baldwin, 1912, c/n 37564, weight 115,000 lb.

series. Most of the KMR order was complete by September of 1905 when cars began to arrive at Klondike City—the balance arrived with the opening of the 1906 shipping season.

There were thirteen box cars, numbered 100, 102, 104, etc., up to 124, and ten flat cars numbered 101, 103, 105, etc., up to 119. All cars were 30 feet in length, and of 15-ton capacity. Anticipated high class freight did not develop, and the company almost immediately began converting box cars to flat cars for bulk hauling. Annual reports to the Federal Government in Ottawa list the following sequence of conversions:

    1906   7 boxcars and 16 flatcars
    1910   6 boxcars and 17 flatcars
    1911   2 boxcars and 21 flatcars
    1912   no boxcars, 23 flat cars.

In making the conversions, it appears the KMR did not identify the new flats in any obvious way—photos show these "new" flats with plain, unmarked, sills.

When the KMR was shut down permanently in 1913, the twenty-three flat cars were parked on the Klondike City line, but were later moved to the section of the main line on Klondike Island. Here they remained, the property of the YCGC, until July, 1942, when they were re-purchased by the WP&YR. Wooden parts had deteriorated and only the hardware was taken, but for some unknown reason, accounts show trucks from only twenty-two cars were retrieved. All were taken to the Skagway shops where, once more, new freight cars were built from them.

Track Car

The KMR owned a Buda track car which was identical, except for being narrow gauge, to Buda's "No. 14 Section Motor Car" listed in the company's 1909 catalog. Powered with a ten-horsepower, two-cylinder opposed, air-cooled engine, it was furnished with a friction/chain-drive transmission which permitted variable power delivery ratios for speeds from four to twenty miles per hour, either forward or in reverse. The remains of this machine were recovered from Klondike City in 1994, and are presently in the locomotive shed in Dawson.

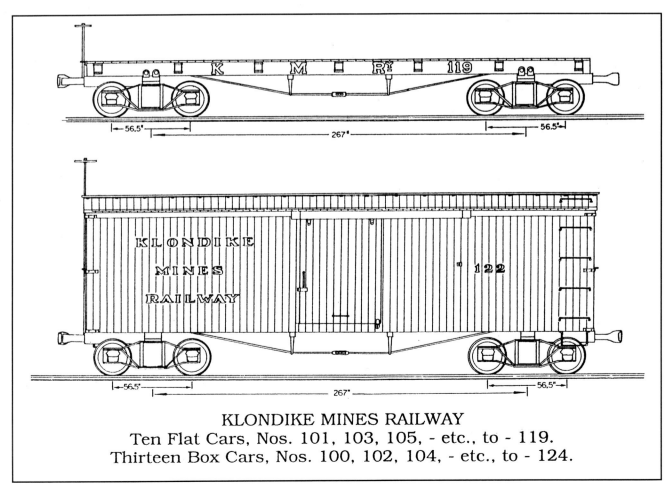

KLONDIKE MINES RAILWAY
Ten Flat Cars, Nos. 101, 103, 105, - etc., to - 119.
Thirteen Box Cars, Nos. 100, 102, 104, - etc., to - 124.

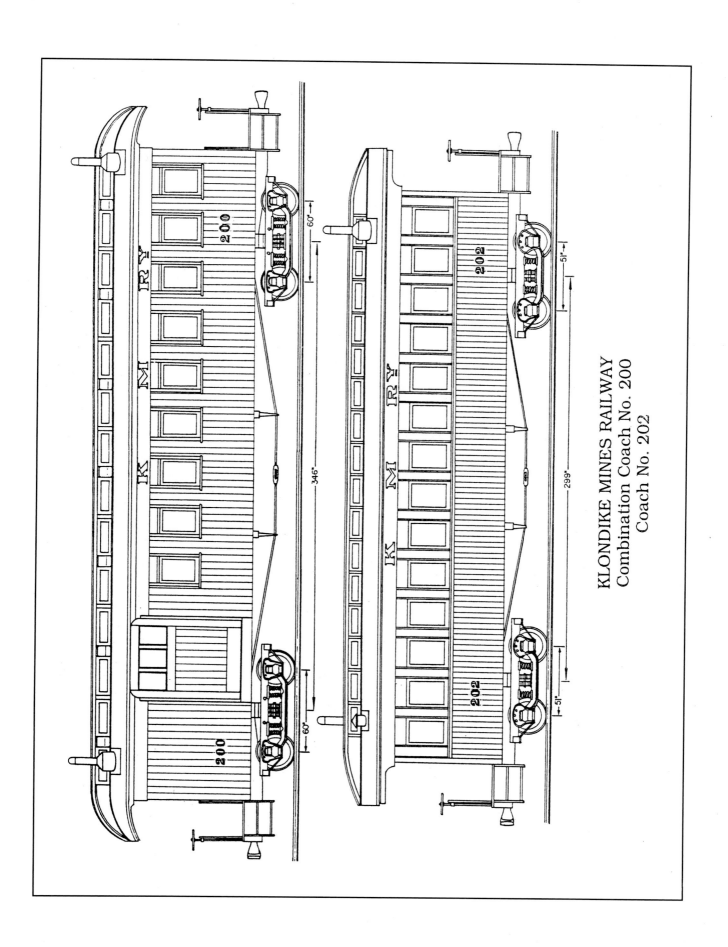

KLONDIKE MINES RAILWAY
Combination Coach No. 200
Coach No. 202

APPENDIX F

THE KLONDIKE RIVER BRIDGE

Summer of 1906: the just-built Klondike Mines Railway bridge crosses the Klondike River just above its confluence with the Yukon River, with the west bank of the Yukon in the distance. The bridge piers, which were formed over wooden pilings, were fifty feet long and aligned with the river current. The bridge, however, crossed the river at a sixty degree angle to the current, thus the bridge spans were parallelograms in plan view. The north (right) span was 100 feet long, the center 140 feet, and the south 80 feet; diagonals of the 80-foot span were of structural iron while of round iron rod on the other two spans.

Eric L. Johnson Collection

KLONDIKE MINES RAILWAY BRIDGE
OVER THE KLONDIKE RIVER

◄— KLONDIKE CITY   DAWSON CITY —►

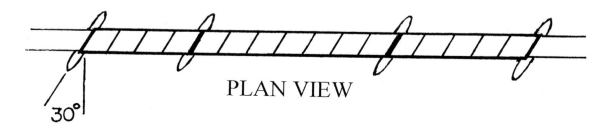

PLAN VIEW

30°

AS BUILT 1906

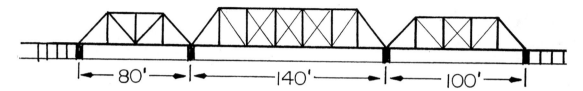

|◄— 80' —►|◄————— 140' —————►|◄— 100' —►|

Diagonals of 80-foot span of angle iron;
diagonals of 100-foot and 140-foot spans of round iron rod.

REBUILT 1911

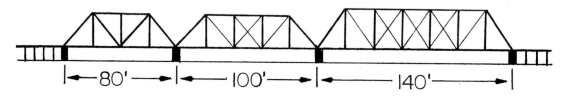

|◄— 80' —►|◄— 100' —►|◄——— 140' ———►|

45-foot span probably of wooden construction.

ABOUT 1920

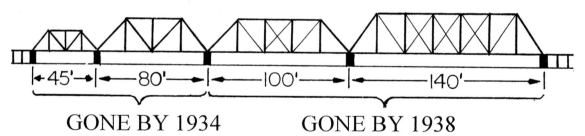

|◄45'►|◄— 80' —►|◄— 100' —►|◄——— 140' ———►|

GONE BY 1934   GONE BY 1938

APPENDIX G

MINING RAILWAYS OF THE KLONDIKE

The Klondike Mines Railway (KMR) was classed a "common carrier"; that is, it was obligated by federal charter to offer its services to any and all customers. In contrast is an industrial railway which is restricted to servicing only its owner's businesses. Three such railways operated in the Klondike district at the turn of the century, all utilizing typically small, saddle-tank, industrial locomotives—and a Shay—running on light, 36-inch gauge, rail. While one of these railways was operated by a gold mining company on placer claims up the Klondike River, the other two railways were operated by coal mining companies; the coal mines were located downstream from Dawson on tributary creeks of the Yukon River. For the fully illustrated story of these railways, see Eric Johnson's
MINING RAILWAYS OF THE KLONDIKE.

The Railway on Cliff Creek:
The North American Transportation and Trading Company

Coal was discovered in the Fortymile region of the Yukon Territory in the 1880s, but it was not until late 1898 that the North American Transportation and Trading Company (NAT&TCo) began developing a mine on Cliff Creek, a tributary of the Yukon River, fifty-eight miles downstream from Dawson City and nine miles downstream from the town of Fortymile. In early 1899 the company began work on a 1¾-mile, 36-inch gauge, railway to haul coal from the mine to the riverside ship-ping terminal. In September a new Porter saddle-tank locomotive and a number of coal wagons arrived to begin operations on the railway. Coal was shipped by barge for use in the Dawson area. Production amounted to about 4000 tons of coal annually, but by mid-1903, coal veins at the Cliff Creek mine were worked out and operations ceased. The NAT&TCo then sold the Porter locomotive to the Coal Creek Coal Company which was just then developing a new coal mine only a few miles south-easterly. The rails along Cliff Creek were pulled up in 1918.

The Railway on Coal Creek:
The Coal Creek Coal Company
The Sourdough Coal Company
The Northern Light, Power and Coal Company

Among several other coal properties discovered in the Fortymile area in the 1890s, one location upstream on Coal Creek was developed in 1903 by the Coal Creek Coal Company (CCCCo). A twelve-mile, 36-inch gauge, railway to connect the mine with a load-out at the Yukon River was finished that summer. Rolling stock consisted of the ex-Cliff Creek locomotive, two well-used 0-6-0 Porter saddle-tankers of unknown origins, and coal cars. The CCCCo had also bought the steamer *Lightning* and the barge *Margaret* to deliver its coal to Dawson City where the chief consumer was the Dawson Electric Light and Power Company. In early 1905 the CCCCo sold the 0-4-0 locomotive to the Tanana Mines Railroad. Under the CCCCo, coal production continued on Coal Creek through 1906.

In late summer of 1906, the Coal Creek mine, the adjacent Sourdough property, railway, steamer and barges were consolidated under the name of the Sourdough Coal Company, which produced coal until late 1908.

In early 1909, the assets of the Sourdough Coal Company were sold to the Northern Light, Power and Coal Company (NLP&CCo). At the mine site, the NLP&CCo would build a thermal-electric generating plant, intending to sell electricity in the Dawson area. To haul in heavy construction material, the NLP&CCo bought a new 2-truck Lima Shay and some flat cars. Installation of the plant and transmission lines were completed in 1910, but the NLP&CCo soon found there was little market in the Klondike for electrical power, and the plant remained idle for most of the next four years. In this time however, two 0-4-0 Porter locomotives and some coal cars were brought to Coal Creek from the Canadian Klondyke

Mining Company's camp at Dawson. Coal for local use was mined until about 1915.

It is believed that the Lima Shay left Coal Creek in late 1912, bound for a gold mine in Alaska. The two 0-6-0 and the two 0-4-0 locomotives were left at the mouth of Coal Creek about 1918 when equipment from the long-inactive power plant and railway were salvaged. In the 1930s or 1940s, one of the 0-4-0 locomotives tumbled into the Yukon River and was lost while the other engines remained on site until 1969 when they were salvaged.

The Railway on Bear Creek:
The Detroit Yukon Mining Company
The Canadian Klondyke Mining Company

The Detroit Yukon Mining Company (DYMCo) was incorporated in 1902 to mine for gold on claims along the Klondike River, a few miles east of Dawson. Initially the company used simple hand-mining methods and a sluicing plant, but in July of 1904, brought in four new 0-4-0 Porter locomotives, lettered D.Y.M.Co. Nos. 1 to 4, and twenty-four mine cars for use on a short, 36-inch gauge, railway at the mouth of Bear Creek. Steam shovels loaded the cars with pay dirt which was hauled to

a washing plant on the Klondike River. The railway operated for only a part of 1904 and into 1905 when the company acquired additional mining claims. In reorganization, DYMCo was absorbed by the newly-formed Canadian Klondyke Mining Company (CKMCo) which promptly installed a dredge, immediately side-lining the year-old railway.

The four locomotives were idle for a time, but found temporary jobs elsewhere in construction. In 1913, DYMCo Nos. 2 and 3 were sent to the coal mines on Coal Creek; their disposition is described above. DYMCo No. 4 was donated to the Dawson Museum in 1961, and DYMCo No. 1 went to southern British Columbia in 1965.

MINING RAILWAYS OF THE KLONDIKE
by Eric L. Johnson, B.C. Rail Guide No. 13, is available from the: Pacific Coast Division
      Canadian Railroad Historical Association
      P.O. Box 1006, Station A,
      Vancouver, B.C. V6C 2P1
for $13.50 Canadian postpaid, or $10 US postpaid.

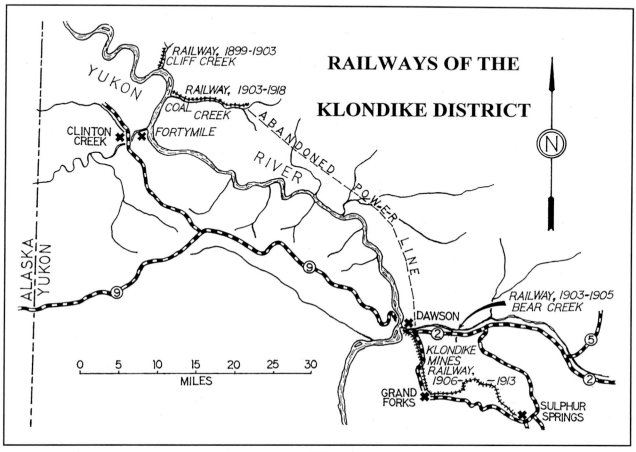

Locomotives of the Mining Railways of the Klondike

Porter (built by the H.K. Porter Company of Pittsburgh, Pennsylvania), c/n unknown, built ca. 1890, 0-6-0T, 25-inch wheels and 7x12-inch cylinders, weight 12 tons, no lettering, no road number while in service in the Yukon.
  present owner, Yukon Transportation Museum, Whitehorse, Yukon, 1993.
  ex-Gunnar Nilsson, Whitehorse, Yukon, 3/1969 to 1993.
  exx-abandoned at the mouth of Coal Creek on the Yukon River, 6/1918 to 3/1969.
  exxx-Northern Light, Power and Coal Company, Coal Creek and Dawson, Yukon, 1909 to 6/1918
  exxxx-Sourdough Coal Company, Coal Creek and Dawson, Yukon, 1906 to 1909.
  exxxxx-Coal Creek Coal Company, Coal Creek and Dawson, Yukon, 1903 to 1906.
  nee unknown, ca. 1890 to 1903.

Porter, c/n unknown, built ca. 1890, 0-6-0T, 27-inch wheels and 8x14-inch cylinders, weight 14 tons, no lettering, no road number while in service in the Yukon.
  present owner, Dick Gilbert, Jake's Corner, Yukon (locomotive located on Venus Place, off Alaska Highway, Whitehorse, Yukon), 1992.
  ex-Harry Cooper, Whitehorse, Yukon, 3/1969 to 1992
  exx-abandoned at the mouth of Coal Creek on the Yukon River, 6/1918 to 3/1969.
  exxx-Northern Light, Power and Coal Company, Coal Creek and Dawson, Yukon, 1909 to 6/1918
  exxxx-Sourdough Coal Company, Coal Creek and Dawson, Yukon, 1906 to 1909.
  exxxxx-Coal Creek Coal Company, Coal Creek and Dawson, Yukon, 1903 to 1906.
  nee unknown, ca. 1890 to 1903.

Porter, c/n 1972, built in March, 1899, 0-4-0T, 24-inch wheels, 6x10-inch cylinders, weight 7 tons, cab lettered N.A.T.&T.Co., probably No. 1 while in service in the Yukon.
  present owner, Friends of the Tanana Valley Railroad, Inc., Fairbanks, Alaska, No. 1.
  ex-display in Fairbanks, Alaska, No. 1, from 1930
  exx-Alaska Railroad, Fairbanks, Alaska, No. 1, 1917 to 1930
  exxx-Tanana Valley Railroad, Fairbanks, Alaska, No. 1, 1907 to 1917
  exxxx-Tanana Mines Railroad, Fairbanks, Alaska, No. 1, 6/1905 to 1907 (note TMR to TVR name change only).
  exxxxx-Coal Creek Coal Company, Coal Creek and Dawson, Yukon, 7/1903 to 6/1905, probably No. 1.
  nee North American Transportation and Trading Company, Cliff Creek and Dawson, Yukon, 3/1899 to 7/1903, cab lettered N.A.T.&T.Co., probably No. 1.

Porter, c/n 3022, built in April, 1904, 0-4-0T, 24-inch wheels, 6x10-inch cylinders, weight 7 tons, originally lettered D.Y.M.Co. on tank, No. 1 on cab.
  present owner, Roger Brammall, Whippletree Junction (3 miles south of Duncan), British Columbia, 1965, No. 1, lettered B.R.R.Co. = Brammall Rail Road Company.
  ex-Yukon Consolidated Gold Corporation, Dawson, Yukon, 1925 to 1965, D.Y.M.Co. No. 1.
  exx-Burrall and Baird, Ltd., Dawson, Yukon, 1921 to 1925, D.Y.M.Co. No. 1.
  exxx-Canadian Klondyke Mining Company, Dawson, Yukon, 6/1905 to 1921, D.Y.M.Co. No. 1.
  nee Detroit Yukon Mining Company, Dawson, Yukon, 4/1904 to 6/1905, D.Y.M.Co. No. 1.

Porter, c/n 3023, built in April, 1904, 0-4-0T, 24-inch wheels, 6x10-inch cylinders, weight 7 tons, originally lettered D.Y.M.Co. on tank, No. 2 on cab.
The fate of this locomotive was in doubt for some time, but new information suggests DYMCo No. 2 was also shipped with DYMCo No. 3 to the Coal Creek mine in July, 1913. When salvaging ceased in 1918 a locomotive was parked on a trestle on the bank of the Yukon River where, for years, it could be seen by passing river traffic. Then in the 1930s or 1940s it disappeared, apparently having fallen into the river when the trestle collapsed.
  ex-abandoned at the mouth of Coal Creek on the Yukon River, 6/1918.
  exx-Northern Light, Power and Coal Company, Coal Creek and Dawson, Yukon, 7/1913 to 6/1918, D.Y.M.Co. No. 2.
  exxx-Canadian Klondyke Mining Company, Dawson, Yukon, 6/1905 to 1912(?), D.Y.M.Co. No. 2.
  nee Detroit Yukon Mining Company, Dawson, Yukon, 4/1904 to 6/1905, D.Y.M.Co. No. 2.

Porter, c/n 3024, built in April, 1904, 0-4-0T, 24-inch wheels, 6x10-inch cylinders, weight 7 tons, originally lettered D.Y.M.Co. on tank, No. 3 on cab.

    present owner, Keith A. Christenson, Eagle River, Alaska, 1981, D.Y.M.Co. No. 3.
    ex-Dan Nowlan, Whitehorse, Yukon, 3/1969 to 1981, D.Y.M.Co. No. 3.
    exx-abandoned at the mouth of Coal Creek on the Yukon River, 6/1918 to 3/1969.
    exxx-Northern Light, Power & Coal Company, Coal Creek and Dawson, Yukon, 7/1913 to 6/1918, D.Y.M.Co. No. 3.
    exxxx-Canadian Klondyke Mining Company, Dawson, Yukon, 6/1905 to 7/1913, D.Y.M.Co. No. 3.
    nee Detroit Yukon Mining Company, Dawson, Yukon, 4/1904 to 6/1905, D.Y.M.Co. No. 3.

Porter, c/n 3025, built in April, 1904, 0-4-0T, 24-inch wheels, 6x10-inch cylinders, weight 7 tons, originally lettered D.Y.M.Co. on tank, No. 4 on cab.

    present owner, Dawson City Museum, Dawson, Yukon, 5/1961, D.Y.M.Co. No. 4.
    ex-Yukon Consolidated Gold Corporation, Dawson Yukon, 1925 to 5/1961, D.Y.M.Co. No. 4.
    exx-Burrall and Baird, Ltd., Dawson, Yukon, 1921 to 1925, D.Y.M.Co. No. 4.
    exxx-Canadian Klondyke Mining Company, Dawson, Yukon, 6/1905 to 1921, D.Y.M.Co. No. 4.
    nee Detroit Yukon Mining Company, Dawson, Yukon, 4/1904 to 6/1905, D.Y.M.Co. No. 4.

Lima Shay (built by the Lima Locomotive Works of Lima, Ohio), c/n 2190, built in July, 1909, two-truck Shay, 26½-inch wheels, and two 8x12-inch cylinders, weight 24 tons, may have been lettered DEL&PCo and may have had road No. 1 while in service in the Yukon. It was originally a coal-burner, converted for wood fuel in 1913, re-converted for coal in 1921, and then to oil fuel in 1928.

    last owner, Biles-Coleman Lumber Company, Omak, Washington, bought 3/1921, scrapped in 1940 at the Omak mill. Lettered Biles-Coleman Lumber Co., at first not numbered but with smoke box plate No. 2; in 1925 became No. 101 (still with front plate No. 2).
    ex-Puget Sound Machinery Depot, Seattle, 3/1921, No. 2.
    exx-Alaska-Gastineau Mining Company, Juneau, Alaska, 6/1913 to 3/1921, No. 2.
    nee Northern Light, Power and Coal Company, Coal Creek and Dawson, Yukon, 1909 to 1913, may have been lettered DEL&PCo, and may have had road number 1.

Although undated, this photo was undoubtedly taken in late 1912, shortly after a large shipment of equipment for CKMCo dredges had arrived. The presence of this DYMCo locomotive, number unknown, here on KMR track at the White Pass docks in Dawson is curious; the KMR had shut down in October, and the mining company was probably permitted use of the line for the delivery of its equipment.

Univ. of Alaska Archives, Fairbanks, Bassoc, 64-92-044

BIBLIOGRAPHY

Berton, Laura. *I Married the Klondike*. McClelland and Stewart,
Toronto, ON, 1954.

Black, Adam & Charles. *Who was Who, 1941-1950*. Adam and Charles Black,
London, U.K., 1950.

Cunynghame, Francis. *The Lost Trail*. Faber and Faber,
London, UK, 1953.

Dodd, Randall M. *Magnificence and Misery*. Doubleday and Company,
New York, NY, 1984.

Government of Canada, Ottawa, ON.
- *Canada Gazette*, 1899 to 1909
- Geological Survey of Canada,
Bulletins and Memoirs, 1898 to 1912
- *List of Shipping*, 1898 to 1920
- *Sessional Papers*, 1898 to 1910

Green, Lewis. *The Gold Hustlers*, Alaska Northwest Publishing,
Anchorage, AK, 1977.

Green, Mervyn T. *Industrial Locomotives*. Pacific Coast Division, CRHA,
Vancouver, BC, 1992.

Hilton, George W. *American Narrow Gauge Railways*. Stanford University Press,
Stanford, CA, 1990.

Hogan, Barbara, and Gregory Skuce. *Klondike Mines Railway*.
Dawson City Museum and Historical Society, Dawson, YT, 1992

Innis, Harold A. *Canadian Frontiers of Settlement*, *Volume IX*.
The MacMillan Company, Toronto, ON, 1936.

Janson, Lone E. *The Copper Spike*. Alaska Northwest Publishing,
Anchorage, AK, 1975.

Johnson, Eric L., *Mining Railways of the Klondike.* Pacific Coast Division, CRHA
Vancouver, BC, 1995

Knutson, Arthur E. *Sternwheels on the Yukon*. Knutson Enterprises,
Kirkland, WA, 1992.

Lavallée, Omer. *Narrow Gauge Railways of Canada*. Fitzhenry and Whiteside,
Toronto, ON, 1972.

Lewis, John E. *Reservation Narrow Gauge*. John E. Lewis,
York, PA, 1980.

Martin, Cy. *Gold Rush Narrow Gauge*. Trans-Anglo Books,
Los Angeles, CA, 1979.

Minter, Roy. *The White Pass, Gateway to the Klondike*. McClelland and Stewart,
Toronto, ON, 1987.

Mitchell, Bob. *Report on the Cultural Resources at Coal Creek*.
Yukon Tourism, Heritage Branch, Whitehorse, YT, 1992.
"   " .   *Chronology of the KMR* (unpublished). 1992

Morgan, Henry J., editor. *Canadian Men and Women*. William Briggs,
Toronto, ON, 1912.

Poor's Manual of Railroads. H.V. and H.W. Poor
New York, NY, 1902 to 1915.

Ross, Brian D. *Chronology of Information Available regarding Thomas W. O'Brien
and the Klondike (O'Brien) Brewery*. Parks Canada, Dawson, YT, 1990.

Sola, Arthur E.I. *Klondyke: Truth and Facts of the New El Dorado*.
The Mining and Geographical Institute, London, UK, 1897.

Taylor, Leonard W. *The Sourdough and the Queen*. Methuen, Toronto, ON, 1983.

INDEX

Figures in italics refer to illustrations or photographs. Appendices are included.

Rusty Spike